|Class and ethnicity

D1422234

RO 0324121 1

THEMES IN THE TWENTIETH CENTURY

Series Editor: Pat Thane, Reader in History,
Goldsmiths' College, University of London

Current titles

Andrew Davies: *Leisure, gender and poverty*
Steven Fielding: *Class and ethnicity*
Junichi Hasegawa: *Replanning the blitzed city centre*

Class and ethnicity

Irish Catholics in England,
1880–1939

Steven Fielding

Open University Press
Buckingham · Philadelphia

Open University Press
Celtic Court
22 Ballmoor
Buckingham
MK18 1XW

and
1900 Frost Road, Suite 101
Bristol, PA 19007, USA

First Published 1993

A catalogue record of this book is available from the British Library

Library of Congress Cataloging-in-Publication Data

Fielding, Steven (Steven J.), 1961–
    Class and ethnicity: Irish Catholics in England, 1880–1939/
Steven Fielding.
        p. cm. – (Themes in the twentieth century)
    Includes bibliographical references (p.   ) and index.
    ISBN 0–335–09993–9 (hb) – ISBN 0–335–09992–0 (pbk.)
    1. Irish – England – History – 20th century. 2. Catholics – English
– History – 20th century. 3. Irish – England – History – 19th century.
4. Catholics – England – History – 19th century. 5. Social classes –
England – History. 6. England – Ethnic relations. I. Title.
II. Series.
DA125.I7F54 1992
942′.0049162 – dc20   92–7401
                                                                    CIP

Typeset by Graphicraft Typesetters Ltd, Hong Kong
Printed in Great Britain by Biddles Limited,
Guildford and Kings Lynn

To Lindsay, who has suffered more than most

Contents

Series editor's introduction		ix
Preface		xii
Acknowledgements		xv
Map of the main districts of Manchester and Salford		xvi
one	Interpretations	1
	Historical perceptions	1
	England's cultural bias	5
	Class and ethnicity	10
	An 'awkward' minority	13
two	Social context	19
	Reluctant immigrants	19
	Places of settlement	27
	English responses	33
three	Church and people	38
	A divided Church	38
	Faith and nationality	40
	The policeman of the Faith	43
	Formal and informal worship	48

four	Catholicism and popular culture	56
	The Catholic family	56
	The parish school	61
	Controlling adolescents	65
	Retaining adults	68
	Mixed marriages	70
	The Church and processions	72
five	The politics of Home Rule	79
	English opposition to Home Rule	79
	The character of Irish Nationalism	83
	Irish Liberals	88
	Catholic education	92
	The progressive alliance	95
	Towards independence	100
six	Labour and the Church	105
	Annexing the Catholic vote	105
	The politics of Catholicism	109
	The Catholic Federation	112
	Labour's Catholic dissidents	118
	Conclusion	127
	Notes	134
	Bibliography	160
	Index	176

Series editor's introduction

A great deal both of everyday conversation, and of everyday academic analysis of contemporary society, embodies assumptions about the past including the quite recent past, for which actual evidence is slight. Indeed the history of Britain in the first half of the twentieth century seems sometimes to have taken on an almost mythic character. This is largely because until very recently social historians have been reluctant to explore history more recent than the First World War. Since British empirical sociology did not take off on a large scale until the 1950s there has been an important gap in our knowledge of the twentieth century, which arguably has distorted our understanding of the whole timespan and limited our understanding of postwar Britain by deracinating it.

Recent work has begun to dispel some widely held convictions about this period though most of it has yet to be absorbed either into everyday consciousness or contemporary social science. It is now clear, to take just a few examples, that there was not a significant movement of women into 'male' occupations during the First World War;[1] that such a shift is not the main explanation for the partial concession of votes to women in 1918;[2] that feminism did not die away after women obtained the vote, but was especially vibrant in the 1920s;[3] that the 1930s was not a time of overwhelming slump, but of contrasting prosperity and recession in different regions;[4] that women were not peremptorily ejected from the paid labour market after the Second World War, but rather exhorted to stay on[5].

The aim of this series of books is to take demythologizing further by subjecting previously un- or underexplored areas of recent British history to empirical scrutiny. Ethnic identity is one such area. Though the Irish have long been a highly important group in the society of mainland Britain, less attention has been paid to them in the twentieth century, especially between the First and Second World Wars, than in the nineteenth, and least of all outside the sectarian redoubts of Glasgow and Liverpool. It seems to have been assumed that elsewhere the Irish lost the distinctive identity they had had in the nineteenth-century city.

Steve Fielding focuses upon Manchester with its large and politically active Irish population, using rich empirical detail to explore questions of more than local importance: the meaning of 'ethnic community', of 'integration' or 'assimilation'. He examines how an Irish identity survived in a long settled community – though it was not a static settlement given the constant movement and exchange of people between the islands. Though surviving strongly, this preservation of identity did not necessarily lead to tensions with the non-Catholic majority as studies which dwell on the sectarian tensions of Glasgow and Liverpool may suggest. But lack of tension did not imply 'assimilation' and loss of the sense of being Irish.

Fielding explores how this sense of self was sustained through his vivid exploration of Irish neighbourhood culture, with its own internal variety and tensions. And also, in keeping with our recent recognition that societies are divided in multiple ways and that individual behaviour is shaped by awareness of multiple identities he discusses how Irish people related their ethnic identity to, in particular, their gender and class identities.

Also important was their religion. Fielding's study of the role of the Roman Catholic Church, and its by no means simple role in sustaining Irish identity, is especially valuable. In general the role of religion in British society since the First World War has been given too little attention. In particular the considerable power of Roman Catholicism has been underestimated, for example in the politics of sexuality, in this case opposing easy access to techniques of birth control when this became an important political issue in Britain in the interwar years. Fielding gives a vivid picture of the relationships, and tensions, between the Church and the Irish population, including its place in the construction of gender roles.

Fielding also breaks new ground in exploring the role of the Irish in Liberal and then in Labour politics during the formative period of realignment between the parties and the emergence of Labour as a major party.

He moves through analysis of the local dynamics of the Irish community – at leisure, at work, at home, at church, at political meetings – to look at their relationship with a powerful international movement – the Church – to discussion of their relationship to structures of national power. In drawing together the political with the cultural and with the economic roles of the Irish at this variety of levels, Fielding uses his local material to focus upon the central issues in this study of ethnicity in modern Britain.

Notes

1 A. Reid, 'World War I and the working class in Britain', in A. Marwick (ed.), *Total war and social change* (London, Macmillan, 1988), pp. 16–24.
2 M. Pugh, *Electoral reform in war and peace, 1906–1918* (London, Routledge, 1978); S.S. Holton, *Feminism and democracy: Women's suffrage and reform politics in Britain, 1900–1918* (Cambridge University Press, 1986).
3 H.L. Smith (ed.), *British feminism in the twentieth century* (Aldershot, Edward Elgar, 1990).
4 J. Stevenson and C. Cook, *The slump. Society and politics during the Depression* (London, Quartet, 1979).
5 P. Summerfield, 'Women, war and social change: women in Britain in World War II', in A. Marwick, *Total war and social change,* pp. 95–118; P. Thane 'Towards equal opportunities? Women in Britain since 1945', in A. O'Day and T. Gourvish (eds), *Britain since 1945* (London, Macmillan, 1991).

Preface

It will be clear to those who progress much further than this preface that the author is no theoretician. Even so, the book's title requires some conceptual definition as it employs terms that are used more frequently than they are explained. 'Class' is deployed in a conventional Marxian manner and is meant to suggest that those who occupied a broadly similar relationship to the means of production shared a common set of economic interests. However, it is not implied that consciousness of these interests was ever fully apparent or that those who neglected to privilege these interests were in some way deficient and in need of enlightenment. There were a number of different but equally legitimate means by which individuals identified with others in society. Class had to compete with, for example, identities based on gender, age, occupation and residence to name but a few. 'Ethnicity', by which is meant identification based on shared cultural traits, was simply another form of social affiliation. Irish Catholics defined themselves around a common set of interests based on a shared national origin and denominational membership. They were hardly unique in 'failing' to put class loyalties before other considerations. It is curious that ethnicity is employed only to describe minorities within society. The English Protestant majority also possessed a distinctive ethnic sensibility. In fact, many of the problems that confronted Irish immigrants originated in the indigenous population's over-developed sense of cultural superiority.

The juxtaposition of class with ethnicity is intended to suggest that neither one nor the other ever held exclusive sway. There was no linear progression from a 'lower' ethnic feeling to a 'higher' class consciousness: they were, in actual, lived experience, organically linked. Moreover, class and ethnic identities were continually contested and redefined. They were protean forms of consciousness, which in themselves possessed no one anterior meaning. Those institutions that sought to represent national, religious and class consciousness constantly attempted to wrest the immigrant population away from their rivals. However, it was up to individuals themselves to map out the best means of reconciling these competitive expressions of class and ethnic sentiments.

The book is principally about Catholics of immediate Irish descent, although the term 'Irish Catholic' also embraces those who might have considered themselves more Catholic than Irish. Irish Protestants have been deliberately excluded from this survey, apart from those occasions when their activities impinged upon the lives of their Catholic counterparts. The experience of Irish Protestants was in most important respects wholly distinct: their relationship with the state was completely different, as were their politics and the meaning of their denominational loyalties. Perhaps working-class Protestant immigrants suffered from no less a number of economic and cultural impediments, not the least of which was the obligation to support Glasgow Rangers F.C. However, their history deserves an author more alert to such peculiarities.

This work is confined to England and so does not refer to Irish immigrants in Scotland. Their experience was too unique to collapse into a broader history, although where it has seemed appropriate common traits have been highlighted. Attention is most firmly fixed upon the adjacent cities of Manchester and Salford, which to save duplication will hereafter be referred to as 'Manchester' unless otherwise specified. This focus has an intrinsic merit, for Manchester was one of the most important centres of Irish settlement and yet has been relatively neglected by those who have written about the Irish in England. Moreover, concentrating on one particular location has the benefit of illuminating in human detail some of the most common forms of experience. It also enables the reader to appreciate the particularity of that experience, the details of which might be lost in a vain attempt to capture the 'essential' nature of the Irish Catholic immigrant experience. This is most apposite, given that one of the main purposes of this book is to demonstrate that it is spurious to suppose that there was any such thing.

Hopefully, this work will be of interest both to those who are studying the history of the Irish in England and others interested in English working-class culture and politics generally. It is unfortunate that, when they are considered, Irish immigrants suffer from a kind of academic ghettoization. Irish Catholics did not exist in a social vacuum: they were an intrinsic part of the working class in England. To amend Edward Thompson's dictum, when the English working class was made Irish Catholics were active participants in the process. Those towns and cities that industrialized first and fastest also attracted the most immigrants. For much of the period

1880–1939 Irish Catholics remained concentrated in those regions most associated with the 'traditional' working class: South-east Lancashire, West Yorkshire, Tyneside and London's East End. Irish Catholics, therefore, should not be seen as minor characters within the history of the English working class. Without them, important parts of the plot make no sense whatsoever.

Acknowledgements

I would particularly like to express my appreciation to Pat Thane, whose efforts have made the publication of this work possible; I hope it was worth the trouble. Tony Mason and Jim Obelkevich, for their supervision of the original PhD thesis, also deserve an honourable mention. If I can write comprehensible English it is due to them. The number of librarians whose time I have shamelessly wasted is beyond calculation. Those at the beleaguered Manchester Central Reference Library, in particular in the Archives Department, Local History Library and Social Sciences Section merit special thanks. I am also grateful to the Bishop of Salford for access to his archive at Wardley Hall, Swinton. Further debts that now call for payment are due to: Mark Clapson Peter Clarke, Andrew Davies, Chris Downham, Chris Ford, Sheridan Gilley, Dermot Healy, Mike Herbert, Bernadette Hyland, Joan Keating, James Kilmartin, Jon Lawrence, Ros Lucas, Mick Stevens, Nick Tiratsoo, Terry Wyke and Barbara Weinberger.

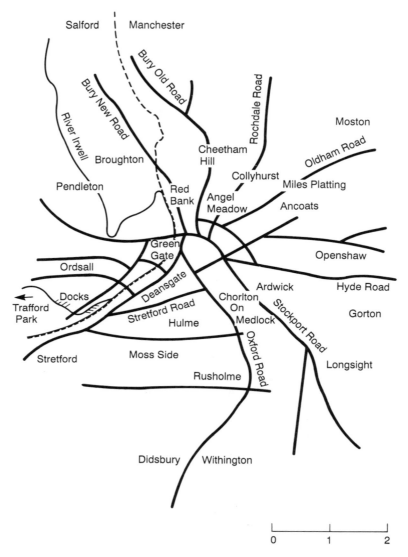

The main districts of Manchester and Salford

one

Interpretations

Historical perceptions

The experience of England's working-class Irish Catholic minority has been interpreted in a number of conflicting, even contradictory, ways. This study aims to chart a course between the most important schools of thought, in the hope of refining some of their insights. Its principal purpose is to establish that Irish Catholics formed a viable and distinct culture that was a compound of class and ethnic influences. Such a culture was intrinsically dynamic: being Irish, Catholic and working class forced individuals to reconcile different demands and particular identities. The nature of these accommodations changed over time and place. National institutional forces, which sought to represent each of these three discrete forms of consciousness, were often in conflict with one another. At various moments, their rivalries threatened the coherence of working-class Irish Catholicism. Matters were further complicated by the increasing importance of generations born in England but raised to think of themselves as members of a nation and faith at odds with most contemporary expressions of Englishness. Moreover, the meaning of Irish nationality changed with the creation of the Free State in 1921 which, Ulster excepted, gave Ireland independence. Thus, the balance between influences of class, nation and faith shifted over time. Yet, despite these fissiparous pressures, few Irish Catholics embraced one expression of their identity to the exclusion of the others; each was an intrinsic aspect of their collective personality that had been adapted to fit the realities that faced a minority culture within the English working class. They were neither simply Irish, Catholic or working class, but an amalgam of all three and, in combining them, they evolved their own ways of expressing this fact. Thus, the Catholic Hierarchy disapproved of their Catholicism; Irish Nationalists in Ireland considered them degenerate members of their nation; many putative leaders of the working class held them in contempt. Nevertheless, the three component elements of the Irish Catholic working-class identity were inextricably linked and remained locked together.

Many historians have written as if ethnic and class identities were mutually exclusive and have suggested that the former had given way to the latter by the end of the nineteenth century. There *was* variation and change: broadly speaking, the further generations moved from their Irish antecedants the less powerful was their willingness to identify with Ireland. However, this process occurred slowly and imperceptibly: an Irish Catholic working class, with all its apparent ambiguities of identity, was still in existence on the outbreak of the Second World War. Even so, a reading of most historical accounts leads one to suspect that they had unproblematically merged into the English working class at least four decades before 1939. To account for this erroneous impression, attention must therefore be given to the historical perception of Irish Catholics.

The most established interpretation of the Irish Catholic experience is associated with an emphasis on the centrality of class sentiment within English society and the crucial importance of the labour movement to working-class culture. This view has given rise to a belief in the ability of trade unions to foster the integration of minority groups into the working class.[1] The lives of Irish Catholic immigrants, viewed from this perspective, seem extremely similar to those of English workers with whom they shared an apparently compelling common class interest. As a consequence, the significance of the Irish Catholic ethnic identity has been diminished, leading to the conclusion that Irish workers and their descendants had been fully incorporated into the English working class by 1914 at the very latest.

Historians who belong to this class-centred tradition make particular mention of England's Irish Catholics only when discussing the period that includes the Potato Famine of the 1840s and its aftermath. These years saw the dramatic flight of Irish peasants to England and their violent rejection by many indigenous workers. The cause of anti-Irish feeling is seen to be the collapse of the Chartist movement as much as the scale and impact of the Famine influx itself. Before its demise in 1848 Chartism is thought to have united English and Irish workers behind a programme that embraced both class concerns and the demand for a liberated Ireland. As a consequence, Irish workers were supposedly some of the most enthusiastic of Chartism's supporters.[2] The strong implication is that if the movement had survived it would have, at the very least, ameliorated those sectarian outbursts that so marred the 1850s and 1860s. Such antipathy has been seen partly as the creation of a middle class intent on dividing workers along ethnic lines for its own economic and political purposes. It is deemed to be no accident that the most vicious expressions of anti-Irish hostility occurred during the period between the fall of Chartism and the assumed revival of socialism in the late 1880s.[3] Thus, the fundamental cause of the perceived decline in sectarian feeling in the late nineteenth century is thought to be the emergence of the modern labour movement. The great strike waves of the late 1880s and early 1890s, which heralded the mass unionization of unskilled workers, is also said to have hastened the social integration of Irish Catholics. Strikes organized by dockers, gasworkers and the like – many of them Irish by birth or descent – are taken to have registered the increased class consciousness of such workers. In contrast with these, increasingly obvious, shared class interests, the importance of distinctions based on nationality and religion, which cut across such loyalties, are thought to have receded. In short, occupational solidarity, when expressed in an organized form, is assumed to have been stronger, ultimately, than ethnic feeling.[4]

So far as many historians are concerned, by 1900 Irish Catholics had become an 'old problem'. Safely ensconced in their unions and solid in support for the Labour Party, they ceased to function as a separate and distinct ethnic group.[5] The dearth of studies dealing with Irish Catholics after this date is clear evidence of such an attitude and the sectarianism so obvious during the mid-Victorian period can therefore be dismissed as an aberration to be explained away by reference to exceptional circumstances. After these fraught decades, Irish and English workers are taken to have recognized the importance of their class similarities over their ethnic differences. In fact, Irish nationality is seen as making many immigrants even more class conscious than their English counterparts. They are said to have provided the working class with, 'a cutting edge of radicals and revolutionaries, with a body of men uncommitted by either tradition or economic success to society as it existed around them.'[6] By the end of the nineteenth century Irish Catholics are thought to have identified primarily with a culturally and politically homogeneous working class. It has even been suggested that the working class at this time should be conceived as a 'singular rather than a plural noun'.[7] This belief has been endorsed by numerous recollections of proletarian life that have emphasized the extent to which working-class experience was unitary and defined by an acute sense of 'us and them'.[8] At the heart of this proletarian world was the labour movement; indeed, 'the world and culture of the working class is incomprehensible without it'.[9] To parody this view only slightly, it seems that by 1939 each and every member of the working class ate fish and chips every evening, went to football matches each Saturday afternoon, fervently belonged to a trade union and instinctively voted Labour. It is clear that there is no room for the Irish Catholic identity within this conception of working-class culture.

There are many reasons to dissent from this view of working-class life. Its most serious flaw is the extent to which emphasis is placed on the cultural impact of the work place and the labour movement. Occupation did not determine each and every aspect of a person's identity. Moreover, the average union density between 1900 and 1940 was only 24.8 per cent of workers. The unskilled remained disproportionately unorganized and the Irish were, throughout this period, predominantly unskilled. Hostility to unions was evident amongst the English unskilled well into the 1930s.[10] In any case, it remains an unproven assertion that trade union membership increased an individual's toleration of cultural difference. Indeed, the failure of unions to overcome racial, national and religious prejudice within the working class has been widely noted, since at least Lenin's time. Even Henry Champion, one of the leaders of the exemplary 1889 London dock strike was tainted by anti-Irish chauvinism.[11] It may well be that union membership gave workers one more form of identification, but only a minority allowed it to dominate their horizons to the exclusion of all others. Moreover, most would have identified with other members of their trade union – not the working class as a whole. Thus, if only a minority of workers attained trade union consciousness after 1889 even fewer transcended this stage of development. The inability of the Labour Party to attract enough working-class votes to win a majority in the Commons before 1945 and the failure to establish a credible Marxist alternative both bear out this suggestion.[12] There is therefore little evidence on which to base the view that the labour movement supplanted ethnic differences.

The general bias towards this type of class interpretation is partly a reflection of the relatively homogeneous nature of English society. Unlike most other industrial countries there was only ever one labour movement and one effective national party that claimed to represent workers. Compared to other, similar, societies, religious divisions and national minorities were less important. In France and Italy anti-clerical radicals fought against Catholic-orchestrated opponents; in Germany the power of the Catholic Church led to Bismarck's Kulturkampf; in Holland religious and political differences within the working class led to what has been described as the 'pillarization' of society. Moreover, within the Irish diaspora, England is almost unique. Both relatively and absolutely it became home to far fewer immigrants and they remained confined to the poorer echelons of the working class.[13] Thus, England gave rise to national political loyalties and institutions almost completely free from ethnic influences: there has never been an equivalent of the American Jewish lobby or Tammany Hall.

The lack of interest in ethnicity and cultural diversity within the working class has, therefore, some grounding in reality. Yet, the existence of comparative homogeneity in the national culture has been too often confused with that of absolute homogeneity. The emphasis on class has obscured the fact that no period of English history has been without immigration on at least some scale. This was invariably modest: between 1901 and 1931 not quite 4 per cent of those living in England and Wales had been born elsewhere.[14] Thus, on a national scale comparison between

England and the United States is hardly worth pursuing. Locally, however, the picture is rather different, for Irish and subsequent immigrant groups won for themselves an important position in many industrial towns and cities. Unfortunately, the two conurbations most associated with Irish immigration are Liverpool and Glasgow, places marginal to the cultural and political life of the nation. They are aberrant precisely because they contained so many Irish immigrants and supported a sectarian culture not seen elsewhere. They are the exotic exceptions that prove the dominant class rule: the more historians discuss ethnicity in these cities, the less relevant it is deemed to be for the rest of the country. In short, it is the way many historians have chosen to interpret working-class history that has led them to neglect the unique nature of the Irish Catholic experience.

England's cultural bias

Historians have not been content just to present the English working class as culturally homogeneous; they have also suggested that Irish and English workers were almost indistinguishable. Those few, relatively insignificant, differences that existed after the Famine are seen to have firmly receded into the background by 1914. Thus, despite forming England's largest national and religious minority until well after 1945, Irish Catholics are seen as constituting the least 'alien' of all the country's ethnic groups. Indeed, their ethnic status seems somewhat in doubt.[15] This, in the face of abiding differences of national origin, religious faith, rural background, political tradition and economic circumstance. Moreover, at least during the early nineteenth century, Jews were looked upon more favourably than Irish immigrants.[16] Such a view has a legitimate basis in the intimate social, economic and political ties that have bonded Ireland to England, largely a consequence of their geographic proximity. Between the 1800 Act of Union and the creation of the Irish Free State in 1921, Ireland was not a colony, nor a foreign country, but actually a component part of Great Britain. Even after 1921 all those who lived in Ireland formally remained subjects of the Crown; Irish citizens resident in England today may still vote in elections and claim welfare benefits. Additionally, Irish Catholics being white, Christian and usually English speakers were unlike most other immigrant groups. This explains why they never suffered hostility in quite the same way as those Jews who emigrated from Eastern Europe in the late nineteenth century or black settlers from the Caribbean and the Indian sub-continent after 1945. Thus, it is understandable that Irish Catholics have been seen as workers first, and their national and religious differences have come a poor second.

It is true that, relatively at least, Irish Catholics had more in common with indigenous workers than those immigrants who came later. However, such an emphasis has obscured the importance of their dissimilarities. It has also concealed the ingrained hostility to Catholics, and the Irish, which was deeply embedded in English society. Irish Catholics were the victims of a cultural bias that castigated them even before they settled in England. Anti-Catholicism effectively began when Henry VIII broke with the Pope and established his own English national church. In fact, it has been asserted that hostility to the Catholic Church was one of the first defining qualities of modern 'Englishness' shared by all members of society.[17] After the 1580s an ingrained popular mistrust of Catholics and their Church was established in many English minds. The individualism that emerged during the seventeenth century was closely related to Protestantism and saw in the Catholic Church a bitter opponent. Thus, episodes such as the Civil War of the 1640s and the 1688 Glorious Revolution were interpreted as part of England's struggle against Romish rule. It became a patriotic truism that Protestantism was the source of England's greatness, whereas continental Catholics were poor, oppressed creatures denied the comforts of roast beef and liberty. More ominously, the Catholic Church was imagined to be at the heart of an international conspiracy, intent on overthrowing England's beloved constitution and restoring the absolutist rule of the Pope. During this time 'popery' popularly stood for darkest evil, although as Daniel Defoe claimed, most did not know whether it was a man or horse. There were also infrequent attacks on Catholic chapels in places as far apart as Liverpool, Sunderland and Bath. The most famous of these anti-Catholic uprisings came to be known as the Gordon riots of June 1780, the last and greatest of London's street disorders, which left 500 killed or injured.[18]

Anti-Catholic sentiment is usually associated with political reactionaries; however, albeit for distinct reasons, it was also evident within English radicalism. For religious dissenters the Catholic Church was the embodiment of all they opposed. John Bunyan's *Pilgrim's progress*, first published in 1678 and widely read well into the nineteenth century, had 'Old Man Pope' warn Christian that, 'You will never mend till more of you are burned'. For the young William Cobbett growing up in rural Surrey the Pope was a terrible bogy, dressed in a robe dipped in Protestant blood. In fact, some of the most violent anti-Catholic rhetoric came from radicals. The Pope, 'the whore of Rome', was a dictator whose worldly corruption masked his spurious claim to have privileged access to God. The Catholic Church was accused of manipulating popular belief in magic and superstition; it was seen as being deliberately obscurantist and anti-rationalist in order to perpetuate its own malign rule.[19] These criticisms remained part of the common sense of nineteenth-century radicals and were inherited by many socialists who joined the Independent Labour Party in the 1890s and the Communist Party in the 1920s.

For those closer to the centre of political power, anti-Catholicism had a slightly different basis. The Anglican Church was part of the state, with the monarch as its head. To symbolize this relationship, since 1689 the Coronation Oath had included the promise to maintain, 'the Protestant

Reformed Religion Established by Law'. As one Surrey gentleman declared in 1828, 'the nation and the church are one . . . the unity of the individual with the nation is to be attested by his unity with the church.' For such conservatives, religious questions assumed a constitutional importance. As a consequence, denominational loyalties held political implications: those who challenged the position of the Anglican Church were seen as threatening government. As Catholics were part of a foreign church, their national and religious loyalties were assumed to be in conflict.

During the eighteenth century some of the more serious doubts about Catholic loyalties were forgotten and a number of punitive prohibitions on their participation in public life were abrogated. However, this was not entirely due to the willingness of the English people or their legislators to see Catholics in a more favourable light. The 1829 Catholic Emancipation Act, which abolished most Catholic political disabilities, was drafted to prevent civil war in Ireland. It was widely opposed in the country and split the governing Tories. Instead of marking the end of feelings hostile to the Catholic Church, the Act possibly exacerbated them, by stoking fears that it was regaining influence.[20]

Anti-Catholicism inevitably coloured reactions to Irish Catholic immigrants, especially as it was actively encouraged by Ulster Orange lodge members who also settled in England. In fact, the English anti-Catholic obsession reached its apex during the mid-nineteenth century, at the same time as Irish immigration also approached its zenith. This was, however, more coincidental than causal, although the latter probably helped reinforce the former. Paranoia had intensified within the political elite after a number of prominent Anglican clerics, grouped together as the Oxford Movement, defected to Catholicism. These fears were seemingly confirmed by the re-establishment of the Catholic Hierarchy and the appointment of an Archbishop of Westminster by the Pope in the early 1850s. The Papal army seemed to be once more on the march and threatening cherished English liberties guaranteed by the Protestant constitution. William Murphy was but the most famous of a number of professional anti-papist lecturers who toured the country during the 1860s and 1870s to exploit such fears. Sponsored by the Protestant Electoral Union, Murphy was part of a small band of highly vocal groups dedicated to defending 'the Protestantism of the Bible and the Liberty of Britain' against 'the yoke of the Romish Priesthood and its abettors'. His message was taken to predominantly working- and lower-middle-class audiences in the industrial north and midlands, where Irish immigration was greatest. In these places he was guaranteed the most opposition from Catholics and therefore the biggest Protestant audiences; that some led to sectarian riots only helped publicize his cause.[21]

As an issue of immediate national importance, anti-Catholicism lacked a future. After Murphy's death in the early 1870s few lived in fear of the Pope, who faced difficulties of his own in a newly-unified Italy. Moreover, there was little likelihood that English Catholics would ever attempt a violent overthrow of the Anglican Church. Abroad, national rivalries replaced those based on religion; it was the military and economic power of the Russian, German and French states that worried English politicians, not their denominational complexion. Yet many in society retained a mistrust of Catholics and their Church: anti-Catholicism was pervasive if, usually, unarticulated. There continued to be something essentially different, even sinister, about Catholics. If Protestants no longer feared them as potential enemy agents they still gained vicarious pleasure in speculating about what exactly occurred during mass and in the confessional. Catholics remained part of the 'other'.[22]

By the late nineteenth century anti-Catholic feeling had been largely subsumed within a broader antipathy to Irish Catholic immigrants. English hostility to the Irish, in fact, enjoyed a lineage even longer than that of anti-Catholicism. Since at least the time of the Norman Conquest those who lived beyond the realm of the Kings of England – the Scots, Welsh and Irish – were roundly despised by the English. In dramas, poems, novels and histories the English depicted these Celtish peoples as primitive, tribal, violent and backward. By the eighteenth century this practice of satirizing the Celts had systematically poisoned the public mind: they could be seen only in a negative light.[23] During this period the 'wild Irish' were favoured objects of ridicule, but the Welsh were also considered fair game by dramatists, who exploited their reputation for criminality. In the sixteenth century it was the Welsh, rather than the Irish, who were the butt of leaden jokes about their alleged stupidity. Gradually, however, Wales and Scotland were annexed, suppressed and forcibly anglicized. This was much harder to accomplish in Ireland and provoked greater resistance; Ireland's place within the United Kingdom was only formally confirmed in 1800. Moreover, the Irish remained more of a threat to the English state than the Scots and Welsh due to their sustained hostility to constitutional incorporation. By demanding Home Rule the Irish were open to the accusation that they sought the destruction of the Empire.[24] Therefore, by the middle of the nineteenth century the English anti-Celt prejudice had been reduced and concentrated into enmity for the Irish. It has even been suggested that one of the causes behind Chartism's collapse was the establishment's depiction of the movement as an Irish conspiracy: this turned patriotic English workers away from radicalism.[25] Thus, the ability of Chartism to promote harmony between the nations seems to have been severely exaggerated.

By the late eighteenth century the Irish peasant and soldier had become a stock character on the London stage, his appearance being the excuse for a lively song or jig. Appearing in farce, comedy or melodrama the Irish were shown to be blundering fools, brutes or buffoons. 'Pat', as this character was invariably called, was presented as a lovable innocent and an occasionally wily, feckless rogue: if he wasn't singing or drinking, then he was brawling.[26] Stereotypes were a common device utilized by contemporary playwrights and music hall performers. They were a shorthand, intended to establish character swiftly, thus allowing the plot to continue apace or the jokes to flow more quickly. They were not only deployed against the Irish, but also exploited popular preconceptions about other 'types', whether based on nationality, region, class or gender. Playwrights and performers did not create the hunger for a particular image but, rather, fed a pre-existing public appetite, and in so doing codified it, making it more firm and definite. Stereotyping was commercially astute and few deliberately avoided relying on it when dealing with Ireland or the Irish. One of the very few exceptions was *John Bull's other island* which was written by Irishman and Fabian George Bernard Shaw and first performed in 1904.

It would be reasonable to suppose that constant exposure to 'Pat' made Victorian audiences less receptive to the notion that the Irish were a sensible people capable of self-government. Although it was not the intention of those who conjured him to life, 'Pat' confirmed the English people's innate sense of national superiority. Yet, an audience willing to be entertained by such a portrayal probably needed little prompting.[27]

If on the stage the Irish were stereotyped as comic buffoons, in cartoons drawn for newspapers and journals they were presented as noxious, ape-like maniacs. The fully-fledged 'simianization' of the Irish occurred during the 1860s. However, the image traded on the long-established bestial reputation of the Celts. The 1860s also witnessed the intensification of the land war in Ireland and saw Fenian bombers perpetrate a number of outrages in England: from this point Home Rule was never far from the domestic political agenda. It was as a way of undermining the Nationalist case that the ape-like image was deployed.[28] It was in the best interests of those who opposed Home Rule to exploit popular prejudice about Irish Catholics. As the *Manchester Guardian* noted in 1895, the case against Home Rule began and ended with an attack on the Irish national character.[29] To demolish the case for self-government the Irish were said to be uncivilized, emotional, irrational, lazy and lacking self-reliance. As one, apparently fair-minded, opponent of Home Rule stated, the Celt was:

> Warm-hearted but fickle; brave but wanting in endurance; brilliant but ineffective . . . with the fierce passions of men, the lack of sober calculation which often limits the power of the cleverest woman, and the unreasonableness of children . . . we love them, but they irritate us; we admire them, but they disappoint us; we would fain trust them, but . . . they betray us.[30]

It should be emphasized that such ideas were not the creation of those who were hostile to Home Rule. They undoubtedly exaggerated them, but for the most part such images had long been common currency.

English hostility to Celts has led some historians to deduce that the Irish were victims of a form of racism.[31] They have gained sustenance from this famous comment made by Karl Marx in 1870:

> In relation to the Irish worker he [the English worker] feels himself
> a member of the ruling nation . . . He cherishes religious, social and
> national prejudices against the Irish worker. His attitude towards
> him is much the same as that of the 'poor whites' to the 'niggers' in
> the former slave states of the U.S.A.[32]

It is certainly true that many contemporaries thought in racial terms, not
just about the Irish but also the Welsh and Scots.[33] Even on the political
left some disparagingly compared the Irish with other 'primitive' races.
Honeymooning in Ireland during 1892 the Fabians Sidney and Beatrice
Webb noted that although 'charming', they detested the Irish 'as we should
the Hottentots'. In the same year Henry Champion, an early stalwart of
independent working-class politics, complained that:

> As I have never had an opportunity of seeing political meetings of
> Hottentots, I cannot say how far it would be a libel on those inhab-
> itants of Africa to compare them to . . . Leeds Irishmen.[34]

However, although couched in the language of race, anti-Irish hostility was
primarily based – as Marx himself suggested – on 'religious, social and
national prejudices'. The English thought the Irish to be a separate and
inferior race because they despised their religion, poverty and demand for
Home Rule. They did not oppose Home Rule because they considered
them racially inferior, although it was useful to suggest that they were.
Moreover, it seems that such specifically racial rhetoric was not used by
members of the working class but by the educated elite. By the late nineteenth century it was the struggle for Home Rule that determined attitudes to the Irish.[35] To English workers, most of whom had accepted the
benign character of the state since the collapse of Chartism, the Irish
demand to be free of Westminster seemed perverse. The Irish recourse to
violence also confirmed popular ideas about their lack of 'civilization'. In
their own struggle for recognition few late Victorian English socialists ever
advocated the revolutionary road to power. Thus, in unaccountably
wishing to win independence from the state Irish Catholics appeared to
be most 'alien' to English eyes.

Class and ethnicity

The weaknesses inherent in the class-bound conception of working-class
culture have been exposed by many critics over the last decade. There is
now an emerging consensus that the working class was not as socially or
politically homogeneous as was previously supposed. Few historians now
place all their interpretative weight behind class. Other forms of identity
of equal or greater influence have been given credence, including those
such as gender, age, region and occupation. If it was not felled over-
night, the 'traditional' working class has suffered death by a thousand

qualifications.[36] The contemporary impact of black immigration has slowly brought the realization that workers can possess a form of class awareness – for example, they may belong to a trade union and vote Labour – and still owe some form of allegiance to their own ethnic culture. In this pluralist model of social consciousness ethnicity has been given a more important role. Perceptions of the place of Irish Catholic immigrants have benefited from this reorientation of focus. As Raphael Samuel has written, 'the Irish can now be seen as one of those minority cultures of which (it could be argued) the "majority" culture of modern Britain is composed.'[37] Now, greater regard is given to the 'peculiarities' of Irish Catholic identity by historians no longer impatient to consign them to a culturally undifferentiated working class.

This new approach begs an important question: what exactly *was* the place of Irish Catholics within the English working class? Increasing attention has been focused upon this difficult matter. As has been suggested, their distinctive experience has often been subsumed within a class-based narrative. However, in reacting against this view it would be incorrect to rush to the other extreme and suggest that, instead, they lived a life apart, isolated from the rest of the working class. This was not the case, because Irish immigrants were not neatly slotted into a vacant space within the working class and kept there by impenetrable boundaries. Immigration was a much more organic, dialectical process, which involved the adaptation of both immigrant and indigenous peoples. The experience of Irish Catholics was partly structured by the culture in which they found a place and that culture was, in turn, transformed by their presence.

Lynn Lees has postulated the existence of a separate 'Catholic workers' culture' in London before 1914, which embraced both the Irish-born and their third- and fourth-generation descendants. At the centre of this subculture was the Catholic Church, membership of which delineated the Irish from the rest of the working class. Although operating at some distance from the general run of working-class existence, this Irish Catholic style of life nevertheless shared many of the indigenous culture's characteristics and institutions. Although mechanistic and functionalist in its implications, Lees's notion usefully undermines the idea that Irish Catholics were unproblematically integrated within a homogeneous working class. Moreover, it allows for the coexistence of cultural attributes, which made them different from and similar to the other workers. Ironically, however, it implicitly assumes the existence of a homogeneous culture for the remainder of the working class. More importantly, it also presumes that the Irish Catholic sub-culture was itself homogeneous, incorporating an all-encompassing Irishness, which uniformly affected each and every member. Therefore, although abandoning one model of a single, dominant, monolithic class culture Lees draws a picture of a series of smaller, but equally homogeneous and static, ethnic cultures. Having been liberated from the box marked 'class', Irish Catholics have been thrown into one marked 'ethnicity'.[38]

One of the advantages of Lees's work is that it grants proper status to the role played by the Catholic Church, something largely passed over by labour historians. Others have credited the Church with preventing the formation of a common platform between Irish and English workers under Chartism, thus further undermining the idea that the movement could have ameliorated ethnic differences.[39] Some have even gone so far as to describe the Church as the 'primary social institution, which fostered the growth of a community identity [and] gave the immigrant Irish a valuable sense of constancy and continuity.'[40] The Church certainly hoped to separate adherents from the rest of society. As will be seen in later chapters, although the Church enjoyed a problematic relationship with its Irish adherents it certainly left its mark upon most of their lives. This contrasts starkly with the anglicized Jewish elite, which sought to encourage Russian and Polish co-religionists to assimilate into local society as quickly as possible.[41]

The so-called 'problem' with Irish Catholic immigrants is that they neither wanted full assimilation nor complete separation from English society. For them class and ethnicity formed a continuum, not mutually exclusive poles of attraction. They have consequently been described as being a 'peculiar minority' occupying a 'curious middle place' in society.[42] That they held an ambiguous position is impossible to deny; however, it is difficult to find an immigrant group that did not do likewise. The Jewish population of late nineteenth-century Manchester demonstrated a similar two-facedness: their experience was the result of a complex interweaving of ethnic and class influences. In that context, feelings of ethnicity were not competitive, but often complementary, with those sentiments evident in wider society, the most important of which was class.[43] Immigrants appear peculiar only when a vain attempt is made to force them into certain categories into which they do not want to go. Thus, Irish Catholics straddle class and ethnic feeling, much to the annoyance of those who wish they had chosen one or the other. An appreciation of the individual, uneven nature of 'acculturation' is required to fully understand the immigrant experience.[44]

Until relatively recently, however, most accounts that took as their principal focus the Irish in England have emphasized the extent to which they lived a life apart from the rest of society. These have echoed the Irish Nationalist Hugh Heinrick's description of Irish immigrants in 1872 as, 'a nation within a nation . . . a foreign and peculiar element resident among a people different in habits, tastes, religion and sentiment.'[45] Of late, however, there has been a subtle change in emphasis. A picture is now emerging of an Irish population alienated, demoralized, dispersed, transient, politically disorganized and barely interested in Catholicism. Not living in ghettos, they lacked the basic constitutive elements that would have allowed them to build a distinct ethnic culture. Nevertheless, they retained a sense of difference that prevented their complete assimilation into English society. Fatally caught between these two imperatives, the Irish were unable to build a community worthy of the name.[46] Such an emphasis usefully qualifies those earlier studies, which went too far in accepting the self-serving claims of Nationalists that the Irish in England had become a, 'mighty power that statesmen must reckon with, permeating, in various ways, the religious, social, and political life of Britain.'[47]

This new view is clearly influenced by the failure of Irish immigrants to emulate their peers in the United States.[48] Compared to their more numerous compatriots across the Atlantic, the Irish in England do indeed appear to have been lacking in a number of important respects; in comparison with them, the Irish in England do not seem to have created a viable culture. However, relative truth should never be confused with absolute truth. The extent to which Irish Americans established a secure and respected place within their adopted society has been exaggerated. Despite capturing the Catholic Church and establishing an important local political voice, most Irish remained poor workers and their rise up the social ladder was slow. Moreover, the success they did achieve says more about the nature of the United States than it does about the Irish themselves. In any case, there remain important unanswered questions about the extent to which immigrants retained a separate identity or were 'Americanized', and whether success in politics and the Catholic Church marked their social alienation or integration.[49]

None the less, there is no real doubt that the Irish in America, by all forms of criteria, were more successful than those in England. Nor can it be denied that they constructed more impressive institutional embodiments of their identity. However, a number of structural factors are held in common by both immigrant groups: as will become clear in Chapter 4, the role of the Catholic Church in England and the United States, on the parish level, was very similar. Although the experience of the American Irish was different from that of those in England there is no reason why this should lead us to denigrate the achievements of the latter. In its zeal to break new ground, the new orthodoxy goes too far, so far in fact that the Irish in England are perilously close to disappearing in a cloud of green smoke, having exploded into thousands of tiny atoms randomly cast about society. Such an approach is patronizing, for it casts immigrants in the role of resourceless, passive victims. It is also in danger of losing sight of the very real organizing principles that articulated the immigrant identity.

An 'awkward' minority

There is much evidence to suggest that the Irish Catholic immigrant identity was an extremely malleable entity, defined by ambiguity and equivocation, with vague boundaries and a variable character. However, this should not lead us to suppose that it did not exist or, more to the point, that competing versions of Irishness and Catholicism could not stand side-by-side. It is, in fact, highly problematic to talk of the immigrant 'identity' and 'experience' in the singular, for this implies a cultural uniformity that did not prevail. Irish Catholics were as divided as any other group and such divisions gave rise to different types of experience and discrete forms of identity.

The Irish seem to have been rather less obviously divided along class lines than some other immigrant communities. In Leeds it was a common complaint that Jewish landlords and masters exploited Jewish workers and tenants regardless of their shared religion.[50] The Irish middle class – such as it was – was involved in the professions and the service sector rather than production. If Irish exploited Irish it was because they were pub landlords and shopkeepers selling watered-down beer and adulterated food. Moreover, many Irish workers were employed by municipal government not by individuals, or found jobs in English middle-class households. There was little direct face-to-face confrontation between Irish people at the point of production. Although class conflict was not common, class differences still existed: the National University of Ireland Dining Club, formed in London in 1928, was as much a socially exclusive body as those English clubs it sought to emulate.[51] As will become clear later, Irish men and women also had different experiences and were expected to conform to different role models.

If the Irish Catholic identity was internally differentiated, the border between Irish Catholics and the rest of society was permeable. This was particularly evident in the case of intermarriage between Irish and English or Catholic and Protestant. One extreme example will suffice to establish this point: John Tomlinson was a devout Catholic who lived in a working-class Manchester parish where Irish adherents had a strong voice. Yet, his paternal grandfather was born a Protestant, whose marriage to a Catholic did not prevent their children being raised Protestants. Despite this, John's father, who followed his parents' example and married a Catholic, brought John up as a Catholic. To confuse matters still further, Tomlinson's father eventually converted to Catholicism, as did – on the verge of death – his grandfather.[52] Although intermarriage was relatively uncommon it would obviously have meant that the offspring of such unions would have had a potentially split identity. This was especially the case in the much larger number of those generations raised in Irish families but born in England.

By the late nineteenth century many of those considered to be Irish had been born in England of Irish parents. In recognition of this, those who calculated the size of England's Irish population during the later decades of the nineteenth century usually doubled the number of Irish-born. American evidence suggests that this rule of thumb was probably accurate.[53] The proportion may even have been higher, for some third- and even fourth-generation Irish still felt their national origins to be important. As time went on, immigration declined but Irish immigrants and their descendants continued to marry and produce children. Thus, those actually born in Ireland comprised a diminishing part of the 'Irish' population. By 1900 the 'culturally Irish' had become an ever-growing majority within the

Irish Catholic population. The Nationalist John Denvir suggested that, 'generally the children and grandchildren of Irish-born parents consider themselves just as much Irish as those born on "the old sod" itself.'[54] Although matters were by no means so simple, due to the proximity of Ireland, the prominence of the Irish issue in English politics, the nature of residence and the attempts of the Catholic Church to isolate adherents it seems that most remained, mentally at least, within the Irish Catholic milieu.

The family was the most important means of transmitting an appreciation of their national heritage to the English-born. Migration had made family life an important source of identity, at least for those mid-century migrants and their children. One contemporary suggested that after an evening meal conversation in such homes inevitably turned to memories of the homeland and discussions of the latest news.[55] Born in Newcastle in 1856, future Labour MP James Sexton's maternal grandmother ensured that he was acutely familiar with stories of the suppression of the Irish rebellion of 1798. He vividly recalled tales, 'of men being hanged, drawn and quartered [and] of an ancestor, hanged from the shafts of his own cart'. Manchester-born Bart Kennedy summarized his Irish mother's thoughts about her son:

> In time he would grow up and become a fine, big Irishman. He was born in England, but that would never make him an Englishman! She wanted him always to remain an Irishman.

South Salford's future Labour MP Joe Toole wrote only half in jest when he suggested that, 'Love of Ireland is, of course, natural to me; apart from that, my Irish grandparents insisted upon it.'[56] Family links between Ireland and England were retained so that children born of Irish mothers might spend their summer holidays in Ireland or, during a parental illness, be sent to Ireland to be cared for by a grandparent. During the Second World War one girl spent a year in her mother's village as an alternative to evacuation.[57] Moreover, living in an Irish district might also have left its own mark. George Brown was born in Lambeth in 1914 to a second-generation Irish father and a Scottish mother. As a child he considered himself Irish, in part, because of the nationality of a large number of his neighbours. Dan McCabe, Liberal councillor for Manchester's St Michael's ward between 1892 and 1919 was born in Stockport and raised in Ancoats yet spoke with an Irish accent.[58]

However, the cultural Irish reacted in a number of contrasting ways to their national background. J.R. Clynes, a Manchester Labour MP between 1906 and 1945, was born in Oldham of Irish parents and claimed to be 'half Irish and wholly Lancastrian.' However, in office he did not seem any more exercized by Irish issues than his English colleagues.[59] Moreover, relations between the culturally Irish and Irish-born were not always amicable. In 1910 a member of a Manchester branch of the United Irish League complained that he was mocked on account of his lack of an Irish accent. Perhaps this response was understandable given that he described the Irish brogue as sounding like, 'spitting pieces of bog turf'.[60] It was a common experience for Irish children to feel ashamed of their accent and culture because of the ridicule it provoked from English friends. As a result, some tried to sound like their peers and others mocked Irish national traditions.[61] Yet, the lack of an accent did not necessarily mean that an individual had lost their sense of Irishness. The author Jack London met a young woman who expressed herself in a Cockney manner, at times expostulating phrases such as 'Lord, lumme' and 'Gawd blimey'. Yet, when asked, she defiantly described herself as Irish.[62] In some cases those of Irish descent asserted national feeling much more aggressively than did the Irish-born themselves. During a wake to mark his grandfather's death, Pat O'Mara's aunt asked her mother:

> 'Would you like to see Ireland again before you go mother?'
> 'No,' scowled my grandmother, 'I remember nothin' in it but poverty! . . . Ireland! Don't talk to me about Ireland. Your father's an Irishman – see what he done! God have mercy on his soul!'
> Then Lonnigan, wiping his beer from his mustache, said, 'Mrs Molloy, Ireland would be all right if she was left alone. It's England . . .'
> 'What do you know about Ireland – born in Manchester as ye was!'
> 'That's all right Mrs Molloy, but I'm an Irishman just the same!'
> 'Arra g'wane! Shut your bloody mouth Joe Lonnigan, don't argue with me now!'[63]

There were also divisions between the Irish-born. Emigrant families having painfully established for themselves an accepted place in society, sometimes resented new arrivals because their ignorance of English urban ways reflected badly upon themselves.[64]

Irishness, like all forms of national identity, was a contested concept. Moreover, those who lived outside Ireland were thought to be wholly distinct from, and inferior to, those who remained. As one English observer wrote in 1892:

> I have always found that the more primitive and less civilised Irish were the best-mannered. The Irish who have been much in England or America are generally ill-mannered, often rude and offensive.[65]

This was not just an English opinion: it was a commonplace among Irish and Catholic commentators. Heinrick considered that residence in England, 'degrades our manhood, and destroys the purity of our womanhood' as it left them vulnerable to the English vice of drink. It was a 1950s immigrant who thought the way some Irish women adopted English idioms 'demeaning'. Second generation Irish Catholics were viewed as even more depraved than their emigrant parents. Thus, Irishness and Englishness were deemed mutually exclusive: the more immigrants conformed to the ways of dominant culture the less 'Irish' they supposedly became. The old Fenian John Devoy felt that, because they had joined trade unions and Liberal clubs, his compatriots had become less 'Irish'.[66] Such attitudes were based on the notion that a certain set of ideas and actions constituted national identity: there was a golden mean from which emigrants somehow deviated.

The Irish in England were, then, considered to be neither completely Irish nor wholly English. They possessed a third cultural identity that fell, awkwardly, somewhere between the two. One girl born of Irish parents in Manchester discovered, when she visited Ireland she was teased for sounding English. Yet, in Manchester she was mocked for her Irish lilt. Another immigrant discovered that despite her poverty in London she was considered affluent in Cork.[67] The failure of the Gaelic 'revival' in Manchester illustrates the extent to which the Irish in England had developed an intermediate way of life. Enthusiasm for things Gaelic began in Ireland during the 1890s with the formation of the Gaelic League and the Gaelic Athletic Association. Their shared aim was to reject expressions of Englishness and replace them with allegedly 'pure' Irish ways. Branches of both organizations were founded in England some time thereafter, in London in 1895 and in Manchester five years later.[68] Although the English Catholic Hierarchy did not encourage such initiatives the movement won enthusiastic support from many Irish priests working in the city.[69] During the early 1900s a few parishes offered Gaelic evening lessons and held occasional services in the language. One priest working in St Patrick's parish even talked of the 'necessity of the Gaelic League'.[70] The *Manchester Catholic Herald* applauded these initiatives and encouraged those 'thousands' in the city who could speak the language to take an interest. Gaelic, in fact, was spoken in a number of public places where the Irish gathered: as late as the 1930s the 'Shamrock' pub reverberated to the sound of it.[71] Thus, there was some reason to hope for success.

However, despite these advantages, the movement was met by a wall of apathy: most immigrants considered themselves no less Irish for their ignorance of Gaelic syntax. Classes were under-subscribed and ran for only a short time; Gaelic services were also poorly attended.[72] Hurling and Gaelic football found little support: there were only two clubs in Manchester before 1914. All five branches of the Gaelic League established in the city were feeble.[73] As a result, the movement turned in upon itself. Activists accused their fellow immigrants as having been corrupted by English ways – they were considered worthless members of the Irish nation. This increasing disenchantment can be seen in the rules of the League's Hulme branch, which in 1906 resolved that those who could not pass a simple Gaelic exam would not be allowed to administer its affairs. A few months later it was decided that a similar test would be required of those who simply wanted to join. Such unwelcoming attitudes were ultimately self-defeating.[74] Those who pursued 'English' ways were attacked. The Church was criticized for allowing children to play English sports such as football and cricket at school. It was even suggested that those who went to the cinema would eventually cease to be 'really Irish'.

In other words, those active in the movement, were completely hostile to each and every aspect of English society. One described Manchester as, 'this woe-begone town to which destiny has chained me – temporarily at least.'[75] Unfortunately for such Gaelic enthusiasts, many of their compatriots sought to establish a more permanent place for themselves.

There was a brief moment after the 1916 Dublin Rising when interest in Gaelic and hurling became more general, but this soon fell away after the creation of the Free State. By the 1930s there was only one small League branch in Manchester and those few clubs devoted to hurling and football were found in middle-class rather than working-class districts.[76] In fact, interest in Gaelic culture had always been the preserve of the Irish middle class. In London and Leicester during the early 1900s the movement appealed only to the literary classes, those who derived their livings from at least menial white collar occupations. They were considered quixotic by most of their fellows as a consequence of their interests.[77] The dominant attitude of most Irish immigrants was expressed in an attack on 'Hibernomaniacs' in the *London Catholic Herald* in 1924. Such people were criticized because they, 'would immolate themselves in the farcical martyrdom of a racial Coventry.' This did not mean that the Irish no longer took pride in their national origin. However, they did not allow any obsession with that identity from preventing them grasping 'all the comfort and prizes and advancement' in the society in which they now lived.[78]

The view taken in this study, in line with some of those who have investigated the lives of Jewish immigrants, is that Irish Catholics were subject to both ethnic and class influences.[79] That this produced what, from the outside, appeared a confusing, incoherent cultural amalgam is due to the preconceptions of the observer and not the culture itself. By standing between a number of poles of attraction, working-class Irish Catholic culture was hardly unique. No culture has been its own product; every way of life is open to competing influences and subject to change. Yet, only Irish Catholics stand accused of being culturally deprived. Suspected in England of being too Irish, and criticized in Ireland because they were not Irish enough, Irish Catholics in England were an almost universally denigrated group. Not as successful as their American cousins, considered too similar to the English majority and often with more than one eye on events in Ireland, they are, incorrectly, seen as failing to constitute for themselves a separate and viable way of life. The following chapters will hopefully make the case for the rejection of such a view.

two

Social context

Reluctant immigrants

Each of the various ways of interpreting the Irish Catholic experience, described in the last chapter, has some grounding in reality. Historians of different persuasions can point to particular examples that support their general analysis: no view is wholly fallacious. This is largely due to the heterogeneous nature of the Irish Catholic experience, and it is this diversity that historians are now concerned to explore further.[1] However, such an appreciation is but a beginning and not an end: whilst cultural difference was obviously significant, it was nevertheless set within overarching patterns and dictated by a common set of circumstances. In its complex detail, each life is unique, but many of the forces that shape individual experience may, in fact, be broadly the same. From this perspective, this chapter will describe the social context in which Irish Catholics found themselves, in England in general, and Manchester in particular. It would be inadequate to assert that Irish Catholics in Manchester were wholly typical of all those who settled in England. Therefore, the prime concern will be to suggest the extent to which Irish Catholics in Manchester differed from counterparts who lived elsewhere. It will be suggested that Manchester found more echoes in the wider Irish Catholic experience than did Liverpool, which, until recently, was mistakenly discussed as if it was the archetypal Irish Catholic city.

Irish Catholic immigration is popularly associated with the great Famine influx of the mid-nineteenth century. However, the Irish were already well-established in English urban society by 1800, especially in ports such as Liverpool, Bristol and London. Nevertheless, it was only after the Industrial Revolution that immigration from Ireland reached truly significant levels. The Irish were not unique in this, for they formed but part of a general movement of agricultural workers into England's towns and cities during this period.[2] The nineteenth century marked a fundamental shift from economic activity based on the land to that of capital. Irish society, being predominantly rural was especially vulnerable to these developments. This was especially so given its subordinate relationship to the English industrial giant, whose government was reluctant to encourage Ireland to build its own competitive industries. The elimination of protective tariffs, which followed the Union in 1800, meant that any nascent industrial activity was swept aside by rampant English capitalism. In particular, the Union caused the collapse of Ireland's textile industry. The economics of the Union meant that Ireland was only able to develop as a market for English goods and as a source of cheap agricultural produce for English towns. Only in Ulster did industry develop, and then as a mere adjunct to the hegemonic English economy.

Some of the earliest Irish immigrants were skilled handloom weavers attracted to Lancashire during the 1790s. At this time handloom weavers were an affluent, elite group within the expanding cotton industry and their skills were in short supply. By the 1820s, however, their position had been disastrously reversed after the power loom had made these skills redundant. In any case, the vast majority of those who arrived in England before the 1840s did so more for negative than for positive reasons. They were responding, first, to the endemic crisis in Irish agriculture and only secondly to the prospect of better paid jobs in buoyant industries. They inevitably settled in those places where jobs were most available. Thus, by 1851 just over 40 per cent of Irish immigrants residing in England and Wales settled in Lancashire and Cheshire, counties at the cutting edge of economic expansion.[3]

Table 2.1 demonstrates that, as early as 1841, 289,404 people of Irish birth lived in England and Wales. Ten years later this population had risen by nearly 80 per cent. This increase was principally due to the collapse of Irish agriculture, the awful apogee of which came during the potato failure of 1846–7. The Famine was followed by an uninterrupted exodus until the early 1930s, when the world depression brought it to a temporary halt. However, emigration soon resumed in the mid-1930s and continued until Ireland eventually began to industrialize during the late 1960s and early 1970s. The zenith of emigration occurred in the 1880s, when as many as two-thirds of those born in Ireland actually lived elsewhere. Even as late as 1926 nearly one-third of native-born Irish resided in another country.[4] The reasons for emigration remained consistent with the earlier period: poverty remained endemic in the Irish countryside while in Dublin's tenements matters were perhaps even worse. The necessity for leaving Ireland might have become less acute by the 1880s – few emigrants actually faced

Table 2.1 Irish-born in England and Wales in relation to total population, 1841–1931

Date	Number of Irish-born	Per cent change	Per cent of population
1841	289,404	–	1.8
1851	519,959	+79.7	2.9
1861	601,634	+15.7	3.0
1871	566,540	– 5.8	2.5
1881	562,374	– 0.7	2.2
1891	458,315	–18.5	1.6
1901	426,565	– 6.9	1.3
1911	375,325	–12.0	1.0
1921	364,747	– 2.8	1.0
1931	381,089	+ 4.5	0.9

Source: *Census of England and Wales*, 1841–1931.

starvation if they remained at home – but it was no less insistent. The Irish still left their homeland, with reluctance, for purely economic reasons.[5] The post-famine exodus was, in the main, composed of rural workers and caused by the reconstruction of Irish agriculture, from labour-intensive subsistence arable production to capital-intensive pasture farming. There were few choices for potential emigrants. For most, the alternative was to remain, only to eke out a miserable living as a landless, under-employed labourer. Indeed, without this enforced emigration Ireland's agricultural economy might well have completely collapsed. Even so, despite depopulation, the Irish harvest remained vulnerable to failure, such as that which occurred in 1878, and this encouraged further emigration. Moreover, exiles helped those who remained: remittances, particularly from the United States, were of vital importance to relatives left in the old country.[6] Thus, emigration and the Irish economy were familiar, but miserable, bedfellows.

The vast majority of those who left Ireland made for the United States. Official figures suggest that an average of 89 per cent crossed the Atlantic during the period 1891–1900, 4 per cent left for the Dominions and only 6 per cent travelled to Britain.[7] The United States was generally the preferred choice of the richer emigrants, but only because they were the ones who could afford the fare. The self-proclaimed land of the free was a much more attractive proposition than England, considered to be the land of the oppressor.[8] However, the proportion of those who settled in England, Scotland and Wales has probably been under-estimated: in reality, such emigrants might have accounted for as many as one in four of those who left Ireland between 1852 and 1911.[9] In contrast, there is little doubt that during the 1920s and 1930s Britain replaced the United States as the principal destination for emigrants. An average of 94 per cent of those who left the Free State between 1931 and 1937 went to Britain. This increase was mainly due to the introduction of quotas by the United States, which, after 1918, was gripped by fears about the repercussions of continued uncontrolled immigration. Being subjects of the British Crown, those living in the Free State were still able to enter the country freely. Thus, despite the inter-war recession, the number of Irish immigrants to England rose for the first time in 60 years.[10] The imposition of American limitations only partly explains the greater willingness of emigrants to settle in England, for the Irish never filled their quota. It has been suggested that after the creation of the Free State they looked on England in a new and positive light. However, there were other considerations: although the English economy was depressed for most of the inter-war period it did not suffer the cataclysm endured by America after the Wall Street Crash. Given the bloody manner in which independence was achieved, and the continued hostility to Irish immigrants in the country, it is unlikely that England was attractive for other than economic reasons. Instead, it may well have been that, with independence newly-won, Irish workers were more reluctant to travel thousands of miles from their homeland.[11]

England was the easiest and cheapest of possible destinations; residence did not entail a complete break with the old country. Thus, those who settled there were among the poorest, least willing and most uncommitted of those who left Ireland. They were also among the most 'urbanized' of Irish, so far as that word had much meaning in Ireland: the majority of immigrants after 1870 came from the north-east and the southern and eastern coast. These were parts of Ireland most economically integrated into northern England and southern Scotland, where most nineteenth-century emigrants settled. Thus, Irish immigrants shared many of the characteristics of English rural migrants who also settled in expanding industrial towns and cities. However, with entry into the United States increasingly circumscribed after 1918 the proportion of more completely rural immigrants to England would inevitably have increased.[12] The inter-war period also saw a general move away from the economically depressed parts of England, principally Lancashire, towards the expanding midlands cities of Coventry and Birmingham, as well as London. The impact of the new pattern of immigration was especially noticeable in Scotland, which had always attracted proportionately more Irish than England. In 1937 there was a net flow of population from Scotland to the Free State. These processes continued apace after 1945.[13]

Despite the geographic and cultural proximity of England to Ireland the distress caused by emigration should not be under-estimated. By no means all were unhappy to leave home, some saw England as a land of opportunity; however, it would be wrong to think such people as typical. One mother declared she would rather bury her daughter than let her go to England. However, the inevitable had to be accepted, albeit with reluctance.[14] For those raised in small, isolated villages England was in almost every sense a foreign country. To such people, the world beyond the nearest mountain might have been alien territory: how much worse that country as many as three days journey 'over the water'? Emigrants still had to endure shocks, new experiences and overcome a sense of loss. Brought up in Mayo and uprooted to Bolton in 1914, the young Bill Naughton was struck by the incessant noise of industrial England, its peculiar smells and the incomprehensible speech of the natives; to him, even the air felt strange. He eventually overcame these feelings of alienation. In contrast, his father was never reconciled to the new society and hated being a miner. To compensate, he determinedly denigrated all things English, deeming them inferior to their Irish counterparts. As Naughton concluded:

> There was a feeling that as a family we had not emigrated but had been transported, and we were in bondage, living in a harsh degraded life, alien in every way to our natures.[15]

Other immigrants from further afield might have suffered more traumas, but the Irish were still struck by the fact that England was a different country which threatened the Irish character. Patrick MacGill has his heroine Nora Ryan declare on her death-bed:

> Never let yer own sisters go to the strange country Dermod, never let them go to the potato squad, for it's the place that is evil for a girl like me that hasn't much sense . . .[16]

There were other, less dramatic surprises in store for new arrivals. When T.P. O'Connor first came to London in 1870 he was struck by the way that poor natives spoke. In Ireland he associated an English accent with the upper classes; to hear London's poor speak in the same manner seemed extremely odd.[17]

Although never pleasant to cross on a cattle boat, the relative ease with which Irish workers could travel to England allowed them to move freely between the two countries. The most destitute of Irish were able to do this, even if it meant stowing away on a small cargo boat.[18] The seasonal labourer was the most striking indication of this process: although described as 'the Pariah of his race' these workers were important figures in both the Irish and English rural economies. In Oxfordshire Irish labourers were, 'as much part of the harvest scene as the corn itself.' These were principally men who tended a small piece of land in the spring and autumn; they came to England during the summer to earn money to subsidize this holding. Whilst this enabled families, especially in Mayo, to live on a very modest acreage it also provided English farmers with labour that only appeared when it was needed most. By no means all seasonal labourers fitted this pattern; some were young sons or daughters whose parents needed another income. For them, work in England was very much like the temporary work they had undertaken within Ireland. It also had the function of an apprenticeship, preparing those who would later settle in

England on a more permanent basis. In 1880 there were as many as 30,000 seasonal workers, upon whom relied a further 100,000 dependants. However, with the mechanization of rural production, demand for their labour declined. Even so, there were still over 10,000 such workers employed during harvests thirty years later.[19]

Whilst some moved between Ireland and England on an annual basis, others worked in England for many years but ended their days back in their homeland. This seems to have been the original ambition of a large number of emigrants, although few ever appear to have realized it. In fact, some immigrant lives were dominated by the desire to accumulate as much money as possible to buy a small farm and return home. This fortunate minority was probably most numerous among those affluent enough to save money, such as the Manchester grocer who retired to Killarney to run a hotel. One expression of the emigrant's continued attachment to home was the custom of sending money back to relatives. Single men were expected to dispatch a weekly amount and supplement this with an especially large remittance at Christmas. By no means all lived up to expectations, however, and came to resent such an imposition despite the consequent guilt.[20] Other emigrants used England as a temporary stopping-off point to make some money before they settled more permanently elsewhere, usually the United States. This seems to have particularly affected Manchester's Irish Nationalist movement, whose members were mainly drawn from skilled workers and the lower-middle class. After twelve years residence, the president of Hulme's Father Sheehy United Irish League branch left to seek his fortune in South Africa; a few years earlier the secretary of another city branch had departed for the United States. At least one Irish-born electrician left his family in Manchester whilst he searched for work in the United States. He returned to the city only after failing to find anything suitable.[21] Thus, England was an imperfect third choice: if it had been possible, emigrants would have preferred to have remained in Ireland. Given the near-inevitability of emigration, they would rather have settled in the United States than England.

Apart from religion, nationality and lack of skill, immigrants differed in other ways from the rest of English society. Youth was one of their defining characteristics: the Famine influx had seen the Irish come over as members of family units, but after the 1860s the typical emigrant was the lone young adult. The 1871 census indicated that 56 per cent of Irish-born men and 48 per cent of women in Manchester's Angel Meadow were between twenty and forty-four years old. This was also a well-established pattern in the United States.[22] However, although immigrants were young when they left Ireland, because of the decline in immigration up to the 1930s, England's Irish-born were as a whole much older than the rest of the population. This was primarily due to the relative absence of Irish-born children. In 1911, only 8.7 per cent of Irish-born living in Manchester were under twenty, compared to 51.9 per cent of those born in Manchester. Above the age of twenty-five the Irish-born were increasingly over-represented, so that 14.5 per cent of Irish-born were sixty-five and over compared to only 1.8 per cent of Manchester-born. Despite this predominance, immigrants were associated with certain 'problems' connected with poor working-class youths, such as alcohol abuse, violence, illegitimacy and prostitution. After the 1880s, women were predominant: by 1931 they accounted for 53.3 per cent of immigrants. There are a number of reasons for this: lack of demand for their labour in the Irish countryside; their exclusion from inheriting land; the custom of large dowries and, in the 1930s, an official prohibition on women working in all but the lowliest jobs. Moreover, as the English economy shifted from heavy to light industry and services female labour was increasingly in demand.[23]

Although immigration was accomplished individually, it was common for immigrants to settle in places where friends and family had already established a presence. The main reason for this pattern of settlement was that their first jobs in England were often found by such acquaintances. One gang laying sewers in Manchester in 1919 was almost entirely composed of men from Irish villages within a five mile radius, from where the contractor also originated. Even after 1918 few immigrants used the formal mechanisms of locating work, such as employment exchanges.[24] The jobs they took were principally those that required few skills and were consequently badly paid. Many young Irish women were employed as domestic servants or performed other menial tasks. These were jobs that all but the poorest English women refused; few women raised in industrial towns were willing to lose their independence and status by taking such low-paid posts. Like others from similar rural backgrounds elsewhere in the British Isles, young Irish women were attracted to domestic service and hotel work because there was usually provision to live-in.[25] Sometimes, however, domestic service left employees open to interference if they wanted to practise their Catholic faith. This was especially the case in Nonconformist households, where servants were expected to participate in family prayers and were prevented from attending Sunday mass. Perhaps as a consequence, a high proportion of Irish domestic servants in Manchester worked for Jewish households, where relations seem to have been very amicable.[26] Those women who did not enter service performed similar lowly tasks. A large number of the maids in Salford's Ladywell Sanatorium were Irish. Because this work carried the danger of contracting one or other of the infectious diseases treated in the institution, staff were actually required to live-in.[27]

Young Irish men often found it difficult to find work other than that involving general labouring, for they had few skills that were at a premium in an industrial town. The Irish were not alone in this: all male rural workers faced similar problems, they all possessed nothing but physical strength and a willingness to work hard. However, country men enjoyed an advantage over unskilled workers raised in the big cities, for even in the 1890s they were reputed to be by far the strongest. If some considered them lazy, by no means all did so and it seems that Irish workers still enjoyed an enviable stature – if only with regard to arduous physical labour:

> . . . Irishmen, whether in England or the Colonies, are among the most hard-working members of the community. Whether as professional men, or labourers in docks, shipyards or ironworks, Irishmen are among the most useful people in England and could be ill spared. Poor though the 'harvestman' is, he is rarely a 'cadger' and many an English harvest would rot on the ground but for his active and willing hands.

The other side of this reputation was the assertion that they were incapable of sustained and regular employment.[28] A few were fortunate enough to be able to exploit knowledge acquired in the country. Before he became a market porter one Irish man traded in horses and donkeys at Manchester's Great Ancoats Street horse market.[29] Most jobs performed by male emigrants did not provide board. As a consequence they lived in lodging houses, many of which seemed to have an exclusively Irish clientele, few of which possessed a salubrious reputation. Such transients could claim, as did Jim Larkin in 1913, that:

> there was not a roadway between Manchester and London that he had not tramped nor a hedge under which he had not slept as a boy. He had hungered in Manchester, slept in railway trucks there . . .[30]

However, after the first few months or years most settled more permanently into a district, married and raised children, although by no means all did so. Some clearly relished life on the road, with its lodging house fights, hard work and even harder drinking. Having freed themselves from the claustrophobic obligations of Irish village life they had no desire to return. Such figures were lionized by Patrick MacGill through his depiction of the character Moleskin Joe. His favourite saying, 'There's a good time comin', though we never live to see it', was underpinned by the assumption that it definitely would never come for the likes of him. Freedom had its price.[31]

Although Irish immigrants were popularly associated with large families and overcrowding it seems that this was more myth than reality. Although pronounced in the immediate wake of the Famine influx, by the 1870s differences in English and Irish household size were marginal. Moreover, although statistical evidence is scanty, as family size declined among the population as a whole in the early twentieth century, Catholic families followed suit, albeit at a slower pace. Certainly, Catholics were subject to much greater public pressure from their Church on the subject of birth control. However, among working-class men and women in general ignorance and distaste for contraception was widespread, particularly among the unskilled. A Mass-Observation survey conducted in the 1940s even suggested that with three children the average Catholic family was the same size as its Anglican counterpart.[32]

Places of settlement

If emigrants in the diaspora shared broadly similar characteristics, being
for the most part unskilled rural workers, their eventual places of settlement were also analogous. In England, the United States and, to a lesser
extent, Australia, they were generally urban and industrial. However,
superficial similarities between places of settlement masked numerous differences of culture, politics and occupational structure. Even in England,
each town, city or district where immigrants established a place had its
own unique character. The very size of an immigrant population created
a different kind of experience: a large community might provoke more
hostility but it would also promote the construction of a more coherent
set of ethnic institutions, which would protect immigrants from its full
impact. Liverpool, home to over 45,000 Irish-born in 1901, stood at one
extreme; the 375 Irish residents in the small market town of Stafford were
at the other;[33] Manchester lay somewhere in between.

Manchester was a large city, which experienced a substantial early Irish
presence that slowly diminished in size after 1861. It was second only to
Liverpool in its proportion of Irish-born; with 28,194 Irish in 1901 it had
the third largest Irish population after London (60,022) and Liverpool. As
in most other big cities, Irish Catholics in Manchester had a politically
distinct voice, but were unable to operate in the independent manner
they did in Liverpool. Moreover, the city's working class was not as overtly
sectarian as it was in Liverpool, although ethnic differences did periodically assert themselves in an open and violent manner. Liverpool was
unique in the severe nature of the divide between indigenous Protestant
workers and those of Irish Catholic extraction. It was such that a 'no-man's
land' was said to separate the two communities.[34] This was not just because
Liverpool had considerably more Irish Catholic residents than elsewhere,
but also because it was home to an exceptionally vocal Orange movement.
Salford's Joe Toole was shocked to discover the extent to which politics in
Liverpool's Everton constituency was determined by religious loyalties when
he campaigned there during the early 1920s.[35] If it was only in Glasgow
that football took on a sectarian meaning, in Liverpool folklore mistakenly
suggests that also did there. In Manchester, in contrast, the rivalry between United and City was bitter, but it was not the reflection of religious
or national differences.[36]

Manchester has been made famous by Frederick Engels's vivid description of the squalor and poverty in Little Ireland and Irish Town during
the 1840s. This has led to the suggestion that, during that decade at least,
the city's Irish were 'ghettoized'.[37] This term is meant to suggest that the
Irish were economically and socially separated from the rest of the city: in
other words, that they lived a life apart. There are other views of the
period that suggest that prior to the Famine Irish and English workers
mixed fairly easily.[38] In any case, it is unlikely that 'ghettoization' was ever

Table 2.2 Proportion of Irish electors in Manchester divisions, 1906–1910

Division	Estimate	Per cent electorate
Manchester South-west	1,000	11.7
Manchester North	1,200	11.3
Manchester North-east	1,000	10.3
Salford South	400	9.6
Manchester East	700	5.5
Manchester North-west	400	3.5
Manchester South	400	2.8

Source: P.F. Clarke, *Lancashire and the New Liberalism*, Cambridge, 1971; F.W.S. Craig, *British Parliamentary Election Results, 1885–1918*, Glasgow, 1974.

completely accomplished; doubt has even been raised about the applicability of this concept in Liverpool.[39] If Irish Catholics found themselves in a ghetto it was not due to their nationality or religion but because of their poverty. Whatever the merits of the term for the 1840s, 'ghettoization' seems a wholly inappropriate way to describe the residential and occupational distribution of Manchester's Irish Catholics by the 1880s. This does not mean that they were not found disproportionately in the poorest districts and the lowliest jobs. Irish Catholics were most numerous in the infamous slum district of Angel Meadow where, in the late 1880s, the death-rate was over twice the English average, prostitution was rife and one-third of residents were paupers. In 1871 one-third of the Meadow's residents were Irish-born; in 1900 at least half were Catholic. Moreover, certain streets were overwhelmingly, if never exclusively, Irish: in 1881 68 per cent of heads of households in Old Mount Street were Irish-born; in Back Simpson Street the proportion was 77 per cent.[40]

Even if the Meadow had been the only place of Irish Catholic settlement it was never quite a ghetto; in fact, by the 1880s, most Irish-born and their descendants lived elsewhere. They were dispersed throughout the city, although most were concentrated in north Manchester, that is in and around Ancoats and the immediately adjacent districts of Angel Meadow, Collyhurst and Miles Platting. In 1887 one-third of the city's Irish lived there.[41] This part of Manchester contained the municipal wards of New Cross and St Michael's, which were dominated by Irish Nationalists. Estimates of the number of Irish voters in particular Parliamentary divisions is, in fact, one means of establishing the distribution of the Irish population across the city.[42] These were hardly accurate and precise, but do give a rough indication of Irish numbers. Contemporaries were too credulous in accepting Nationalist claims, which over-estimated the total of those of Irish birth and descent. However, this is more than compensated for, because the pre-1914 franchise excluded all women and discriminated against Irish men. These estimates confirm that the Irish were most

Table 2.3 Proportion of Catholics in certain Manchester districts from the late nineteenth century to 1939

District	Date	Per cent Catholic
Angel Meadow	late C19th	56
Chorlton-on-Medlock	early C20th	28
Hulme	1927	36
Ancoats	1937	30
Ancoats	1938	46
Moston	1939	30

Source: M330/2/6, M100/1/7, M383/1/9/2, M45/1/14/1, Misc/847, M274/2/1/1, available Archives Department, Manchester Central Reference Library.

numerous in unskilled working-class districts (Table 2.2): the South-west division contained Hulme; the North included St Michael's ward, while Manchester North-east encompassed New Cross ward; Salford South was dominated by Ordsall and the docks. In contrast, Ardwick, the preserve of skilled engineering workers, lay in the East division; North-west was essentially Manchester's commercial district plus Cheetham Hill and the professional middle-class residential districts of Rusholme and Moss Side comprised the South division.[43]

The city's Catholics, most of whom were of Irish descent, were similarly concentrated. This residential pattern was demonstrated by surveys conducted under the auspices of the Catholic Church. Each year priests were expected to estimate the number of parishioners; in 1900 the Salford diocesan census also called on them to calculate the proportion of Catholics within their parish boundaries. As with estimates of the Irish vote, such calculations have their weaknesses. However, while priests are not famous for their statistical prowess, the resulting figures confirm the general picture. Thus, in 1890 nearly 40 per cent of all Catholics lived in seven parishes located in north Manchester. Moreover, according to the 1900 census, within this area about 20 per cent of the population was Catholic. As might have been expected, there was wide variation between parishes. Those in the poorest districts had the greatest proportion of adherents: from 50 per cent in St William's, Angel Meadow; 38 per cent in St Patrick's, Collyhurst and 12 per cent in St Edmund's, Miles Platting. The 1900 census also revealed that in the southern middle-class suburbs of Stretford, Withington and Chorlton-cum-Hardy, Catholics comprised at most 5 per cent of the total population. Many of these would have been domestic servants rather than members of the city's middle class.[44] As Table 2.3 demonstrates, this residential pattern has been further verified by religious surveys conducted by rival denominations during the period.

Manchester's Irish Catholics were not alone in being concentrated in poorer working-class districts: it was a familiar experience wherever they settled. London's East End was the reception point for most of the capital's immigrant groups, of which the Irish were the largest. In 1881 they were over-represented in the most poverty-stricken riverside areas. In the district of Whitechapel 36 per cent were Irish-born; in neighbouring St George-in-the-East the figure was 40 per cent. Yet, one mile north, in Bethnal Green, no more than 6 per cent were Irish-born and further north, in Hackney, only 3 per cent of residents had been born in Ireland.[45]

There is some evidence that as the twentieth century progressed Irish Catholics became more residentially dispersed both in Manchester and elsewhere. By 1939 less than one-quarter of Catholics lived in the seven north Manchester parishes already described. The principal reason for dispersal was not any sudden social improvement, but slum clearance: because they lived in the worst housing, so Irish Catholics were most affected. Due to the extension of the railway and spread of warehousing the population of Angel Meadow was already in decline during the 1880s. By the 1930s the Meadow had virtually ceased to exist as a residential district.[46] Thus, when Catholics started moving into Chorlton-on-Medlock in enhanced numbers during the 1920s, it indicated the collapse of the district's lower-middle class tone rather than their own rise into the ranks of clerkdom.[47]

Irish Catholics were disproportionately located in slum districts, not as a consequence of their nationality or religion but because the vast majority of immigrants were poor and unskilled labourers.[48] Most of their descendants remained in such districts because, like their mothers and fathers, they remained in the lower reaches of the proletariat. Even in the United States, hailed as a land of opportunity, Irish social mobility was modest.[49] England was an even more rigid class society. Movement beween the classes was rarely accomplished, whatever the individual's ethnic background. It was because of the virtual impossibility of progress up the social ladder, that poverty was deemed to be a natural and inevitable part of life by the unskilled working class.[50] Lees has demonstrated that, during the mid-nineteenth century, Londoners of Irish birth slowly moved up the social scale, between 1851 and 1861 such movements were 'small and statistically insignificant'. This seems to have been the case subsequently and generally across the country: any improvement was achieved within the working class. Thus, although the Irish predominantly remained manual workers the nature of that work became more permanent and better paid. In Lancashire, between 1851 and 1871, there was a general, if uneven, decline in the number of Irish-born household heads returned in the census as simply labourers. In Oldham this fell dramatically from 34.6 to 13.9 per cent; in Manchester the decline, from 16.1 to 15.1 per cent, was more modest; in Salford the proportion of labourers actually increased from 11.1 to 12.4 per cent.[51]

Writing in 1892, John Denvir suggested that the Irish in Manchester were more prosperous than counterparts in Liverpool because of the superior type of employment provided by the city's textile factories.[52] He did not appreciate that, although Manchester had fewer casual trades than Liverpool, Irish-born workers were largely excluded from secure factory work.[53] Moreover, by the late nineteenth century Manchester was no longer predominantly a cotton town. By 1900 it had been transformed into an economically diverse city, increasingly involved in services and distribution rather than production.[54] Although Manchester's remaining factory production was increasingly relocated in the city's expanding margins, the Irish were left behind in the inner-city. Thus, by the 1890s Ancoats, once the centre of the city's industrial activity assumed the character of a Klondike with all the gold mined out.[55] The Irish mainly lived in districts where insecure, unskilled trades and therefore poverty were most common. In the 1880s, 42 per cent of the population of Ancoats were unskilled labourers, 85 per cent of these were designated 'poor' or 'very poor'. During the 1930s unemployment among adult males in the district was as high as 40 per cent.[56]

The single most important employer of Irish Catholic labour was Smithfield Market, 'the great emporium of Lancashire', which dominated north Manchester. Irish Catholics were found in all levels of activity, including merchants and stall holders, but were most numerous among the lowly porters and general labourers.[57] An army of Irish street traders and hawkers also depended on the market: in 1904 17 per cent of those living in St Michael's ward derived their paltry livings from this activity.[58] The Irish had always been well-established among street traders and stall holders in the city: during the 1830s three-quarters of Manchester's stall holders were Irish-born. This association was also evident in both London and Glasgow.[59] Occupations of this sort commonly indicated poverty rather than enterprise: livings were eked out selling rabbits, fish and vegetables from street to street helped by the unpaid labour of children.[60] The street was also the place for Irish singers to make some kind of living: *Poor Robert Emmet, Southdown Militia* and *I'll take you home again Kathleen* echoed around Manchester's poorer districts.[61] Irish labour was also prominent in public service. As in many American cities, and in London, many Irish men were employed on the expanding public transport networks. These supplied low-skilled but secure jobs for which rural experience was no impediment.[62] A large proportion of Manchester's police officers were also of Irish origin. Earlier in the nineteenth century, these were predominantly Ulster Protestants; however, two inter-war Irish Catholic Labour councillors, who represent St Michael's ward, were both former police men.[63]

Most Irish Catholic Mancunians, therefore, would have disagreed with Denvir's optimism. They realized that most of their number were predominantly unskilled and many of those had experience of poverty.[64] When Dan McCabe became the first Irish Lord Mayor of Manchester, in 1913, his elevation was celebrated by Catholic and Irish alike. They used it as a measure, not so much of the extent of the community's social progress but more of the lack of it.[65] Orange lodge members gathered in Manchester's Athenaeum in 1912 were asked of Irish Catholics: 'when they

Table 2.4 Number of Catholics resident in New Bridge Street
Workhouse, 1881–1914

Date	Catholics	Total	Per cent Catholics
1881–9	1,750	3,396	52
1891–9	2,913	5,702	51
1900–9	2,042	4,339	47
1912–14	695	1,409	49
Total	7,400	14,846	50

Source: Religious Creed Registers, New Bridge Street Workhouse, Manchester Township,
available Archives Department, Manchester Central Reference Library.

come over here where [do] we find them particularly? Why, in our workhouses and gaols.'[66] There was more than a grain of truth within such
inflammatory rhetoric: Catholics *were* over-represented in Manchester's
workhouses and prisons. New Bridge Street Workhouse served Manchester Township, which covered Angel Meadow, Ancoats and Collyhurst, where
Catholics constituted no more than one-third of inhabitants. However, as
Table 2.4 clearly demonstrates they usually formed a majority of inmates.
The 1900 diocesan census also revealed that Catholics comprised 31 per
cent of those in Crumpsall Workhouse, 22 per cent in Chorlton and Salford
workhouses and one-third in Strangeways Prison. As late as January 1929,
35 per cent of children in the care of the Manchester Union were Catholic.[67] In London, Catholic children were twice as likely to be defined as
'very poor' than non-Catholics while non-Catholics were over 50 per cent
more likely to be deemed economically 'comfortable'.[68] Thus, it was in-
disputable that Catholics of Irish descent were born poor and remained
poor.

   While most Irish Catholics performed unskilled tasks and lived in low
status districts, by no means all did so: there were a number of skilled, lower-
middle-class and professional middle-class Irish.[69] However, this was a fairly
modest elite group, mainly composed of teachers, publicans and shopkeepers, most of whom served within the Irish Catholic milieu. Some
shopkeepers were not much more than permanent street traders: second-
hand clothes dealers were not exactly at the summit of their profession.
Others might have traced their economic origins back to acting as middle-
men within the Irish communities, that is lending money, running shops,
finding jobs and places to live for their compatriots.[70] Yet, by the turn of
the century a solid, prosperous shopkeeping class was emerging in Manchester, as elsewhere in Lancashire.[71] The Catenian Association was formed
in Manchester in 1908 to further commercial co-operation between
members of this developing Catholic middle class. Those who joined were
involved in business rather than the professions, particularly in printing,

textiles and construction.[72] Some were aided in their social ascent by the patronage of the Catholic Church, whose churches and schools needed to be built and maintained: the critic and novelist Anthony Burgess had two uncles who seemed to specialize in installing lavatories in presbyteries.[73]

English responses

In his account of life in central Salford during the first two decades of the twentieth century Robert Roberts firmly stated that, 'differences of race, religion, culture and status kept the English and Irish apart'. He described the character of working-class culture as essentially hierarchical, principally based on differences of income and occupation but also on that intangible quality 'status', which was not necessarily dependent upon economic circumstances. Within Roberts's part of Salford, artisans, shop-keepers and publicans stood at the top of the social pyramid for all three reasons, whilst the unskilled, in which the Irish were disproportionately represented, lay at the very bottom. Moreover, even within this lowly stratum Irish Catholics were considered to be inferior in status due to their religion, nationality and rural background.[74] Roberts's view has been confirmed in other accounts of industrial working-class life during the first decades of this century. In Oswaldtwistle, Lancashire, the Irish stood on the 'lowest possible rung of the social ladder', being 'regarded with supreme contempt as utterly beyond the pale.' The Irish who settled in the Hunslet district of Leeds during the inter-war period have been described as living a life apart, huddled together as they were in a few streets with their own school and pubs. They were seen by locals as constituting a separate caste, with its own alien culture, which involved large families, excessive drinking, public brawling and being dominated by Catholic priests. St Helens also had its own 'Irish quarter' where housing was the very worst the town could offer. In such closed, parochial 'urban villages', where status was all, the Irish were seemingly easily marked off as being both different and inferior.[75]

However, even Roberts's own account contains numerous cases that inconveniently contradict his bold assertions. His father enjoyed a friend-ship with a fervent Irish Nationalist; Roberts himself established relationships with boys of immediate Irish Catholic descent.[76] Others who have recalled life in Manchester during this period have also indicated a wide degree of variability in attitudes. Although one woman stated that during the 1930s Irish Catholics in north Manchester were 'under a kind of sense of siege', her Irish mother's best friend was, nevertheless, a 'very staunch' English Protestant. An Anglican who dwelt in Trafford Park stated that, 'with the Catholics . . . the community was so tight, and there was always "them and us". And of course they said the same thing – "them and us". It was always "them and us", "them and us".' In contrast, a Catholic from Ancoats recalled that, 'we were all neighbours.'[77] Therefore, in Manchester at least, there was no one immutable reaction to Irish Catholics that was set in stone. There was some cultural freedom, which allowed contrasting reactions to exist side-by-side. After the height of immigration, there might have been few riots outside Liverpool, but it was not the case that small fights and verbal abuse did not continue in the back streets after closing time. This could be seemingly petty in its expression. The son of an Irish police constable stationed in west Lancashire recalled that after he had left for work, a neighbour would often stand outside the family home and shout 'You Irish buggers'. The neighbour only stopped this harassment after a punch from his father persuaded him to see the error of his ways. Certain emotions might have been more pervasive than others – the cultural bias against Irish Catholics remained an omnipresent, if latent, force. Superficially, relations might have been friendly, but underneath there was still a marked sense of difference.[78]

Although there was no one, set, indigenous response to Irish Catholics, reactions could be crystallized around questions of nationality, religion and occupation. It was at such moments when biases hidden beneath surface feeling were exposed. The effect of national differences in the realm of politics will be dealt with in Chapters five and six. It is enough to note, for the present, that St Patrick's Day was an occasion for Irish and English school children to fight each other in Cumberland, Jarrow and St Helens, even if in some cases, 'it was just something our dads had done before us . . . [we did it] more in fun than anger'.[79]

The absence of a strong Orange movement was important in influencing how relations were conducted. Newcastle had the reputation of being a tolerant city largely because of the strength of local Liberalism and the apparently complete absence of an Orange tradition. This meant that there were few who sought to exploit those differences that existed between Irish and English.[80] Manchester, in fact, was the place where the first Orange lodge was established in England in 1798. The country's first Orange riot also took place in the city in 1807. For the subsequent three decades each July was the time for sectarian street brawls in the city.[81] It seems that after this point Ulster Protestants no longer settled in the city in great numbers, preferring Liverpool and, later, Glasgow. Thus, by the 1880s Orangeism's orbit had shifted firmly to Liverpool, where lodge members were at least eight times more numerous than in Manchester; by the early 1920s there were only 200 active members in the city.[82] As one last flourish, Manchester's Orange movement provoked a brief riot during July 1888 when up to 150 processionists paraded through an Irish part of Miles Platting. If they had wanted to provoke a violent response from residents they were not disappointed. After stones had been exchanged, a mêlée developed, which required forty police officers to disperse. The local press comforted itself with the thought that such an incident was an aberration in such a tolerant city.[83] It was not as broad-minded as some seemed to believe: 'bits o' tiffs' continued to occur on July 12 in Collyhurst, where Manchester's few Ulster Protestants were most numerous. However, such sectarianism, as elsewhere in urban England, was never on the scale of Liverpool or Glasgow. There were never enough Ulster Protestants to influence relations throughout the city and they barely formed a distinct and coherent community. Instead of attacking one another, the Orange and the Green in Manchester lived in the same streets, and even drank in the same pubs.[84]

Religious questions, at least those couched in doctrinal and theological abstractions divorced from social loyalties, enthused only members of the middle class. The population as a whole was left cold by such matters. However, when religion was intertwined with a sense of territory emotions were more easily mobilized. In 1902 an attempt was made to burn down a temporary chapel in the newly-created parish of Sacred Heart in Gorton. During this initial period it was also common for local youths to break the chapel's windows. In Collyhurst, Protestants were similarly keen to prevent the establishment of the Catholic parish of St Malachy's during the 1920s. To make their point, they firebombed a temporary chapel three times, twice whilst mass was in progress. When proposals were put forward to build a parish school in the district residents signed a petition in protest and sent it to the Board of Education.[85] The ability of religion to arouse sectarian feelings remained, therefore, a force to be reckoned with. In 1897 Manchester Watch Committee tried to stop Joseph Slattery, author of works like *Secrets of Romish Priests Exposed*, addressing a meeting because it feared he would provoke a riot. When Alexander Ratcliffe, a member of Scotland's Protestant League, delivered a series of lectures in the north-east of England on themes such as the life of a Carmelite nun, his meetings were broken up by Catholics.[86]

In the immediate aftermath of the influx of Irish workers there were numerous conflicts between immigrants and indigenous workers over the distribution of jobs. Hostilities followed the ebb and flow of demand for labour and were determined by the nature of the local job market. When Irish workers moved into trades that had previously been deemed English then the spark to conflict was usually lit.[87] There was, in fact, some real cause for complaint, for when Irish workers moved *en masse* into a trade they brought down wages or, at least, impeded their increase. The long-term effect of their presence is much more doubtful. Moreover, their impact was limited to certain trades and occupations within the unskilled. One of the factors in Liverpool's abiding sectarian conflict was the dominance of insecure unskilled jobs associated with the docks, which meant that Irish and English were in permanent, daily competition.[88] Elsewhere, however, the fall in immigration and the stabilization of the division of labour between Irish and English largely accounted for the decline in such conflicts – they were no longer in competition for the same jobs.[89] The informal way of finding jobs through friends and family practised by Irish and non-Irish led to a gradual ethnic dominance of certain trades.[90] Moreover, through the influence of Irish contractors, Irish labourers could effectively monopolize certain kinds of work in a locality.[91] Despite stabilization, the threat of Irish immigrants flooding the English labour market remained a potential political weapon in the hands of opponents of Home Rule. Liberals even tried to turn this argument on its head by suggesting that Home Rule was the only guaranteed means of ensuring that Irish workers remained in Ireland.[92]

One of the factors that had some impact on keeping the Irish in such lowly occupations was discrimination. By the nature of such matters, it is almost impossible to quantify the effect of prejudice as it usually operated in ways difficult to detect. This was not always so: before 1914 it was not uncommon to see notices posted outside factory gates declaring, 'No Irish Need Apply'. This persisted into the 1950s in certain parts of the country. A rhyme popular with Manchester's Irish residents during the inter-war period attempted to turn this into a rather grim joke; '"No Irish need apply", Whoe'er wrote this did write it well, The same is written on the gates of Hell, "No Irish need apply"'.[93] Prejudice was usually more discreet, being more evident in small family firms where personal preferences were more likely to be expressed. Discrimination was also sometimes applied to those of Irish descent: during the 1920s two Catholic brothers were denied work on a building site because their surname was Riley. To avoid such feeling some changed obviously Irish surnames. Whilst employed in a tea warehouse in London's East End during the 1880s Ben Tillett worked with an Irish man who assumed the name Fleming, although he had been born Flannagan. Others modified their names by simply dropping the 'O' from O'Hanlon. Some, with ambitions to enter white collar occupations, also tried to lose their accent. These pressures did not just affect the socially mobile: trade unionist and Social Democratic Federation member Patrick Curran felt it necessary to be known as Pete.[94]

There were times when English Protestants also felt that discrimination prevented them getting certain jobs. A St Helens woman recalling the inter-war period suggested that, 'it couldn't be proved, but jobs seemed to go to Catholics' through the influence of Catholic councillors. In parts of lumpen London anti-Irish sentiments were far from uncommon, 'You never get no Irishmen round there ... They've given the Paddies all the pubs – but you try and get one'. In Bermondsey during the same period it was assumed that it was advantageous for applicants for Council work to be Irish Catholic.[95] The prolonged inter-war depression exacerbated such paranoia, especially in Scotland, which was most severely effected.[96] In Manchester, in 1922, a deputation of unemployed men complained to the Council about the use of Irish labour in building Manchester City's new Moss Side football stadium. The British Union of Fascists exploited these popular fears. During their Manchester campaign of the early 1930s they blamed both Jewish and Irish immigrants for causing unemployment.[97]

When Irish immigrants decided to settle in England they usually did so with some reluctance and by no means saw it as a permanent step. However, having made the trip over the water, most became enmeshed in the banalities of everyday life, such as marriage, raising a family and trying to make ends meet. They generally lived in particular parts of a town and worked in distinct areas of the economy, although they were never completely cut off from the rest of society. Occasionally stigmatized for their religion and nationality, they were never actually or mentally 'ghettoized' but lived between two worlds: Ireland and England. Although important, residence and occupation do not, in themselves, explain how Irish Catholics in England made sense of their lives. Where individuals lived and how they earned their living provided the skeleton of existence, around which other elements took shape and form. In the case under discussion here, they are but the first steps towards an appreciation of the nature of Irish Catholic working-class culture.

three

Church and people

A divided Church

The Catholic Church was the most important institution within Irish Catholic working-class culture. Although this chapter will concentrate on its social influence, it should not be forgotten that at least some of the Church's power derived from its claim to be the necessary intermediary between the individual and God. However, this was not the principal reason why many Catholics attended mass or felt allegiance to the Church. Few working-class adherents became Catholics because they had been intellectually persuaded so to do – the vast majority had simply been born into the Faith. Membership of the Church was a seemingly natural consequence of family and national origin: it was an unquestioned, unremarkable constitutive element of a person's identity. The main consequence of this was the unwillingness of most adherents to allow their Catholicism to dominate the rest of their lives. To most, attending mass was something that one did, if not without thinking, then without needing to appreciate quite why it was so.

Catholicism did not just comprise this vague feeling of belonging, but also included a bureaucratic institution with it own set of interests, which were articulated and enforced by appointed officials – the Hierarchy and clergy. To these men, amorphous emotional stirrings were inadequate if unaccompanied by strict conformity to the letter of Church law. Thus, despite the allegiance of thousands of members in the working class, the Church engaged in a ceaseless struggle to win acceptance for its own idea of good Catholic devotional practice. This chapter will focus on the relationship between official and popular Catholicism in Manchester, in an attempt to delineate the limits of the power of the Church and measure its influence upon the lives of ordinary working-class adherents.

Manchester lay in the south of the predominantly industrial diocese of Salford, which also contained most of eastern Lancashire and parts of north-east Cheshire, including cotton spinning and weaving towns such as Blackburn, Burnley, Bolton and Rochdale. The diocese was dominated by Manchester, which, in 1900, accounted for one-third of its 300,000 adherents. The Bishop's cathedral was St John's, in the city of Salford, and many of his concerns were centred on the metropolis. The vast majority of adherents were working class and the diocese boasted only one aristocratic Catholic family, the de Traffords, who owned estates in rural Lancashire to the south and east of Manchester. Sir Humphrey and Lady Annette de Trafford played a minor role within the Church, mainly through making charitable donations, attending public meetings and lending weight to their friend the Bishop. Some clerics earnestly looked to the family to provide lay leadership but, so far as most adherents were concerned, they remained distant figures. Moreover, in the years immediately prior to 1914 the family moved its centre of orbit to London and ceased to play any role in Manchester's Catholic life.[1]

The numerical strength of the diocese was the result of nineteenth-century Irish immigration. Unlike Preston to the north and the Fylde coast to the west, few indigenous English Catholics lived in the region prior to 1800. In 1690 a mere two adherents resided in Manchester; as late as 1767 there were only thirty-five. Yet, by 1890 Manchester contained nearly 98,000 Catholics, who accounted for 14 per cent of the city's population. It was a common assumption that the vast majority of these Catholics were Irish. John Denvir went so far as to suggest that of the city's 90,000 Catholics in 1881 80,000 were of Irish extraction.[2] This was something of an exaggeration: by the end of the century only about one-third of Catholics had been born in Ireland. Taking into account those of immediate Irish descent, perhaps as many as four-fifths would have considered themselves to be Irish. However, due to falling immigration, this proportion was in constant decline: of the city's 130,000 Catholics in 1931 only one-sixth were Irish-born and no more than two-fifths of immediate Irish descent. Thus, an increasing number of adherents were so far removed from their Irish antecedents that they would have considered themselves to be English. This is an important consideration, because the Irish were Catholics primarily because of the association between their faith and national identity. The Church was inextricably linked to a sense of national difference and was used by immigrants as a means of asserting Irishness. Yet, because loyalty to the Church was transmitted through the family, despite a diminishing sense of Irishness, the number of Catholics in England continued to increase. If Irish Catholics owed a divided allegiance to the Church, because of their nationality, such 'English' Catholics did not. Thus, it was with no sense of irony that one Catholic lodging house keeper in turn-of-the-century Angel Meadow derogatively referred to all his Irish guests as 'Paddy'.[3]

In the United States, the Catholic Hierarchy was soon monopolized by Irish immigrants and continued to be so, despite the later influx of Catholics from other parts of Europe. In England, the Church was ethnically divided and the Hierarchy remained almost exclusively the preserve of English Catholics. All but one Bishop of Salford was English, the exception being a second generation Italian: Herbert Vaughan (1872–92) was from a landed recusant family; John Bilsborrow (1892–1903) came from an old Catholic family on Lancashire's Fylde coast; Louis Casartelli (1903–25) was the son of an Italian middle-class immigrant; Thomas Henshaw (1925–38), although born in Manchester, was thoroughly English.[4] This ethnic division was also evident in other spheres: although nominally part of the same Church, most Catholics looked to their own particular parish as the centre of activity. Parochial character was inevitably variable, for it tended to reflect the social composition of the district it served. For the sake of simplicity these can be divided between middle class (and hence usually English) and working class (and therefore often Irish) parishes. Thus, during the inter-war period, St Anne's in Crumpsall enjoyed the use of its own tennis courts whilst, in Miles Platting, Corpus Christi cancelled a bazaar because unemployment amongst parishioners meant that there was little to sell.[5] There were also keenly contested rivalries between neighbouring parishes, such as 'posh' Holy Name and 'poor' St Wilfrid's. Despite the superficially monolithic character of the Catholic Church, the popular meaning of Catholicism was extremely variable.

Faith and nationality

Despite being largely ultramontane in its doctrinal sympathies, the Hierarchy used every opportunity to emphasize the Church's patriotic English character.[6] This was only partly a natural corollary of its ethnic complexion. It was also one way of counterbalancing those Protestants who continued to see the Church as a mysterious, threatening, unEnglish force.[7] However, the fundamental reason behind the campaign to establish the Church's patriotic credentials was the hope that one day Catholicism would resume its position as the country's established religion. Innumerable articles in the Salford diocesan journal the *Harvest* were devoted to English recusants; 'Faith of our Fathers', the hymn sung at virtually every Catholic public ritual, told of their oppression. Catholic school children were taught that their Church was more English than that of the Anglicans, which was merely the creation of bad King Henry VIII. The building of Westminster cathedral and the campaign to remove the anti-Catholic clauses in the monarch's accession oath were all part of this effort. As Cardinal Manning stated, 'the constitution of England, with the Crown, Lords and Commons is a Catholic creation and a Catholic inheritance.'

Canon Richardson, of Manchester's St Augustine's parish, even went so far as to state that adherents were *English* – rather than Roman – Catholics.[8] National events were used to implant the impression of a national church-in-waiting. During celebrations of Queen Victoria's 1897 Diamond Jubilee, Bishop Bilsborrow declared to the congregation, which included most of Salford Corporation, that 'Catholics have ever been obedient to the laws, devoted to the commonweal, and faithful in our allegiance to the throne of this country' precisely because of their adherence to the Church. On the day of the funeral of George V the Church held special services, echoing those held by Anglicans.[9] Despite this propaganda the Church remained, for the most part, mistrusted and isolated. As Bishop Bilsborrow complained in 1893:

> . . . every day of the year the public press was reproaching her [the Church] for her insolent claims, for her usurpation of liberty and of civil rights, for being an enemy of progress and loving darkness, and for being hostile to Sacred Scriptures. They need not be surprised at those charges, nor must they be sick at heart to find the Church they loved so well reviled. Their Lord said that if they were of the world the world would know its own and would love them. But because they were not of the world but of God, therefore the world hated them.[10]

Therefore, Irish Catholics became part of a Church that, despite its best efforts, was detached from the rest of English society. Despite this, the Hierarchy looked on the Irish presence with alarm and tried to obscure their numerical importance. Historical accounts of the mid-nineteenth century Catholic revival in England, known as the 'second spring', emphasized the conversion of intellectual Anglicans, the renewal of faith within indigenous adherents and the efforts of the Papacy, at the expense of the significance of the Irish influx. The only contemporary account of the Church in Manchester managed to devote a mere two pages to Irish immigration. If, in print, leading Catholics tried to ignore the Irish presence, in person the response was sometimes more direct. In 1939, one Irish resident of north London protested that he had heard compatriots described by priests as an 'undesirable element' and a 'corrupting influence'. After remonstrating with a cleric for making such comments he was informed that he was 'unwelcome in this respectable district'.[11]

In turn, Irish adherents did not entirely approve of the Church's English emphasis. Nationalist leaders were concerned that the Church's attempt to anglicize Irish children threatened their political position. Some Irish priests were also unsympathetic with the Church's ambitions: in Bermondsey, one incumbent would 'forget' to include the obligatory prayers for the monarch.[12]

Yet, the Church could not alter demography. In Manchester, as in most other parts of industrial England, it served a population in which English adherents were in the minority. By 1900 north Manchester not only contained many Irish Catholics but also adherents from Italy, Poland, Lithuania and the Ukraine, all of whom had their own needs and identities. These the Church tried to accommodate without compromising its attempt to project an English image to the rest of society. About 1,000 Italians lived in the parishes of St Michael's and St Alban's in Ancoats before 1914. During the 1920s priests endorsed Mussolini's Blackshirt movement, whose members were prominent lay activists; Fascist literature was even displayed in vestries.[13] Poles and Lithuanians formed part of St Casimir's parish, so named to avoid offence to either of these two antagonistic groups: Casimir was both patron saint of Poland and a prince of Lithuania.[14] These minor nationalities were fairly easily accommodated within the Church either because they had no political disagreement with the state or because they were small in number; this cannot be said of Irish Catholics. However, the Hierarchy still tried to mollify Irish adherents while at the same time imposing an interpretation of the meaning of Irishness that best suited its organizational ends. Although Cardinal Vaughan was well known for his hostility to Home Rule, as Bishop of Salford he regularly addressed St Patrick's Day gatherings. On one occasion he declared that:

> I am not an Irishman in blood, but in heart I am an Irishman. My heart has gone out to you, and yours have to me. We are closely united in affection. My cause, the cause of our Holy religion, is your cause, and your cause is mine.[15]

He appealed to the Irish on the basis of their mutual faith, thereby effectively ignoring their distinctive national origin and all that it entailed.

Irish nationality could not be so easily overlooked as most in the Church realized. Thus, Irishness was appealed to, but only as a way of further impressing upon adherents the importance of their faith. The Irish in Manchester were told that only by being obedient to their Church would they be true to their nation. Both English and Irish priests exploited the widespread, if rather erroneous, notion that Ireland was a devout nation and compared the supposed corruption of England with the religiosity of the homeland. Immigrants were exhorted to live up to this noble Catholic heritage. In 1932 Father Edwin of St Patrick's made this, by then familiar, claim:

> He reminded the congregation of the traditional fervour of the Faith of the Irish and their steadfastness to moral principles, but they must not live in the past or on the past. Their Faith and their moral principles were being assailed as never before. They must live their Faith and courageously proclaim it to the world, only in that way would they be the true sons and daughters of St Patrick.[16]

Such rhetoric deliberately flattered Irish adherents. It gave them a sense of moral superiority over the English and suggested they channel all their efforts into improving the place of the Church in England. If society denigrated them for their poverty and their nationality, the Church asserted that their religion was a positive advantage. Thus, Irishness was used to encourage adherents to conform in ways approved by the Church. Irish women were praised for being more innocent than their English counterparts whose habit, after 1918, of smoking and wearing bobbed hair brought shivers down priestly spines. This rhetoric was no doubt intended to ensure that Irish women remained 'pure'.[17] Attempts to mobilize Irishness on behalf of the English Church were accomplished with varying degrees of subtlety. One of the most blatant examples occurred in 1935 when Bishop Henshaw announced that if he was Irish he would 'feel very much ashamed if I did not contribute something to the [building of the] new St Patrick's.'[18]

The Church celebrated St Patrick's Day by holding masses and blessing sprigs of shamrock in special ceremonies. This was done to infuse the occasion with Catholic, as opposed to Nationalist, sentiments. During the 1880s St Patrick's Day had been commemorated by a mass meeting in the Free Trade Hall organized by the Salford diocesan temperance crusade. Alcohol abuse was widely linked by contemporaries to poverty: some thought that the former caused the latter. Although Catholics tended to be rather more circumspect in their analysis, drink was still widely seen as a contributory factor to the break-down of family life and an impediment to regular devotions. Moreover, it was broadly accepted that a Catholic population that drank heavily would remain poor and, by remaining poor, would impede the Church's accumulation of status within society. In this light, Cardinal Manning instituted a 'Truce of St Patrick', which granted indulgences to those who abstained on 17 March, a traditional time for inebriation among immigrants.[19] The opportunity was also taken to propagandize on behalf of Catholic schools and promote the message that, 'Nationality was a very good thing but religion was a better.' Some even attempted to wrest Irishness completely out of the hands of Home Rulers. On St Patrick's Day 1901, at the height of the Boer War, Father Bernard Vaughan of the Holy Name suggested that Ireland's sons, 'were as Catholic as they were intelligent, generous and brave. Their bravery they were even now displaying on many a field in South Africa.'[20]

The policeman of the Faith

The relationship between the English Hierarchy and the Church's Irish adherents was mediated by the parish priest. He was the human bond between the institution and the people and reflected the concerns of them both. In contrast to the bishops, a sizeable proportion of priests had been born in Ireland. During the late nineteenth century 38 per cent of clerics working in the Salford diocese were Irish, a proportion which increased to 46 per cent by the 1920s.[21] Moreover, so far as most Catholics were concerned, the most important figure in the Church was not a bishop, cardinal or even Pope, but their own priest. To some Protestants the priest appeared a sinister character who wielded untempered power over his flock. The supposed priestly conspiracy in politics was occasionally 'exposed' by concerned citizens and lurid tales of their alleged exploitation of young women were propagated by William Murphy's successors. Although such fears were increasingly expressed in the form of off-colour jokes, they still pointed to the alleged 'otherness' of Catholics. Ernie Benson, raised in Leeds before 1914, recalled that if his gang:

> . . . happened to meet an RC priest in the street and the RC kids said 'Good morning father' the others would mimic them in the hearing of the priest or start ragging them by saying 'If he's your father he must be kept busy' or 'does your dad at home know he's your father?' . . . Quite often this would lead to fighting.[22]

Protestant suspicions were founded on an exaggerated idea of the priesthood's influence. Although this was reinforced by an Irish belief in the magical abilities of clerics they were, after all, only human. Despite their reputation, priests were neither omnipotent nor omnipresent but limited by a physique that could collapse under the considerable strain of administering a working-class parish. Much of their time was spent finding ways of financing the parish: in 1890 only five out of 155 parishes in the Salford diocese was not in debt.[23] Moreover, a great variety of individual temperaments existed within the clergy: some were outgoing, others were more restrained; if one gently persuaded another fell back on bluster and bombast.[24] This variability in character was sometimes exploited by canny members of their flock. When denied absolution for his sins by one Holy Name priest Anthony Burgess simply confessed again to a more lenient colleague.[25] Thus, priests were in an unrivalled position to influence how adherents lived their lives and practised their faith. Yet few, if any, were able to force their adult parishioners to do that which they did not wish to do. For example, it seems that, within a modest margin, priests could alter the extent of attendance at mass. Nevertheless, those who advocated temperance were unable to persuade even the most devout of Catholic working men to abstain from drinking beer.[26]

As a general rule, priests preferred the laity to passively obey their will.[27] This did not mean they received blind obedience even from parochial activists: those incumbents expecting such submission were sadly disappointed. During the decade prior to 1914 St Patrick's parish suffered two contests between priest and laity, both of which provoked the intervention of the Bishop of Salford. In 1904 members of the Old Boys' Association were banned from mass after a disagreement. Some years later another priest attempted to wrest control of the Boys' Sunday School from the hands of the Confraternity of the Christian Doctrine. He accused members of exhibiting 'disrespect and disregard of his authority' when they resisted.[28] Resentment of such a high-handed demeanour seems to have been not uncommon among parishioners who wished to make an active contribution to the life of the Church. One of the aims of the Catholic Federation was to introduce a more democratic framework into parish life. It felt that the priest's monopoly of power inhibited the participation of trade unionists, who were used to administering their own affairs. However, the Federation's attempt to dismantle the existing 'autocratic arrangement' floundered at the hands of a priesthood jealous of their power. A Federation branch could not be established without a priest's permission and it relied on his support thereafter. It was no accident, therefore, that in St Wilfrid's, where one of the Federation's severest critics was incumbent, there were never more than forty-five members.[29]

A priest's principal function was to maintain some sort of influence over adherents who might require the occasional prod or sharp shove back into devotional conformity. The assumption was that, as Cardinal Vaughan put it, 'A house-going priest makes a church-going people', an aphorism that was taken very seriously.[30] Father Timothy of St Alban's visited local pubs on Saturday nights to ask patrons whether they had recently attended confession. He also visited homes on Sunday mornings to cajole reluctant adherents into attending mass. In the mining communities around Whitehaven, in Northumberland, Catholics who missed mass were visited by the following Tuesday at the latest to discover the reason for their absence.[31] The most regularly exercised duty performed by priests, outside of church, remained calling at Catholic homes to enquire after the health, welfare and mass attendance of family members. In most parishes Catholic homes were visited at least once every four weeks – even those of 'backsliders'. One Manchester family continued to be visited despite their resolute failure to attend Easter communion for seven years.[32]

As they walked through their parish some priests made a striking impression indeed. Father Tim of St Augustine's strode through Manchester's mean streets wearing 'bell-bottomed trousers and a big trilby, all in black and [carrying] a walking stick which was more like a shillelagh.'[33] The incumbent at St William's, Angel Meadow, described one such round of home visits to middle-class readers in the early 1890s:

> 'Good morning, Father.' 'Good morning, child.' 'Hallo! Good morning Mrs Smith.' 'Good morning, Father,' and so on all day round the Meadow . . . There is evidently a pleasure in seeing the priest as he passes by with a cheery word and a friendly nod, while the mere glance of the eye will at once detect whether the occupants of the house belong to the household of the Faith, or to that vast army of 'don't go anywhere' class of people so often met with.

Having entered such a household, he merely 'gently' reminded adherents about the importance of mass.[34] If this picture is at all accurate, and it has an admittedly roseate glow about it, it was by no means completely representative of the clerical method. Parishioners in St Augustine's were said to have attended mass during the 1920s out of fear of the pugnacious

Father Keegan.[35] Anxiety about priestly retribution seems to have been more common among Irish immigrants than those of Irish descent. This is perhaps a reflection of the greater degree of authority enjoyed by priests in Ireland itself. It is certainly true that priests of Irish birth are remembered as being by far the most tough and fearsome of clerics. Furthermore, if he was Irish, the priest had little regard for the privacy of the Englishman's castle: he would often enter a household without knocking. This presumption was resented by some who managed to put a stop to it; others, afraid of the consequences, allowed it to persist.[36]

This occasionally enforced familiarity was necessary to the full performance of another of the priest's duties. This was the protection of families, and especially children, from anti-Catholic influences. One of the most important tasks with which a priest was burdened was to ensure that each child born to a Catholic was at least christened and educated in a Church school. This was vital in the case of mixed marriages, where Catholic offspring were in particular danger of being lost to the Faith. One Protestant resident of Ordsall recalled such an intervention in the marriage of her mother's best friend some time before 1914. Born a Catholic, this acquaintance had lapsed and married an Anglican, who had insisted that both their children be christened in his church. Having slipped through the Catholic net, she came to the notice of the Church because the birth of their third child had required the attention of a local midwife, who happened to be Catholic. It seems the midwife informed a priest from St Joseph's about these lost souls, for he quickly began a campaign of harassment:

> The Father went that often and told her that her two children she'd already got were bastards and she was living in sin . . . In the end she came to my mother and said could she sleep at our house, because she wasn't sleeping with Harry any more – that was her husband – until he turned and married her in church.

Harry eventually yielded to this pressure: the couple were remarried at St Joseph's, the two older children rechristened Catholics and all subsequent offspring attended St Joseph's school.[37] It was this sort of interference which caused the Anglican Archbishop of Liverpool to complain of the 'coercion' of Protestant partners within mixed marriages.[38] Even in exclusively Catholic families a priest sometimes felt it necessary to intervene in order to protect one member against the malign influence of another. After arguing with his priest a member of St Patrick's was branded a Communist and had his name so blackened that old school friends cut him dead in the street. Priests also began to visit his home more frequently, afraid he would turn his devout sister against the Church.[39]

Priests not only tried to influence family affairs but also attempted to impose a more respectable form of civic conduct. This seems to have often led to them breaking up drunken fights. Father Thompson of St Anthony's was especially known for this:

. . . he was a fat, very jovial man, you know. Any trouble, especially on a Saturday night, any trouble boozing – 'Send for Father Thompson.' And Father Thompson'd soon have it settled.
How would he settle it?
Just tell them off. Oh, they'd take notice of him, even the Protestants. Oh, he was a by-word for that kind of thing in Trafford Park. He'd settle any business, any trouble.[40]

In this instance, Catholic and Anglican clerics shared a similar function. In Miles Platting Reverend Catterall and in Greengate Canon Green were known for their ability to disperse a street brawl. Both sides of the sectarian divide seem to have accepted the inter-denominational nature of such peace-keeping. It was an Anglican who described a Catholic priest as better than the police when it came to calming intoxicated disputes.[41] If it suited their own ends, Anglicans also used a priest's authority in other areas of life. When a shopkeeper was told that a Catholic customer refused to pay her bill she went to the local priest. After hearing her complaint he is said to have remarked that, 'The first thing they're taught to do in this Church is pay their way.' By the following morning the bill had been settled.[42] While they encouraged honouring debts, priests also tried to discourage money-lending within their flock. One Liverpool priest refused to give absolution to a dying moneylender until she paid back interest to her customers. Under the circumstances, it was understandable that she did not waste much time in obeying his orders.[43]

Although their main priority was to ensure spiritual salvation, priests also attempted to look after the material needs of Catholics by representing their interests to officialdom.[44] Perhaps more importantly, the priest was also a source of charity for the indigent. At the Holy Name Bernard Vaughan was regularly visited by unfortunates asking for some form of financial assistance. Hard-pressed mothers would also send their children to beg for money from clerics. There were clearly priests who had no interest in their own material self-interest. As Charles Booth noted of some London incumbents, 'if they have a shilling in their pocket no one in want will ask in vain.' One such figure was Canon Byrne of St Michael's, on whose death in 1907 it was said:

He robbed himself even of necessaries and wore his clothes till they were something more than shabby, so that he might be able to assist the poor. He was always reluctant to refuse any one seeking alms, and this naturally led him to be the victim of much imposition. Beggars met him and knew that their appeals would not go unheeded if he could possibly assist them, and the demands on his purse were far unequal to his means.[45]

A priest's funeral revealed what sort of place he had carved out for himself in the lives of parishioners. At his death, Byrne had been attached to St Michael's for twenty-five years. The Sunday prior to his burial an unprecedented number attended mass and communion whilst 3,000 copies of his portrait had been sold in less than three days. When Canon Toole died in 1892, after serving for nearly half a century in St Wilfrid's, even Protestants paid their respects. Thousands gathered outside the church and lined the route to the cemetery; shops shut as a mark of respect. When Canon Liptrot of St Anne's, Ancoats, died a year later 6,000 people filed past his coffin, the equivalent of the entire parish.[46] These were clearly exceptional men whose long tenure had helped establish an unrivalled position in the affections of locals. Even so, they demonstrate what was possible for priests to accomplish, although few colleagues managed to emulate them. The meaning of such exhibitions of affection is difficult to disentangle, although the participation of non-Catholics suggests that such priests were seen as individuals first and representatives of the Catholic Church second. Moreover, notwithstanding the efforts of such paragons, priests probably no more than checked bad conduct; they were unable to instil permanent improvement.[47] Like a police officer, the priest could encourage those who were afraid of breaking the law not to do so, but could not prevent those who paid little heed to such considerations. Yet, the priest was more than simply an agent of conformity; his very presence in Catholic homes expressed their difference from non-Catholics. By accepting his authority, however grudgingly and imperfectly, Catholics confirmed their allegiance to another power.

Formal and informal worship

One of the most time-consuming duties performed by the clergy was the maintainence of religious conformity. Although widely presented as a religious paragon, rural Ireland before the 1850s was far from that. Most peasants were wholly ignorant of doctrine, whilst only about one-third regularly attended mass. From that decade, however, the Church in Ireland is said to have 're-made' Catholics by emphasizing the importance of formal devotions and sacred duties. Henceforward, the rural Irish became, outwardly at least, a much more devout people.[48] The English Church was faced by an even more acute problem during the 1840s and 1850s: Irish immigrants' low level of formal devotion declined further in England's urban slums. The Church responded with a campaign along lines similar to that of its Irish counterpart. As with the Irish campaign, this has been credited with improving levels of religious conformity. One estimate is that prior to 1918 as many as 60 per cent of Catholics in England regularly attended mass. Others have suggested that the proportion was more modest, being in some working-class parishes as small as 20 per cent.[49] Whatever the actual proportions, the Church constantly struggled not just to maintain but also increase levels of religious conformity.

It is extremely difficult to establish the real extent of religious worship among Catholics, the few statistics to hand being infamously unreliable. In any case, attendance at church was by no means the only index of popular religious sentiment, although the Church treated it as such. There were many adherents who identified with Catholicism, yet did not attend mass regularly, if at all. There are no figures for mass attendance in Manchester, although details are available for attendance at Easter communion throughout the city in 1900.[50] Easter was one of the most important periods in the Catholic calendar and the Church considered non-attendance to be a very serious offence. During the inter-war years, priests from St Patrick's made special home visits during the holiday to ensure adherents had performed their duties.[51] As a consequence of this pressure, many adherents who rarely went to mass, attended church at Easter. Some even felt that this alone kept them true to the Faith.[52] The 1900 census covered thirty-one parishes in the city, encompassing just over 89,000 Catholics; of these, 43 per cent attended communion. This places Manchester in an intermediate position within the diocese: 32 per cent of Catholics in nearby Bury and 49 per cent in Bolton attended mass at this time. Likewise, in Newcastle in 1882 attendance at Easter communion was 39.1 per cent.[53]

There were large differences in levels of attendance across the city: from 24 per cent at St Edmund's, Miles Platting to 82 per cent in St Alban's, Ancoats. Most parishes, however, hovered between an attendance level of one-half and one-third of parishioners. Class seems to have been the most important factor in influencing these figures. Three of the four parishes that reported attendance in excess of 70 per cent were in the city's middle-class southern suburbs. There were also differences between parishes of apparently similar social composition, which cannot be explained. It is also interesting to note that Irish nationality did not in itself appear to have encouraged higher attendances. The predominantly working-class St Patrick's, which anecdotal evidence suggests was the most Irish of all parishes, had the eighth worst attendance level of 36 per cent. Such differences and variations are clearly due to a number of obscure factors. Even so, in broad terms, the census provides an invaluable snapshot of the state of formal devotions in the city.

A more sustained picture has been provided by St Wilfrid's, Hulme which recorded attendance at Easter communion between 1914 and 1937. These figures suggest that levels recorded across the city in 1900 did not diminish by much during the subsequent forty years. In 1900 48 per cent of the parish attended communion at Easter; the average for the twenty-three years after 1914 was 53 per cent. This consistent level of attendance is clearly illustrated in Table 3.1. The vigour of Catholic levels of formal devotions during this period was evident across the country.[54] This suggests the existence of a solid body of faithful, regular attenders. However, the averages listed in Table 3.1 conceal a year-by-year variation, from a low of 44 per cent in 1937 to a high of 69 per cent in 1925. Instead of a large cohort of habitual attenders, this shows that there was a substantial turnover in those attending communion.

The most important cause of this variation was the parish mission: in

Table 3.1 Attendance to Easter duties at St. Wilfrid's, Hulme, 1914–1937

Date	Average attendance	Percentage of parish
1914–19	3,162	47
1920–5	4,044	60
1926–31	3,690	54
1932–7	3,548	52
1914–37	3,611	53

Source: St Wilfrid's Parish Log Book, available from the church.

mission years between 10 and 15 per cent more parishioners participated in communion. All parishes periodically held a mission: St Wilfrid's had one about every five years. The mission inaugurated a period of evangelical activity meant to penetrate even the poorest alley, transforming a parish church into a vibrant centre of activities designed to renew popular devotions. For a few weeks special mid-day conferences and evening sermons were held, while confession was heard morning, noon and night. Although evangelical in method, the intention was not to convert non-Catholics but to bring non-conforming Catholics into line. As the St Wilfrid's figures suggest, these tactics had a fair degree of success: churches were often crowded during campaigns while membership of confraternities, guilds and other parochial bodies all increased.[55] However, popular zeal was not sustained: the Easter after a mission at St Wilfrid's attendance fell back to its usual level.

The Hierarchy considered attendance to be unacceptably low and strove to improve it. Yet, compared to Anglicans, even the worst attended Catholic parish was a centre of spiritual ardour. Although Easter did not hold quite the same significance for Anglicans as it did for Catholics, it was still an important time of year. Figures available for the number of participants in Easter communion in St Andrew's parish, Ancoats, in 1902 indicate that only 5 per cent of Anglicans attended church.[56]

Rowntree's research in York, where the Irish Catholic population was overwhelmingly working class, indicates a wide difference between male and female levels of formal devotions. It seems clear that, although as children there was little to choose between them, after leaving school women attended mass much more often than men. This explains why in 1935 one-third of all males, but only one-quarter of females who attended mass in York were under seventeen years old. In 1901 59 per cent of those over sixteen attending mass were women, a proportion that had barely changed by 1935. York was not unique, for the disparity seems to have been all but universal. Evidence for 1930s Liverpool generally endorses these findings, although there the proportion of men was rather greater, perhaps because the number of middle-class Catholics was larger.[57] There are a number of explanations for this difference: women lived longer than men; there were also more female Irish immigrants. Moreover, although men were encouraged to be more devout, it was expected that Catholic wives would be more religious than their husbands because they were supposed to be the guardians of their children's souls. Thus, the Church concentrated its attention on women rather than men. Even so, proportionately more Catholic men attended church than did their Anglican counterparts – in 1930s Liverpool 8 per cent more.[58]

The Church's emphasis on mass attendance was in some respects fallacious because by no means all those who went to church were actively engaged by the ceremony. As one priest complained in 1924, 'the undivided attention of congregations today was seldom guaranteed.' This certainly seems to have been true of the young Anthony Burgess, who found mass 'boring and incomprehensible'. For him, the most noteworthy aspect of mass at St Edmund's in Rusholme was that 'people always seemed to be farting'.[59]

Despite such diversions, a devout minority sat carefully listening to the priest's words. This can be seen from figures for mid-week mass attendance, which was also calculated as part of the 1900 census. Overall, average attendance at mid-week mass was 4 per cent in Manchester, which was consistent with Bury's 5 per cent and Bolton's 6 per cent. As with Easter attendance, those parishes with the highest levels were predominantly located in middle-class districts, the lowest in working-class areas. The highest figure was recorded in St Anne's, Stretford, where 18 per cent of the parish attended mid-week mass; the lowest was registered by St William's, Angel Meadow, where 0.4 per cent did so.

Confraternities were another means for devout Catholics to demonstrate their adherence to the Faith. These were organizations, divided along lines of gender and age, which encouraged doctrinal conformity in every respect. The vocation of the Children of Mary, which enrolled women and girls in their later teens, was conceived as, 'one of sheer battling against unworthy worldliness and of striving for a higher ideal than those that worldliness has to offer.'[60] Members undertook collectively to attend mass, communion and confession at least once a month. Some also attended mid-week mass once a week, as did 400 members of St Anne's Men's Confraternity in Ancoats during the 1890s and a similar number of men from St Patrick's during 1910. Members also participated in Sunday afternoon meetings, which discussed matters of concern. During the autumn of 1929 members of Holy Name's Children of Mary listened to talks on Pius X, Church dogma and the position of the Church in Mexico.[61] These activities were not wholly spiritually-centred: members attended social evenings and went on trips together. For those of the appropriate class they were also a useful way of establishing business contacts. They were also a means of bringing young members of the opposite sex together in respectable circumstances. Adolescents in St Patrick's Children of Mary and the Christian Doctrine held modest house parties, with piano recitals in front parlour rooms. Participants were charged 6*d.*, which was donated to the Church.[62]

The proportion of parishioners who were confraternity members seems to have been in the order of between 10 and 20 per cent. Paradoxically, given their under-representation at mass, men were preponderant: in St Wilfrid's before 1914, 59 per cent of members were male, 73 per cent of these being over fourteen years of age.[63] Membership varied between parishes: during 1910 about 8 per cent in St Anne's in Ancoats, 12 per cent in St Wilfrid's, 21 per cent in St Patrick's and 26 per cent in both the Holy Name and St Augustine's. For all but one of these five parishes membership declined after 1918: the inter-war years saw a fall of between one-third and a half of members. Impressionistic evidence suggests that most of the devout were from the lower-middle class, middle class and skilled working class and that, therefore, those of Irish birth or immediate descent were under-represented. This is partly confirmed by the low proportion of priests born in the Salford diocese with obviously Irish surnames, for the sons of the devout were an especially fecund source of novices. The Catholic devout, in other words, were socially little different from their counterparts in other denominations.[64]

One of the main tasks assigned to confraternity members was to help save the religious faith of their poorer co-religionists. As the social composition of the Holy Name parish became increasingly working class during the 1920s, confraternities were seen as:

> ... best suited to provide the frame work for the social and charitable activities which are often needed on behalf of the poorer – and still, more, the younger – sections of this 'floating' Catholic population.[65]

Working-class adherents were viewed with great concern. It was reluctantly accepted that economic circumstances sometimes prevented them conforming in ways approved by the Church and, at Salford, Cardinal Vaughan noted that short-term slumps resulted in a fall in mass attendance. The consequence of economic hardship was one reason why he was such an insistent advocate of thrift and temperance: Vaughan felt that an affluent Catholic would inevitably be a conforming Catholic. However, these were long-term hopes: the Church had to still face the fact that at least one-quarter of those born Catholic were 'nominal only'.[66]

Poverty in itself did not cause non-attendance. Yet, the consequences of being poor made going to church more difficult, awkward, even embarrassing. The lack of disposable income also inhibited participation in parochial leisure activities so favoured by the devout. The poor were also denied much of a role in Catholic ritual and ceremony. The parish May Queen had to be the 'right type of girl', which meant that she needed to have parents who could afford to pay for her costume and floral accompaniments.[67] The poor themselves explained their non-attendance by referring to their embarrassment about their inadequate state of dress. Clothes were an important indicator of status and this was exaggerated by the widespread practice of dressing up for church. Children, happy enough in their 'weekday rags' saw them as a 'badge of shame' when worn at mass.[68] Some priests thought such complaints a mere cover. Others were more sympathetic, recognizing that during periods of unemployment Catholics 'are unable to appear as they think fit [so] they often miss Mass for a while.'[69] However, by no means all poor Catholics remained outside church; they attended mass, but only after doing what they could to hide their modest circumstances. Women used shawls to hide cheap clothing whilst men who did not own a Sunday best suit still wore a collar and tie.[70] Unfortunately for them, once inside church economic status was not cast aside: instead, it was emphasized. Those with money could buy themselves the best seats in the house. It was also expected that those attending mass paid for the privilege. In 1902 it was stipulated at the Holy Family, Chorlton-on-Medlock that those taking 11 o'clock Sunday mass paid 3*d.* if they sat on the floor of the church, 2*d.* if they sat in the centre gallery and 1*d.* anywhere else. During the 1920s the Holy Name reserved places near the front of the church with cushions and kneeling mats. Poorer Catholics had to sit at the back. By no means all priests were happy with this. In 1908 one complained that pew rents were still widespread throughout the diocese, and asked:

> Look at the matter from a democratic point of view. Why should there be any class distinctions? I believe in poor and rich mixing together and sitting wherever they wish. Pew rents cause a deal of unpleasantness amongst the parishioners.

Nevertheless, he concluded that it would be difficult to abolish them altogether. Just as the priest had to accept the drinking habits of working-class adherents, so the better-off were allowed their vices and pleasures.[71]

Catholics did not necessarily consider themselves to be any the less Catholic because they did not attend mass and had not done so for decades. Although they would have been dismissed by many priests as lapsed or nominal, such people retained an abiding affiliation to the Church into which they were born. In any case, the Church would have played some part in these lives, even if it was simply at birth, the start of adolescence, marriage and death. A child's first communion marked the end of their childhood and as such, was considered the most important event in many lives, even if the Catholic stopped attended mass immediately afterwards.[72] Of an Irish road sweeper it was said: 'Mr S. is a Roman Catholic and he says that it is the only true religion, but enquiry elicits that he himself has not been to church for more than twenty years.'[73] He was an extreme example. However, it is doubtful that outside the ranks of the devout many Catholics were much concerned with fulfilling the exact letter of canonical law.

The price Catholicism paid for being an integral part of everyday working-class life was that it was forced into a shape that could be accommodated by that culture. As a consequence, various customs existed side-by-side with the Catholic faith, despite the fact that they appeared to the outsider to be logically incompatible. Just as some Anglican mothers thought that christening babies increased their chances of survival, so Catholics thought that drinking from the chalice cured whooping cough and used the altar as a place to swear oaths. It was deemed sufficient by James Sexton's mother that he had been baptized under a tap. In Mary Bertenshaw's extended family all the women had their ears pierced to keep evil spirits from their eyes. During the 1950s Catholic women in Liverpool's slum districts regarded birth control as a sin but saw abortion before three months as perfectly legitimate.[74]

The homes of non-attenders were often furnished with religious arte-facts that expressed the family's adherence. In the Catholic homes in East London images of the Last Supper, the Crucifixion and the Holy Family were all displayed. In Angel Meadow were hung pictures of the Pope, Sacred Heart or Virgin Mary; in Ordsall pictures of the boxer Joe E. Sullivan were displayed along with those of Christ; houses also contained statues of Mary.[75] Such items held a significance that was perhaps hard for the outsider fully to comprehend. An old Catholic couple forced to pawn and sell various domestic items to forestall their incarceration in the workhouse, saw their house lie bare rather than remove a Crucifix hanging on the parlour wall.[76] Altars were even constructed in some Irish homes. Ancoats-born Mick Burke recalled of his Irish mother that:

> Although she never made me go to church, she had an altar in the front room and would go on her knees in front of the crucifix. Father would say, 'You're a bloody old fool Maggie. There's nobody listening to you,' and she'd reply, 'And you're a bloody heathen!'

She would also pay itinerant barrel organists to play *Faith of our Fathers* on their machines.[77]

There was a thin line between official Catholicism and the world of superstition, spirits and magic, a difference that the Church often ob-scured. The popularity of the shrine at Holywell in north Wales, sup-posedly the scene of a medieval miracle, was encouraged. It became extremely popular with Catholics, who visited the shrine on summer day-trips. Some no doubt hoped to become part of that steady, if modest, crop of cripples and other unfortunates allegedly cured by a visit.[78] Lourdes was a more fecund, if distant, source of fascination. Afflicted and disabled members from the diocese made annual pilgrimages, which were avidly reported by the local Catholic press. In 1934 one apparent recovery from paralysis made the front page of the *Manchester Catholic Herald*.[79]

Catholics were freer than other denominations to exploit their adher-ents' love of show and beauty to encourage popular devotions. In contrast, the Anglican church was still under the surveillance of the Protestant League on the look-out for 'Romish practices' during the early 1900s.[80] This aspect was deliberately emphasized. Cardinal Vaughan recognized that the letter of the dogma was not enough and sought to encourage services in which, 'all is cusp and bright rather than uncertain and tediously

slow.' He also encouraged the introduction of more congregational singing because of its popularity.[81] As Bart Kennedy of St Anne's, Ancoats,
recalled of mass:

> The altar was ablaze and glowing with lights and the shrine of gold.
> The priest chanted forth sonorous words. Old, old words that had
> come down through the ages. 'Kyrie eleison! Kyrie eleison! Christie
> eleison!' The boys on the altar in their white robes gave out their
> responses and in the air were solemn organ-tones.
> And when the stoled priest held aloft the chalice to expose the
> Sacred Heart! How breathless was the hush that came over all as the
> sound of the bell told of the presence of the Body of Christ![82]

Sometimes Catholic ritual was so splendid that even the favourable attention of curious Protestants was aroused.[83]

The Hierarchy's attempt to encourage Irish immigrants to identify with
its own organizational interests was, in many ways, successful. Adherents
came to accept its authority in a number of matters and identified with
some of the Church's concerns. However, the campaign to reinterpret
Irishness in a manner amenable to English society seems to have
floundered. Similarly, the effort to transform the Catholic body into one
in which conformists prevailed had disappointing results: such Catholics
formed a small band. Yet, those who deliberately avoided any contact with
the Church throughout their lives were also a small minority. The great
majority stood somewhere between these two positions: most felt some
sort of attachment to their Church, although this sentiment owed more
to loyalties of family and national origin than doctrine. Nevertheless, they
considered themselves Catholic and usually attended mass and Easter
communion once in a while. It is invidious to put numbers against these
categories, but a sensible guess would be: the devout accounted for 5 per
cent of Catholics, those who frequently attended to their devotions
amounted to 35 per cent, those who infrequently did so, 40 per cent,
whilst those who rarely if ever attended mass came to 20 per cent. Therefore,
so far as formal devotions are concerned, levels do not suggest much of
a 're-making' of Catholicism in England except in the negative sense:
there was at least no collapse in the number of those attending church.
Moreover, if measured in other ways the cultural significance of the Church
was far greater than mass attendance might suggest. The Church was an
organic, accepted feature of working-class life. This wider cultural impact
of the Church is further explored in the following chapter.

four

Catholicism and popular culture

The Catholic family

The Catholic Church's principal purpose was to tend to the spiritual welfare of adherents. However, wanting to direct the fate of the soul, the Church felt it also needed to control the mind and body, and consequently sought to dominate the life of every Catholic. Each parish tried to build the framework for a life apart. Where possible parishioners were provided with their own educational, welfare, health and leisure facilities. Within this separate world the Church tried to mould adherents' thoughts and activities, in the hope that it would also 'improve' their civic, moral and – most importantly – religious conduct.

While this aim was pursued with a unique vigour, the method was not exclusively Catholic. Evangelical philanthropic and religious bodies employed similar means to persuade sections of the English working class to adhere to their particular views of the world. The Church, however, saw matters primarily in defensive terms: it merely hoped to extend its sway over those born Catholic and had little desire to convert Protestants. In fact, the separate Catholic world was intended to protect adherents from the malign influence of rival religious and political bodies. The Catholic Church in England was an insecure institution: it felt that society was inherently anti-Catholic. This was made clear in an article that attempted to explain why so few young Catholic men raised their hats to show respect to priests when they passed them in the street:

Brought up, perhaps, in a Protestant atmosphere, in which every mean method was used to ridicule and misrepresent Catholic doctrines, practices, nations and individuals . . . you, poor little weakling, became mortally ashamed of your race and faith when you were a child, and you find it difficult, even now, to overcome the tendency to bow down, mentally at least, in the presence of the supercilious condescension which deigns to admit you, as a fawning sycophant, to the circle of alien adorers.[1]

This was a conspiracy the Church hoped to combat by encouraging members to withdraw behind protective barriers. The English Church was not alone in being possessed by these fears: in Europe, the United States and throughout the Irish diaspora Catholics had protective 'structural fences' raised around them.[2]

The values promoted behind these Catholic barricades largely conformed with those advocated elsewhere in society. Although some members of the clergy talked of 'the vanity of all dreams of earthly happiness' and the 'blessing of poverty' others referred to 'scroungers' and complained of 'being pestered by beggars'. Individualism, self-improvement, temperance and thrift were all keenly encouraged – not contentment with one's lot.[3] Yet, it would be simplistic to describe the Church as a 'bourgeois' institution intent on encouraging adherents to internalize capitalist doctrines. Cardinal Manning advocated temperance because he felt that if the Irish abstained from alcohol they would rise up the social ladder and thereby strengthen his Church.[4] Catholic leaders reasoned that working-class adherents who were sober, moderate in their habits and obedient to the rule of law would help advance the Church's cause in a hostile world. Yet, in seeking to impose its authority the Church, nevertheless, endorsed middle-class ideas and practices (like those listed above) with little or no relevance to the lives of the majority of its working-class adherents.

The Church had an enviable reputation for its ability to influence even its poorest members. Non-Catholic middle-class contemporaries, frustrated at their own inability to mould the working class in their own image, were impressed by its aptitude in this regard. In London, the Church was credited with preventing adherents from turning to disorder and political agitation. M.C. Bishop considered:

> That the Irish do not figure yet more largely than they do in the criminal statistics of our great cities, that this alien million is not an advanced cancer in the English body politic, is due not to the policeman, but to priests . . .

According to Charles Booth the Church's control of adherents was, 'carried to a degree of perfection and stamped with a thoroughness which make all the Protestant methods seem pinchbeck in comparison.' Even some Irish Nationalists assumed that the Church was able to promote temperance and saw its attempts to culturally isolate adherents as a means of preserving the Irish identity in England.[5]

The main focus of the Church's social activity was the family, which was seen as its most important prop. Although this view was prevalent throughout other voluntary organizations, the family was the centre-piece of a specifically Catholic form of analysis.[6] This was the amalgam of a romanticized view of the character of English Catholicism before the Reformation and Pope Leo XIII's Rerum Novarum of 1891. The Middle Ages were seen as a period when the state was subordinated to the Catholic Church. This, in turn, held sway over a civil society comprised of independent, self-regulating corporate bodies; pre-eminent among these was the family. This view was consistent with Leo's proposition that because the family was historically prior to the state it should enjoy precedence over it. The main thrust of these ideas was that it was the Church's duty to oppose most, if not all, attempts by government to interfere in family life. This point was made most forcibly in the Catholic Social Guild's *A primer of social science*, first published in 1913. There it was stated that:

> The family is the primary product of nature, and is self-contained. Into the family the state has no right of entry except to maintain rights not otherwise defensible. The children, until they grow up, belong to the parents, as being a part and a continuation of themselves.[7]

For ideological, historical and deeply practical reasons the Church looked with apprehension on the seemingly ineluctable extension of state power. It was afraid that the state would eventually interpose itself between the Church and adherents as a means of destroying Catholicism. These suspicions were especially acute after the return of the 1906 Liberal government, which was committed to increasing public control over denominational schools. This was interpreted as a way of introducing state education, seen by Cardinal Vaughan as, 'a violation of the law of nature, a destruction of the rights and responsibilities of parents' who alone had been given charge of their children's 'immortal souls'. It was in this light that Bishop Casartelli warned Catholics that Liberal proposals were part of an attempt to, 'absorb family rights, to instil a state despotism in your homes.' Some imaginative Catholics even suggested that once the ability of parents to send children to the school of their choice had been denied by government a collapse of parental responsibilities would follow and cause the destruction both of Church and society. Perspectives had not changed much by the 1930s.[8]

The Church was, therefore, a liberal institution in the sense that it saw the state as an unnecessary and probably malevolent influence upon the individual. In the wake of the First World War middle-class Catholics established the Mothers' Defence League. Their aim was to frustrate what was taken to be the state's attempt to control the family through an, 'invasion of the homes of working-class mothers by a legion of health officials and welfare workers.' Yet, this was a liberalism that was not applied to the actions of the Church. For, whereas the state was attacked for entering Catholic homes it was deemed perfectly natural and right for priests or Catholic voluntary workers to cross the threshold.[9] The truth was, of course, that the Church saw in the state one of its most powerful rivals intent on encroaching into its own sphere of cultural influence.

Before it could be protected from external threats, the family needed to be put on a proper, Catholic, basis. This meant, first, that adherents should only marry those of the same faith and, secondly, that the authority of husbands be accepted by wives and children. Marriage was seen as a way of channelling a man's energies towards self-improvement. Legal union diverted his gaze away from those 'alluring vices that have no place in his eye or mind when his attentions are centred upon a devoted wife.'[10]

The marriage had to be of a certain sort: those between partners from different denominations were, 'a disaster, a fearful misfortune – in the vast majority of cases full of dreadful misery in this world and the world to come.' Even those mixed unions for which a Catholic had taken the trouble to gain a dispensation were celebrated with a truncated ceremonial, as mark of the Church's disapproval.[11] The 1900 Salford diocesan census revealed that priests considered mixed marriages 'most pernicious', 'unwholesome' and 'a curse'. Impressionistic evidence, recorded elsewhere in the census, suggests that these attitudes were an expression of strongly-held, but nevertheless erroneous, prejudices. Mixed marriages were by no means always detrimental to Catholicism. In St Sebastian's parish, Pendleton, out of a total of eighty-nine mixed marriages one was described as 'good', seven as 'fair' and eighty as 'bad'. In Corpus Christi, however, such unions were seen in a rather better light. There, 50 per cent were defined as 'good', 30 per cent were said to be 'fair', 10 per cent in 'great danger' and another 10 per cent 'practically lost'. Clearly, there was a wide disparity between what individual priests thought made a good Catholic marriage. Moreover, the impact of a mixed marriage on the faith of the resulting children was uncertain. The St Sebastian's incumbent felt that those parents who neglected their children's religion within a mixed marriage would have done the same if married to another Catholic. Moreover, two priests from St Chad's in Ancoats and English Martyrs in Urmston, considered that if the Catholic partner was devout, such unions were actually advantageous, as they led to the Church gaining an Anglican adult as well as all their children.[12] Despite this positive aspect to mixed marriages the Church as a whole discouraged them.

Once established, the Catholic family was to take a patriarchal character, for 'If order and peace are to prevail, there must of course be a head, a ruler, a director. And that head, no doubt, is man.' Such domestic order was ordained by both the authority of nature and of God. This did not mean that a husband was given free rein to abuse his family. He had to take his responsibilities seriously, eat all his meals at home and spend his leisure hours there. Men in pubs were exhorted to spend their wages on their families and not on beer. Yet, if marriage was a partnership it required that each side adhere faithfully to assigned gender and generational roles. Within the family:

> The father's power should rule, and the mother's sweetness direct;
> the children's obedience to their parent's commands should be per-
> fect in simplicity, and the mutual love for one another should be
> stronger than death.[13]

In particular, importance was placed on the submission of women to men.
Cardinal Bourne opposed the 1922 Care of Infants Bill because he considered that it treated wives as joint heads of the family; this he could not
accept.[14]

Despite urging men to take their duties more seriously, the Church still
saw wives as responsible for the real burden of domestic life. It was the
woman's duty to maintain the family's integrity and ensure that her children remained good Catholics and attended a Catholic school.[15] The
Virgin Mary was widely employed as a role-model for Catholic women, being
meek, mild and obedient to authority. The relationship between women
and Mary was expressed each summer when each parish chose its own
May Queen. The selected girl was dressed in virginal white and concluded
her procession by crowning the statue of the Madonna. Mary was by no
means the only saintly virgin used by the Church to emphasize favoured
female characteristics. Saint Winifred of the popular shrine at Holywell
allegedly died rather than be seduced before marriage.[16] Whether the
Church's emphasis upon a woman's subordination made Catholic women
more subject to male oppression than others of their sex is open to question. A large number of secular female figures were used by non-Catholics
to reinforce men's position over women; it was widely accepted that men
held the position of authority.[17] However, the nature of the authority ex-
erted by the Church over female adherents meant that its views may have
been taken more seriously.

Irish women might have been more susceptible to the notion of female
subordination and inferiority because of the ingrained belief in the 'natural'
division of labour in rural Ireland.[18] As the novels of Patrick MacGill
indicate, popular Irish conceptions of masculinity and femininity were
extremely rigid. He describes his heroine, Nora Ryan, as 'small, frail and
tender', and continually refers to her as a 'little angel' whose pure soul ill-
prepared her for life across the water. In contrast, MacGill presents the
hero, Dermod Flynn, as forceful and active. He successfully relies on his
physical strength, something from which his sweetheart Nora also gains
much comfort. Thus, whereas MacGill defines an Irish woman's life as
being comprised of 'dreams, sorrow, love and self-sacrifice', Dermod is
made to declare that 'as a true Irishman, I could have spent all day long
looking at fights'.[19]

The Church also seemed more zealous in its desire to see the subordination of women than perhaps any other religious body. Some clerics
seem to have suffered from a paranoid fear of those women who slipped
free of the bonds of wifely obedience. Ironically, due to its reliance on
female teaching staff the Church provided some women with the means

of avoiding marriage. In 1893 a St Alban's priest bemoaned the 'spirit of female domination', which he blamed on young women teachers. He even attributed one family's irreligion to the wife's usurpation of domestic authority. It was, he suggested, time to 'bring women into lawful subjection to men.'[20] These fears were brought to a head in the aftermath of the First World War, when it seemed that young female factory workers were unwilling to resume their God-given place behind men. Bishop Casartelli declared that when such women were paid high wages their moral sense degenerated. By separating husbands and wives, the war had:

> . . . brought about an abnormal state of mind especially to our young people of both sexes. It broke down a great deal of maiden's reserve, both in speech and conduct. The years unsettled their minds.

In 1921 a general mission was held in Manchester to restore pre-war order to Catholics who had got 'out of hand'.[21]

If all Catholic women suffered as a consequence of their faith, working-class wives suffered most. This was, in part, due to domestic economic realities: it was so much harder for a Catholic woman to uphold her duties in a proletarian context. In addition, unskilled Irish labourers were infamous for beating their wives. According to Pat O'Mara it was only his mother's 'very Catholic conscience' that kept her in a marriage with a drunken and violent husband. Her priority was to remain within the 'rigid laws of the Catholic Church in the matter of marriage' and raise her offspring to be good Catholics.[22] More prosperous Catholic women enjoyed an active life within the parish and some were even able to represent the Church on public bodies. In the late 1880s Rose Hyland stood as a Catholic candidate for the Manchester Board of Guardians and became the first woman to win election.[23] By no means all female teachers were prepared to accept their subordinate place; a minority supported female suffrage and publicly debated with clerics, who felt they were incapable of making rational political decisions.[24] In 1911 a small number of middle-class Catholic women formed their own suffrage society, although this only seems to have established branches in London and Liverpool. Nevertheless, despite the moderation of their programme, which remained hostile to any reform of the divorce law or the promotion of birth control, the Hierarchy refused to support it.[25]

The parish school

Parish schools were seen by the Church as the most influential means of creating a separate Catholic identity. These were much more than places of education: they were a means of ensuring the existence of a Catholic culture. As in the United States, Church schools lay at the heart of the parochial network. A parish without a school was like a parish without a church: it was simply inconceivable.[26] If the Church was adamant about no other aspect of conformity it was attendance at school: 'Catholic children will go to Catholic schools – or nowhere', declared Cardinal Vaughan.[27] Priests were willing to sacrifice every other cause to pay for the construction and maintainence of their schools. The importance attached to Catholic schools within the clergy was reflected in the attitudes of most ordinary adherents who, if they demonstrated their Catholicism in no other way, ensured that their offspring attended a Church school.[28] Parents came to see them as an expression of their own identity and helped finance them through innumerable raffles and collections.

In Lancashire at least, emphasis on the importance of denominational education was shared by Anglicans: on this issue even Catholics and Orange lodge members could agree. It was an Anglican Bishop of Manchester who wrote that, 'Church and school were twin sisters . . . and of the two sisters, school was often the more favoured.'[29] Immediately prior to 1914 a majority of Manchester's working-class children were educated by either Anglicans or Catholics. Throughout the city as a whole, 48 per cent of children were taught at Catholic (13 per cent) or Anglican (35 five per cent) institutions. In working-class districts this proportion substantially increased: in north Manchester Catholic schools alone provided places for 48 per cent of children, while 38 per cent were accommodated in Anglican establishments. During the inter-war period the Church of England allowed municipal schools to assume responsibility for education. However, by 1938 the Catholic Church had actually increased the proportion of Manchester children under its tutelage to 20 per cent.[30]

Despite their important place within immigrant culture, conditions inside Catholic schools were often very unpleasant. Before the 1902 Education Act augmented local authority grants, Cardinal Vaughan accepted the accusation that his schools were among the worst in England. As Bishop of Salford, he had been forced to oppose building improvements because the diocese could not pay for them.[31] Even after 1902, many schools remained in a decrepit state because Catholic authorities were unable to increase spending. During the 1890s overcrowding was such in St Edmund's that the Schools' Inspector twice considered withdrawing state funding; forty years later the situation had not much improved.[32] Schools were also short of trained staff. Before 1914 there was an average of only one certified teacher for every hundred pupils in Manchester's Catholic schools. The resulting strain on some members of staff was obvious: in the early 1920s two teachers left St Anne's, Ancoats, after both apparently suffered nervous breakdowns.[33]

Many of the lessons taught in Catholic and Anglican schools were very similar, and Catholics used text books that glorified England at Ireland's expense. Bart Kennedy characterized his education as being:

> . . . taught a great deal about the glory of God and the glory of England, and very little about the art of reading and writing . . . It was a great privilege to be born in England, the teacher said.

Pat O'Mara in Liverpool had a slightly different experience: he recalled that, while teachers praised the Empire, they were silent about England's misdeeds in Ireland. Despite the imperialist emphasis of some Catholic teachers, it is improbable that, as in Anglican schools, denominational education promoted Conservative sympathies. Given the Irish background of many pupils this would have been extremely unlikely, although they do seem to have made some Irish pupils feel inferior to the English. There were, in any case, a number of Irish teachers, such as the head of St Wilfrid's, who were active Nationalists. Such staff would not have passed over Ireland's history without comment.[34]

Catholic and Anglican schools were also as one in relying on corporal punishment to enforce discipline. However, perhaps because of their vital role in forming young Catholic minds, Catholic schools were rather more enthusiastic to impress on their charges the power and influence of the Church. Pupils were punished not just for misdemeanours committed during lessons, but also for those perpetrated outside school. Boys from St Joseph's, Ordsall, caught stealing in the street were caned in front of the entire school; street fighting was punished at St Michael's and also in Ancoats, St Patrick's upheld cleanliness with the threat of a caning. Thus, in an extremely crude way, teachers demonstrated to pupils those values that made a good Catholic. It is perhaps not surprising that it was the punishment, rather than the reasoning behind it, which impressed itself on children: J.R. Clynes's abiding memory of school was his fear of the cane. Moreover, some pupils became more than a touch cynical about the relationship between religion and pain. During the inter-war period boys at St Patrick's sang about their head teacher, 'Jock MacIver is a very good man. He goes to church on Sunday. He prays to God to give him grace to whack the kids on Monday.' In 1932 the Manchester Education Authority was so concerned about the extent of corporal punishment at St Edmund's that a representative was despatched to discuss the use of 'positive' rather than 'negative' disciplinary measures.[35]

The main obvious difference between a Catholic and non-Catholic education was in the realm of religion. In 1888 the Hierarchy issued precise instructions on how priests were to ensure that schools exuded the appropriate devotional tone. It was, for example, felt important that class rooms displayed 'objects and pictures of piety'.[36] There is a strong suspicion that in the eyes of some priests secular lessons were much less important than spiritual teaching. In 1925, Dean Murray of St Wilfrid's praised his late head teacher for realizing that:

> The true function of a Catholic teacher was to train the soul of the child for Heaven and that the foundation of that training should be the moral teaching of Christ as explained and interpreted by the Catholic Church. He had intense love for his Church . . . He excelled in loyalty to the clergy and in respect for their office, and he instilled that into the children from their earliest years.[37]

Teachers seem to have been selected less for their professional competence and more for their devotion to the Faith. Nuns taught in nineteen Manchester parishes, whilst lay teachers were often church organists, choir masters and presidents of confraternities and sodalities. A similar priority made Catholic schools in the United States less educationally effective than others. It may not have been the intention, but this emphasis on religion may have been at the expense of secular lessons.[38]

Much useful school time was spent ensuring that children had attended to their devotions. Each Monday teachers held a mass register; to discourage lying some churches distributed tickets at services. If a pupil consistently missed Sunday services punishment followed: non-attenders were detained after school had finished at St Augustine's before 1914; girls at St Patrick's in the 1950s were sent in disgrace to the back of the class and were allowed to sit at the front only after they had been to confession. During his official monthly visits the parish priest consulted attendance registers and confronted consistent offenders.[39] Fortunately, for the Church, such recalcitrants were in a small minority: in 1930s Liverpool attendance at mass by Catholic school children was said to be virtually universal.[40] For whatever reason, most parents were only too willing to force their children to attend mass.

After leaving school, however, attendance – especially among boys – became much more irregular. The disappearance of outward conformity should not obscure the way that much of the Church's message had been internalized. A survey conducted during the 1940s revealed that the public's ideas about religion deviated wildly from orthodox dogma. However, Catholics emerged as being in greater harmony with their Church's teaching. As Booth had noted in the early 1900s, the aim of the Catholic school was to instil Church principles so firmly into the child, 'that these may be accepted not loosely, as a garment to be cast off, but as a natural inheritance never entirely lost.'[41] Despite all that followed childhood, this appears to have largely been the case.

Even so, the most important result of Catholic education was not knowledge of theological precepts. The teaching of dogma officially occupied only a small part of the school day, although it seems that some institutions taught it during time scheduled for other subjects.[42] Instead, the most significant effect of schooling was the way it socialized children within an exclusively Catholic atmosphere. Parish schools reinforced a child's awareness of his or her distinct cultural identity. Just as it reinforced prevailing identities of class and gender, so denominational education also underlined loyalties of faith and nationality. As in the United States, it bred sectarian rivalries within the young.[43] Schooling was an experience that united Catholic with Catholic and divided them all from Protestants, pitching the two groups into deliberate rivalry. Inter-school sport, for which St Patrick's mainly Irish scholars significantly wore green jerseys, was a favourite arena of battle. Catholic–Anglican football games in Trafford Park had a special competitive edge; any contest between St Bartholemew's and

St Joseph's in Ordsall was apparently a 'needle match'. Outside school hours, children also gave vent to sectarian loyalties: St Patrick's pupils fought street battles with children from Abbot Street Board school. Anthony Burgess has also described conflicts between Catholic children at St Edmund's and their Church of England neighbours. Each side had their own rhyme: Anglican children would chant, 'Cat lick, Cat lick, going to Mass, riding to Hell on the devil's ass', only to be met by, 'Proddy dog, Proddy dog on the wall, a small raw spud will feed you all. A ha'penny candle will give you light to read the Bible of a Saturday night.'[44]

Controlling adolescents

During the late nineteenth century the Church was possessed by a sense of crisis, with the realization that a number of its adherents were increasingly beyond control. These were working-class adolescents who had just left the protective atmosphere of school and were about to enter the world of work and youth street culture. This reflected similar concerns expressed outside the Church: youth was widely defined as a social 'problem'.[45] Deemed to be most exposed to anti-Catholic influences, adolescents were also the group which most obviously rejected the Church's authority.[46] Because it was assumed that girls stayed at home, they were thought not to be as vulnerable as their male peers. Such an assumption was largely illusory, in Lancashire at least, because young working-class women were not excluded from street culture and fully participated in the world of work.[47] Nevertheless, due to these misconceptions adolescent males remained the focal point of the Church's activities.

In moving into youth work the Church was responding to a number of putative threats, in particular the proselytizing initiatives of other denominations intent on attracting young men into their ranks.[48] St John's in Salford held a summer camp in 1901 only because rival denominations did so. The Church also wanted to divert youngsters' attention away from certain 'evils' endemic to working-class life. St Aloysius's established a football team as a means of encouraging those under seventeen to give public houses a wide berth. More positively, it hoped to isolate adolescents from the rest of society and thereby improve them socially, morally and spiritually. A parochial Boy's Brigade was meant to be:

> A Centre of Catholic loyalty and Catholic activity; each a refuge from the allurements of Socialism, the temptations of the streets, [and] the poisonous companionship of the loafer.

When reformed, a Catholic young man was to become 'a lily among thorns' within the working class.[49]

Lack of available resources meant that initiatives were piecemeal and depended on the philanthropic inclinations of the few wealthy lay adherents. As a consequence, the number of Catholic Lads' Clubs in Manchester was always less than that deemed desirable.[50] The most concerted effort to organize Catholic youth was made in St William's parish, Angel Meadow, a district widely thought to be on the margins of civilization. This was also where Irish Catholics were most concentrated: if Catholic youth was in danger anywhere, it was in the Meadow. Youth work in the area was financed by Edward Caulfield, a wealthy Catholic merchant and Justice of the Peace.[51] Caulfield established the first Catholic Working Lad's Club in the Meadow during the late 1880s. By the early 1890s there were two clubs, one for 'better class' boys, able to pay a small subscription, and another for those unable to afford even a nominal fee. By 1894 this latter club had enrolled about 300 members. Girls had to wait until 1894 for their own place and that only after they had protested about Caulfield's neglect to the Bishop of Salford.

The clubs were intended to improve the spiritual and social life of members. The former point was made by one boy who told his Bishop that Caulfield's aim was for each to realize that, 'Though we are poor we are none the less loyal to our Church and we glory and boast in being Irish Catholic young men.' Boys were expected to attend mass every week, something ensured by a visit from members of the parochial Guild of the Sacred Heart on Sunday morning. The clubs also tried to inculcate wider social values. It was claimed that they had brought about a decline in street fights, something Caulfield, as a member of the Bench, was obviously keen to encourage. To publicize his good work he even brought fellow magistrates to the clubs. However, the effect of his efforts is open to doubt. If they were anything like their Protestant counterparts, boys would have joined for practical reasons: the clubs provided free trips, gifts and recreational opportunities beyond police interference. Moreover, Caulfield was unable to enforce temperance, while gambling for small stakes was also permitted. It was also suspected by some that club members still participated in gang violence.

The Catholic Boys' Brigade movement was seen as another means of transforming irreligious Catholic roughs into devout citizens. This also followed a model established by other denominations. The first two Catholic companies were formed in the slums of Dublin and Southwark during the 1890s. As with those of other denominations, the brigades were not popular with the urban poor. One major problem was that a full uniform cost the equivalent of a labourer's weekly wage. Moreover, the movement's associations with the military were criticized by a number of Irish parents. By 1910 only two companies had been formed in Manchester, these being in the relatively prosperous parishes of Holy Name and Mount Carmel, Blackley.[52] However, after winning the official endorsement of Bishop Casartelli, 4,000 Catholic boys had been enrolled into forty units throughout the diocese by 1914. Unfortunately, the First World War wiped out many of these recruits: of eighty members of Mount Carmel's scout troop all but four enlisted and nearly half were either killed or wounded.[53] Inter-war financial pressures forced the diocesan brigades to affiliate to the

Lancashire Territorials as a means of claiming funds from the War Office. This merely confirmed Irish suspicions of the militaristic nature of the movement, at a time when British forces were alleged to have been committing atrocities in Ireland. By 1924 Manchester had only one company, which disbanded six years later. The Catholic scout movement fared little better: by 1933 there were only four troops in the city with a mere 259 members.[54]

Despite various punitive efforts to discourage them, Catholic children still attended clubs sponsored by rivals. Hugh Oldham Lads' Club, located a few yards from St Patrick's church, had many Irish members; the Salford Lads' Club was similarly patronized by boys from all denominations. The cultural impact of membership of such institutions was probably not as disastrous as the Church feared: a boy could attend Hugh Oldham's and become a practicing Catholic in adulthood.[55] In any case, after 1918, a declining number participated in denominationally-organized youth activities, whether Catholic or Protestant. In 1918 41 per cent of adolescents were connected with such bodies, but by 1940 this had fallen to 28 per cent. The possible cause of this fall was the increasing appeal of commercial leisure.[56] This was especially the case in working-class districts. In Hulme, for example, barely 10 per cent of adolescents attended denominational clubs by the late 1930s; St Wilfrid's was especially backward in this regard.[57]

In contrast to the decline in the popularity of denominational leisure, the appeal of the street was universal and undiminished. The street was where adolescent girls spent 30 per cent of their time during the summer. Not being expected to help in the home, boys of the same age were able to spend even longer there.[58] This, despite priests seeing the street as encouraging 'vulgarity and coarseness in mind and heart'. To combat its influence one Liverpool cleric imposed a curfew on children in his parish playing outside the home after half past seven in the evening. Although initially effective during winter, it is unlikely to have been widely observed once nights grew lighter and warmer.[59] In alleys and highways children and adolescents mixed with little reference to their parents' prejudices. One of Robert Roberts's boyhood friends was Sid Carey, whose father was an unskilled labourer of Irish descent. Although the Careys were regarded as 'low class' by adults, Sid was accepted by their offspring. In a similar manner, a boy named Monaghan was a gang member, although his English peers referred to him as 'Irish'.[60] Such street socialization created a group solidarity among working-class children which, temporarily at least, overcame sectarian differences.[61] Not being residentially ghettoized, young Irish Catholics were active participants in this process. They accepted and shared one of the most powerful normative values taught by such association: loyalty to the street or immediate neighbourhood. Such local patriotism, one of the commanding features of working-class districts, inevitably cut across rivalries established at school, thereby partly neutralizing the Church's work.[62]

The most dramatic form taken by this type of allegiance was the often violent activities of street gangs which, in the late nineteenth century, went under the name of 'scuttling'. Such gangs were predominantly composed of unskilled and semi-skilled males in their teens or early twenties, who enjoyed nothing better than battling with rivals from neighbouring districts.[63] Each gang had its own uniform; members of the Napoo, for example, were especially fond of red neckerchiefs and buckled belts. This particular group was formed by the sons of carters, porters and stall hands from Smithfield Market and operated in the Oldham Street area between 1910 and 1920. Given their residential and occupational origins, it was hardly accidental that they were at one time led by a youth named Logan. In fact, many scuttling gangs followed young men with Irish antecedents: in the 1890s there was Broughton's Jimmy O'Neil, Red Shelley from the Adelphi, Jerry Hoddy in Greengate and the 'king' of Hulme's scuttlers was Thomas Calligan.[64] In complete contrast, inter-war Glasgow had Catholic and Protestant gangs which fought battles across more clearly marked sectarian boundaries.[65]

Gang fights were most intense when residential patterns reflected racial differences. This is probably why the principal victims were Jewish rather than Irish.[66] Despite their shared minority status, Irish Catholic working-class youths were as anti-Semitic as their English peers. Roberts has recalled how Sid Carey's father, a former leader of Salford's Hope Street gang, once gave vent to such an outlook:

'We stopped them bloody Yids moving into the district', he once reminisced. 'Once them bloody "noses" get into a neighbourhood, they take it over. The place is no class at all!'[67]

The Napoo proudly upheld these sentiments. During the Battle of the Somme, and annually for two or three years thereafter, they fought Jewish boys from Cheetham Hill, who they blamed for the First World War because of their German-sounding surnames. After 1918 the gang also pursued a campaign to 'protect' Christian girls from the clutches of Jewish boys.[68]

Retaining adults

Adults were less subject to the Church's attempt to modify conduct. This was mainly because it was assumed that by the time they reached maturity most Catholics were, for good or ill, beyond change. Most men who participated in Church-provided leisure activities and organizations were already devout Catholics.[69] However, married women of child-bearing age were seen in a rather different light because of their presumed influence over children. The Catholic Women's League, whose members were mainly middle class, formed a Mothers' and Babies' Welcome in St Anne's, Ancoats.[70] The aim was to:

Educate our mothers in the proper method of feeding, clothing and general care of their children, and to encourage them to take a more serious view of the physical welfare of their little ones.

In its first year 100 mothers regularly attended the Welcome, although by 1912 this number had fallen to sixty. Expectant mothers were given free milk; they were also encouraged to join a thrift fund to which for every shilling saved a penny was added. The Welcome was also concerned with the spiritual well-being of mothers because of its effect on their children. Meetings began with a hymn and concluded with a prayer; irregular mass attenders were encouraged to modify their conduct. This example was emulated in parishes throughout the city, although paucity of resources impeded wider progress. As with the St William's Lads' Clubs, the St Anne's initiative would have been impossible without the support of a concerned and wealthy Catholic, in this case Rose Hyland. Moreover, by the 1920s these Welcomes also began to fall foul of the law; the St Anne's prototype was closed in 1924 because it was unable to meet conditions established by the Board of Education.

For some working-class women the parish provided a cheap and collective form of leisure. As one labourer's wife recalled of inter-war St Alban's:

> There was always something going on at the church, either a potato pie party – all the women would make a potato pie and you'd have a piano going or a fiddle or something – and Whist drives. In the summer we'd have a days outing.[71]

During a period when most women were restricted to spending their time in the home or street, the parish church must have become something of a refuge. However, it is unlikely that parochial activities completely supplanted neighbourhood loyalties, which were especially important to married women with children. Due to poverty, working-class mothers combined their collective resources, thereby making possible what the individual was unable to achieve. By no means all Irish Catholics participated in these self-help networks. One Irish-born woman who lived in inter-war Hulme claimed she remained isolated from her English neighbours. Most, however, found some sort of place, although this did not mean that hostility completely disappeared on the part of those non-Catholic women with whom they co-operated. This following example, concerning attitudes about two Irish Catholic women, has been recalled by an Ordsall woman born of English parents:

> They were never invited [to pay respects to a dead neighbour], never especially. They weren't allowed into anybody's house in fact. They were tolerated in our street. They were always drunk, rowing and they'd rather drink than spend money on the children. Or they'd send [it] to Mother Theresa's statue; the widow's mite they called it . . . They weren't outcasts because if they really needed help both Maria and Sarah Jane Wilkes would have gone into them. [The respondent had

earlier cited an example of how neighbours helped the two women while they were pregnant.] Immediately they came out of the house me mother would have gone and stood in the back kitchen, stripped herself off, washed herself clean, put clean clothes on and the other clothes would have gone straight into the sink, into disinfectant, because they were dirty [with lice].[72]

It is difficult to disentangle the factors that contributed to the lowly status of these Irish women: poverty and intemperance rather than nationality seem to have been most influential. There is, however, an evident distaste for their religion. Yet, despite such misgivings, neighbours still rallied round: affiliation based on street loyalty, rather than ethnicity, ultimately carried the day.

Mixed marriages

When it came to marriage, national, and especially religious, differences firmly reasserted themselves. The Church's attitude to mixed marriages was well-known and was obediently reflected in attitudes expressed in most working-class Catholic homes. This does not appear always to have been the case, as mixed marriages were much more common during the middle of the nineteenth century. In Bristol in 1851 two-fifths of Irish spouses were married to English-born partners; in York in 1841 the proportion was as large as 71.4 per cent. These figures come from a period when the Church had hardly begun to build its separate institutional network. After the 1850s mixed marriages become more infrequent: in Stafford between 1862 and 1871 only one in three Irish Catholics married an English partner; in York the proportion of mixed unions fell by half in the thirty years after 1841.[73]

The unusual gender balance within the immigrant population probably promoted inter-marriage among the Irish-born. In 1931 53.3 per cent of all Irish immigrants were female. Manchester and Salford were even closer to a perfect match between the sexes, with their respective Irish-born populations being 51.3 per cent and 50.9 per cent female. However, due to the nature of the labour market in other parts of the country male and female immigrants were not always so equally balanced. In Newcastle, only 44.8 per cent were female, a proportion that had been as low as 39.4 per cent thirty years earlier. In contrast, in London 61.5 per cent of the Irish-born were women. Thus, in such cities the pressure for men and women to seek partners beyond their national group, if not outside their religion, must have been intense.[74]

British historians have not systematically explored the extent to which Catholics married outside their own group. Work undertaken in the United States, however, suggests that they would have usually married fellow adherents.[75] More impressionistic local evidence also indicates that

Manchester's Catholics rarely looked beyond the sectarian divide in their search for potential spouses. The Irish-born also usually married those either of Irish birth or immediate descent; in the United States, this preference was especially pronounced.[76] Oral testimony provides numerous examples of young Irish workers leaving Manchester to marry a partner from their home village only to return to the city to start married life. The city's Irish clubs also provided places for Irish youth to meet prospective partners without having to travel back home.[77] Religion could overcome national differences: it was a regular practice for men in Anthony Burgess's English Catholic family to marry Irish Catholic women.[78]

One study of north-west Lancashire has concluded that it was 'fairly rare' for religious differences to complicate emotional relationships. Alternative evidence drawn from the same area has led another historian to conclude that 'only exceptional couples married outside their religious groups'. This latter impression seems to be nearer the mark and is reinforced by Robert Roberts's suggestion that, in Salford, even slum Protestants suffered a loss of status if they married an Irish Catholic.[79] The popular view is that, whereas Catholics faced formal sanctions enforced by their Church, Protestants were subject to informal constraints imposed by friends and family. In fact, it seems that both sides were exposed to the same sorts of pressures, the only difference being one of degree. Anglican clerics were not exactly sanguine about mixed marriages. At various times the Bishops of Burnley and Blackburn both warned against their inherent dangers.[80] Popular Catholic opinion was also firmly opposed to mixed marriages: in 1916 Labour councillor and Catholic Tom Fox called them an 'evil'. One adherent dryly recalled that if she had taken a Protestant boy home to meet her father 'he wouldn't have been made terribly welcome'; two devout Catholic sisters of marrying age just after 1918 could not recall even one friend from St Patrick's marrying a non-Catholic.[81] A mixed marriage could mean that one or both partners were permanently ostracized by family and friends. This, despite tortuous compromises, such as christening children Catholic yet sending them to an Anglican school, or vice versa. Even if there was a reconciliation such unions often left abiding scars on relations with family, friends and neighbours.[82] As a consequence of such factors, therefore, mixed marriages were fairly rare, in some places at least. A 1927 Hulme survey revealed that, although 56 per cent of households were Anglican and 36 per cent Catholic, only 5 per cent were 'mixed'.[83]

Some of those raised within the Irish Catholic milieu indisputably married out of it, despite the Church's best efforts. Youth street culture provided an opportunity for members of the opposite sex to meet one another. The further removed a generation was from Irish birth and the more distant a family became from the Church the more likely offspring were to marry regardless of religion or nationality. Although Mary Bertenshaw had been sent to a Catholic school her parents rarely, if ever, went to church; she was something of a black sheep in class due to her own non-attendance. It was hardly a surprise, therefore, that she married a boy she had met during her hours playing in the street. In Plymouth, James Callaghan's petty officer Catholic father married a Protestant in 1902 despite initially being refused permission to do so by the Catholic naval chaplain. As a consequence, he gave up the Church, and allowed his two children to be raised as Baptists. However, his Irish roots were located in the dim past and, having left home at a very early age, he was free from any family pressure to conform.[84]

The numbers of mixed marriages seem to have been on the increase after 1914. In Bermondsey one-quarter of marriages in 1881 were mixed, but this proportion had doubled by 1928. In 1931 a priest from Leeds claimed that half the marriages conducted in the city's cathedral were mixed. He further complained that, 'Many young people regarded mixed marriage as quite within their rights, and got a shock when informed that they were strictly forbidden by the Church.' This might have been scare-mongering, something priests were prone to over this issue. Even if mixed marriages were on the rise they still involved a minority, albeit an ever-growing one. As late as 1935, the *London Catholic Herald* estimated that mixed marriages were 'very high', by which it meant a rate of 30 to 40 per cent. If this was correct, then not much had changed since the late nineteenth century.[85] Moreover, there were still families where it was almost impossible to contemplate marrying outside the bounds of Catholicism. As one man, who grew up in Preston during the 1930s and 1940s, recalled of the idea of marrying a Protestant:

> It was talked about as an abhorrent thing, and it would certainly mean eternal damnation if you did. People who did were talked about impersonally as 'them' or 'that thing'.[86]

The Church and processions

The Catholic Church used religious processions and ceremonial to rein-force adherents' sense of belonging to a separate culture. They comple-mented, in ritual form, the Church's more mundane attempts to raise structural fences around Catholics. As part of this process, adherents were also reminded of the centrality of the Church to their lives: they or their children literally marched behind Catholic banners. Furthermore, whilst emphasizing the distinctive nature of the Catholic identity processions were also meant to show non-Catholics the power and influence of the Church. In particular, they were to demonstrate that Catholics were an upright, ordered body of citizens who demanded respect for themselves and their Church.

While these were the intentions of those who organized Catholic pro-cessions, for participants and spectators their meaning was rather differ-ent. In particular, Irish Catholics used them to assert their national as well as religious identity. England provided few moments for the Irish to publicly celebrate their national heritage. On those few occasions when immigrants took to the streets it was to protest against England's misdeeds in Ireland. Even on St Patrick's Day the Irish were usually hidden from general view, as they celebrated privately, in homes, pubs and churches away from the general gaze. Apart from a few sprigs of shamrock worn in the streets few of those born outside Irish Catholic families would have known that it was St Patrick's Day. Elsewhere in the Irish diaspora St Patrick's Day was the excuse for immigrants to express both a pride in their national origin and also celebrate achievements made in their adopted country. In the United States, Civil War veterans and the Stars and Stripes were as prominent as the green and shamrock; non-Catholic civil dignitaries were also involved in celebrations. In Australia, St Patrick's Day was dominated by sports contests and musical evenings in which the non-Irish were encouraged to participate.[87] In England, however, St Patrick's Day was used by Nationalists to mobilize support for Home Rule. As such, their celebrations were not intended to win the approval of an already-hostile indigenous population. In 1905 one Irish writer went so far as to suggest that St Patrick's Day was, 'an occasion of offence to persons who were not fortunate enough to be born in Ireland.'[88] Moreover, due to their demand for Home Rule, any Irish expression of loyalty to England would have been qualified at best. This remained the case even after 1921 for, due to the bloody manner in which the Free State was created, most Irish had little reason to celebrate their place in England.[89]

St Patrick's Day was popular with the English public only once. This was during the Boer War when the success of the Irish Guards led to their compatriots in England being viewed in a uniquely favourable light. For St Patrick's Day in 1900 town halls across the country flew flags in honour of the event. In Manchester, such was the English demand for shamrock that its price rose so high that many members of the Irish working class could not afford a sprig. They had to make do with wearing anything that was green, including cabbage leaves. This favourable climate of opinion was short-lived, as most Nationalists criticized England's part in the South African conflict. By 1902 the Irish were once again deemed to be unpatriotic and St Patrick's Day passed without English comment. At least this meant that those Irish who wished to celebrate could afford to buy some real shamrock.[90]

Therefore, when Irish Catholics took to the streets it was usually to ostensibly express their Catholic faith rather than Irish nationality. Prior to 1914 even the poorest of churches held at least two annual parochial processions. These could be often grand and elaborate in their execution. The 1907 May Queen at St Francis's, Gorton, enjoyed the services of forty-eight page boys; in 1923 more than 2,000 participated in St John's Trinity procession.[91] Across industrial Lancashire, Cheshire and Yorkshire, the most important Catholic procession was the annual Whit parade, or 'walk'.[92] During Whit week both Anglicans and Catholics processed; competition was therefore to the fore of organizers' minds. The walks were also appropriated by members of the Irish and English working class, who took the spirit of sectarian rivalry a violent stage further.

Whitsun was a traditional period of revelry, the time when working-class parents bought their children new clothes which, if worn on Whit Sunday, were thought to bring good luck.[93] Late eighteenth century evangelicals had introduced the walks to try and wean Manchester's expanding population away from drinking and gambling. This they largely failed to do, although they did succeed in establishing the walks as an integral feature of the week, awkwardly juxtaposed as they were with less elevating activities.[94] Initially, the walks were organized by an alliance of Anglicans and Non-conformists. In 1801 denominational competition led to the creation of two separate Sunday school parades. By 1844 the Catholic Church had entered the fray and, by the last decades of the century, Non-conformists had largely abandoned the walks, considering them vulgar and irreligious. Thus, by the 1880s they had become a ritual and largely pacific means for Anglicans on Whit Monday and Catholics on Whit Friday to express their respective sectarian identities.[95]

Before 1887 the Catholic walk had begun at New Cross in Ancoats, the centre of Irish Manchester, and continued south and east through Ardwick, up Oxford Road, concluding at Piccadilly. After that date, contingents gathered in Albert Square, the very centre of civic affairs, dominated as it was by the city's Gothic Town Hall. This was a move of obvious significance. All parishes in the city were eligible to walk, although urban growth and population dispersal meant that some were unable to do so. By the early 1900s twenty-two parishes usually walked in any one year, representing a total of about 85,000 Catholics. Each parish contingent was led by priests and any magistrates or elected officials who belonged to the church. They were followed by school children and confraternity members, the rear being brought up by adult members of the general laity. Having squeezed into the Square, processionists sang *Faith of our Fathers* as they faced the Town Hall and received benediction from the Bishop. They were then led up Deansgate, Market Street and eventually to Piccadilly where contingents dispersed and made their way back to their own districts where celebrations continued.

Unlike the Anglican walk, which remained a procession almost exclusively composed of Sunday school pupils, the Catholic walk was meant to represent the entire body of adherents. Despite this, a majority of the 20 per cent of all adherents who walked in any one year were school children. In some parishes the number of participants was especially impressive. Before 1914 St Patrick's was often reported as being represented by a contingent 3,000 strong, which amounted to nearly one-third of all parishioners. The Church was especially keen that adult men walked because they, 'give an air of solidity to the Faith . . . The men claim respect for Catholic interests . . .'[96] However, the response of Catholic males was always less than that hoped for and they probably never accounted for more

Table 4.1 Size of Catholic and Anglican Whit walks, 1900–1938

Year	Catholic	Anglican
1900	18,000	25,000
1904	18,000	30,000
1910	20,000+	24,000
1920		25,000
1922	25,000	
1938		20,000
1939	20,000	

Source: Local press reports, 1900–1939.

than about 15 per cent of participants. This modest presence was not just due to lack of interest. Many had to work on Friday because, unlike Whit Monday, employers did not consider it a holiday. Thus, male Catholics continued to work both at Smithfield Market and on the municipal trams. Yet, to non-Catholic eyes, the number of male processionists always appeared to be one of the most impressive aspects of the walk.[97]

In any case, the participation of a child entailed considerable financial commitment on the part of most working-class families. If a Catholic child was to be allowed to join their school contingent they had to possess appropriate and, if possible, new clothes. Moreover, children were also required to wear co-ordinated attire, while parents were obliged to buy head dresses, crooks, rosettes and sashes from their parish. Clothes were used as a way of raising capital in working-class homes and for this purpose placed in pawn shops immediately after Whit week. However, participation in a walk often depreciated the value of these items: when it was wet they were damaged and during hot weather melted tar from the road's surface ruined shoes. Despite this, it was rare for Catholic parents to rescue their children from a downpour once the walk had started as this would have destroyed the Church's famed discipline. In contrast, Anglican parents had little compunction in dragging their charges out of the wet. Many Catholic parents did so in 1932, but only after youngsters began to cry as dye ran out of their garments.[98]

The walk was always considered to be much more important by the Catholic than Anglican churches. Between 1904 and 1920 the Anglican Bishop of Manchester did not deign to participate in his procession. Press estimates suggest that Catholics came close to matching Anglicans in size, despite their much smaller population (Table 4.1). The Catholic walk was also generally considered to be the more elaborate and orderly of the two. Discipline amongst school children was the result of weeks of hard drill and the exclusion of those under seven who were considered incapable of taking orders.

The walk gave Catholics a chance to publicly assert their individual and collective self-importance in the midst of a society where it was usually denigrated. The singing of the hymn *Faith of our Fathers*, which told the tale of the persecution but eventual triumph of Catholicism, should be interpreted in this light. The widespread English Protestant view of the Catholic Church as inferior and alien was at least temporarily turned on its head.[99] Whit also gave each of Manchester's Catholic national minorities an opportunity to express their distinct identity: Italians, Poles and Ukrainians all made their particular contribution to the parade. These ethnic groups provoked little hostility: this was not the case with the large Irish contingent. Church officials tried to keep the expression of Irish identity within certain bounds: for the most part only sentimental, anodyne expressions of Irishness were allowed. There was a plethora of green flags, banners and kilted pipe bands; more conventional bands played tunes such as *Killarney* and *The wearing of the green*. It was said of the 1935 walk that:

> Most of the tunes were Irish airs. One had seen a banner with the legend 'God Save Ireland – 1899', and Irishness again and again drew attention to the processionists. It was no surprise, therefore, to find the stirring tune rousing spectators to sing was that *Old Ireland shall again be free*, or when that had finished to see a few steps of the jig performed in the side streets behind the spectators' backs.

Even this expression of Irishness was criticized by some Protestant spectators. During one pre-1914 walk one declared, 'You'd think we were in bloody Ireland wouldn't you. Why the 'ell don't they play something English?'[100] In contrast, when it came to expressing loyalty to England the Church was less restrained. During the Boer War both St John's and Holy Name dressed boys as soldiers and girls as nurses and had them march behind the Union Jack.[101]

During Whit in 1921 it was noted that, despite all the troubles between Irish and English, during the holiday, 'happily, people forget racial or religious differences'. The walks actually had the reverse effect, as they forcibly reminded people of their sectarian differences. This realization took many forms, some of them apparently trivial: one Protestant woman refused to wash her front doorstep on Whit Friday, as was the custom at the start of the weekend. In some parts of St Patrick's parish during Whit weeks in the 1950s Catholics placed pictures of the Pope in their windows whilst Anglicans put those of the Queen in theirs to make an already bitter rivalry more obvious.[102] The state of the weather was a more usual cause of conflict. Manchester's infamous rainfall could ruin a procession and lay waste even to the best prepared of displays. On both sides, Divine intervention was often prayed for. People were ingenious in explaining away unfavourable weather: 'If it was raining on one day and sunny on the other, all you could hear was "God knows his own" or in defence they would say "God always waters his little flowers . . ."'[103] Usually, however, good weather was seen as a sign from God, especially if in the same week it rained on the opposition. As one Knott Mill resident recalled of the period before 1914:

> . . . say Whit Monday was a nice day and it rained on Whit Friday, oh there was terrible, it'd be terrible, there'd be fights all over the place, because the weather hadn't been good for Whit Friday. And it was the same if the weather was good for Whit Friday and it was bad for Whit Monday.
> *Who would be fighting?*
> It was fighting amongst neighbours. There was always a punch-up, like [. . .] just a scrap between you. It'd be forgotten, like you'd meet in a pub and it'd be forgotten.[104]

When the two main features of Whit week – excessive drinking and increased sectarian consciousness – came together the mixture was potentially explosive. As a member of St Patrick's recalled:

> . . . there certainly was quite a lot of bigotry in those days which became manifest at Whit Monday and Whit Friday, after the Whit walks took place, when the bitterness crept in mostly caused by people drunk as lords who attended no religious service from year's end to the other, and only knew what religion they belonged to because they had been born into it . . .[105]

Despite its fearsome reputation for dominating the lives of adherents, the Church's attempt to isolate working-class Catholics and transform their way of life ultimately failed. There is little evidence that Catholics became any more 'respectable' than non-Catholics. In particular, it is highly doubtful that the Church modified the conduct of even young male adolescents, the principal focus of many of its efforts. Yet, although unable to accomplish its primary aim, the Church did encourage a sense of difference among Irish Catholics. This was something that probably needed little enough amplification.

Most adherents continued to consider themselves Catholics and yet failed to think and act in ways approved by the Church. The gap between popular and official Catholicism, so obvious in devotional practice, was also apparent in social conduct. The Catholicism most prevalent within the working class was the embodiment of personal, familial and national identity. It had little to do with theological preferences. This is not to say that the Church's influence was weak. Relatively, at least, it was strong: no other church had the ability to relate to so many members of the working class. Given that membership of the Church was inextricably linked with family identity, popular Catholicism was most clearly expressed in relation to attitudes to school and marriage. Children were sent to a Catholic school because that was where their parents had gone. They were expected to marry another Catholic because the family was Catholic. These tendencies were inevitably encouraged by the Church's attempt to create a separate culture. However, this conservative and self-reinforcing logic, if logic it can be called, was not the creation of the Church. Moreover, this culture's impermeability and hostility to change acted against the Church in other respects. Hence the failure of the Church to transform working-class adherents into models of middle-class rectitude.

There was undoubtedly a growing number of those born Catholic for whom Ireland was a distant memory and Catholicism an increasingly tiresome family habit. Given the alternative social influences to which Catholics were subject, it is remarkable that the Church retained a hold on working-class Catholics for so long, even if it chastized itself for not having a firmer grip.[106] With the decline in Irish immigration, the number of those Catholics who thought themselves more English than Irish increased. This was the main threat to the Church's position, for Irishness gave the Church an unrivalled legitimacy within working-class families. Yet, in the face of this danger, it is the success of the Church, and not its failure, that seems most striking.

During the lives of working class Catholics different pressures asserted themselves at various times. At some moments religion seemed paramount; at others it appeared completely irrelevant compared to those of class. Yet, none was ever asserted to the permanent exclusion of the other. The Church's fear that, on entering work, an adherent ceased to be a Catholic was misconceived: occupational consciousness not all-encompassing. Working class adherents still largely married within the Faith, at least occasionally went to mass, mostly sent their children to Catholic schools and bought them new clothes so they could participate in Church processions. Moreover, as will be seen in Chapter 6, despite voting Labour in impressive numbers after 1914, Catholics contested proposals made by certain party members to introduce birth control and secular education.

five

The politics of
Home Rule

English opposition to Home Rule

The period after 1880 has generally been seen as a time during which
loyalties of class, as opposed to those based on religion, increasingly influenced working-class political affiliations.[1] The formation of the Social
Democratic Federation (SDF) in 1881, the Independent Labour Party
(ILP) in 1893, the Labour Representation Committee (LRC) in 1900 and
the Labour Party in 1906 is presented as evidence of this process.[2] Due to
their preoccupation with Home Rule for Ireland, as well as the influence
of the Catholic Church, Irish Catholics are presented as being out of step
with these developments. Most historical accounts see the Irish determina-
tion to pursue Home Rule as wholly at odds with attempts to create
independent working-class parties.[3] This is because Nationalist leaders urged
their followers in England to support pro-Home Rule Liberal candidates
rather than socialists, many of whom actively sought the destruction of
Liberalism. Nationalists are therefore seen as opposing politics based on
the common class interests of all workers. Such a view is fallacious on at
least two counts. First, the extent to which class determined political
loyalties among non-Irish workers has been exaggerated. By no means all
trade unionists, supposedly the most fervent supporters of the Labour
Party, were convinced by its programme before 1914. Furthermore, most
Labour MPs elected in the general elections of 1906 and 1910 were
politically indistinguishable from Liberals. Co-operation rather than conflict defined the relationship between the two parties prior to the First

World War.[4] Moreover, well into the inter-war years many unskilled workers remained hostile to Labour, despite the party's claim to represent their economic interests.[5] Secondly, and most importantly, Irish national and class loyalties were not as exclusive as they have been made to appear.

Nationalists were obviously exercized by the fate of Home Rule and before 1914 the Irish vote in England was mobilized by three organizations whose principal object was self-government for Ireland: the Irish National League of Great Britain (INL) was formed in 1883 after the collapse of the Home Rule Confederation of Great Britain, itself only ten years old. The INL was eventually reformed into the United Irish League of Great Britain (UIL) in 1900. All three bodies were dominated by leaders in Dublin, who saw the Irish in England in entirely instrumental terms. This leadership expected emigrants to obediently raise money for Nationalists in Westminster, vote only for candidates who won their approval and ignore political issues other than those associated with Home Rule. Members were not allowed to belong to English political parties and branches were barred from participating in local elections.[6] Moreover, Nationalist leaders in Ireland were predominantly middle-class figures, whose support for Home Rule was unaccompanied by any desire for fundamental social and economic reform. During the 1913 Dublin dock strike, for example, they almost universally sided with the employers.[7]

Despite these official prohibitions the Irish in England did not, in practice, reserve all their political energies for the battle for Home Rule. They were essentially Janus-faced and looked not only to matters in Ireland, their notional homeland, but also to those in their country of residence, England. Thus, by the mid-1880s the Irish had become Liberals because of that party's support for Home Rule. Yet, Irish Liberals were more sympathetic to the labour movement and independent working-class candidates than most of their fellow party members. This pronounced radicalism was in part due to the fact that most Irish voters were working class. In the Oldham branch of the INL speakers criticized conditions in the mills; it was there that J.R. Clynes, who eventually became a Labour cabinet minister, learnt public speaking. The union leader and future Labour MP James Sexton claimed that it was in the Liverpool Nationalist movement, 'that I imbibed most if not all of my progressive ideas.' In Leeds the INL and Socialist League held a joint meeting in support of a tailors' strike.[8] The leftward inclination of Irish Liberals was also related to their belief that English working-class voters were potentially more committed to Home Rule than many Liberals. Local Nationalists realized that Home Rule could not be won simply by mobilizing Irish voters in England and Ireland. English MPs elected by English voters had to be persuaded that Home Rule was worthy of support. Thus, while on the one hand confirming Irish national differences, Nationalists tried to construct an electoral alliance with English working-class voters. This is why, far from trying to isolate Irish immigrants, the Home Rule movement actually attempted to promote their integration into English politics.

Those who have previously studied Irish Nationalism in England have emphasized its ineffectiveness.[9] It is certainly true that the movement faced a number of potentially debilitating difficulties. The main obstacle was that, until 1910, there was no solid Home Rule majority in Parliament. Between 1886 and 1906 the Conservatives held a tight grip on office, a dominance only punctuated by one brief and weak Liberal ministry. Despite the Home Rule Bills of 1886 and 1892 limited independence for Ireland proved a depressingly illusory goal. Moreover, even when elected in 1906 the Liberals fought shy of embracing an issue whose unpopularity had been demonstrated time and time again. It was only when they were forced to rely on the votes of Irish Nationalist MPs in 1910, that the Liberals were finally won round. Even then, Prime Minister Asquith deferred implementation of the 1914 Home Rule Act as a means of forestalling threatened civil war in Ireland. This fundamental problem was compounded by numerous others: the movement was confronted by a restrictive franchise, which was prejudicial to unskilled workers and a registration process that discouraged participation. Thus, while it is possible that as many as one in six Irish men were entitled to vote, only one in ten ever did.[10] Moreover, despite contemporary claims to the contrary, Irish voters were distributed in a way that gave them little opportunity to affect the result of the vast majority of Parliamentary contests. Apart from T.P. O'Connor in the Scotland division of Liverpool, the Irish in England were unable to elect a Nationalist as MP. Although Nationalists in Manchester were especially well-organized even their influence was limited to three of the city's six divisions. These were Manchester North and North-east, both of which included Ancoats, and Manchester South-west, which embraced Hulme. Such external constraints were compounded by internal divisions, which emerged between Nationalist leaders based in Ireland. The most famous and traumatic of these was provoked by the exposure of Charles Parnell's affair with Kitty O'Shea in 1890. This scandal led to nearly ten years of bitter conflict, which in turn led to many Irish in England abandoning the cause of Home Rule in despair. Given such structural and self-inflicted misfortunes, the relative ineffectiveness of Nationalism in England seems much less striking than the ability of Irish immigrants to sustain a viable Home Rule movement at all.

One of the principal external obstacles that determined the fate of Nationalists in England was the innate hostility of most English voters to the idea of Home Rule. Politics in England was largely based on competing ethnic, rather than class, identities. This was especially so in those places where the Irish were most concentrated. In Lancashire, English working-class voters living in areas with large numbers of Irish Catholics showed a pronounced preference for Conservative candidates until at least the early 1920s. It seems that when confronted by a group with a different ethnic complexion to their own, English voters turned to the party of church, monarchy and empire in an attempt to assert their cultural superiority.[11] The Conservatives had successfully exploited these sentiments since the 1860s, using hostility to Irish Catholics as a means of solidifying their support among the English working class. The maintenance of the Union and opposition to Home Rule brought cross-class support to the party. In fact, support for the Union was possibly the only dogmatic principle to which the party unquestioningly committed itself.[12] It remained a well-used part of the Tory armoury well into the twentieth century. In 1892 the future Prime Minister, Arthur Balfour, assured his East Manchester audience that:

> If we have to choose between injustice to Englishmen and Scotchmen and injustice to Irishmen, I, for my part, am prepared to go for injustice for Ireland as the least of two evils. – (cheers).

This hostility was expressed in cruder terms by a Conservative candidate for the city's New Cross ward fourteen years later. During a meeting, perhaps not surprisingly disrupted by Irish members of the audience, he asserted that:

> It is a disgrace to have Irishmen coming into your own town and filling your berths – (laughter and continued disorder). If I thought I was going in on an Irish vote I would not go. I am an Englishman, an Imperialist, and a Conservative; we try to do our best for you but you won't have it. – (Cheers and groans). Will you submit in your own town to this hooliganism and rotten system?[13]

These feelings were exacerbated when Home Rule was placed to the fore. In an era when the empire was a central element in English national identity, even partial Irish independence was a highly unpopular issue, for it cast doubt on the ineluctable nature of imperial expansion. When Gladstone embraced Home Rule in 1886 he did not, as has been suggested, give legitimacy to the Irish claim. Instead, he split his party and threw those who remained loyal to his leadership into an unpatriotic light. The Liberals were subsequently condemned to nearly twenty years continuous opposition. In Manchester, Home Rule was a liability in all but the North division, the only seat in the city the Liberals managed to retain in the 1895 general election.[14]

Conservatives successfully defined Home Rule as a measure that would bring full independence to Ireland. Home Rule, they alleged, would undermine the economy, imperil national security and place Ulster Protestants at the mercy of Catholic bigots. This, despite the fact that Gladstone's proposals were much more modest and were intended to keep Ireland within the United Kingdom. As a consequence, Home Rulers came to be perceived as preaching, in the words of the leader of Salford's Conservative Labour Party, 'what seemed to us poor natives to be treason and strife.'[15]

The character of Irish Nationalism

Historians consider that the membership and organization of the various Home Rule organizations were extremely unimpressive. Nationalism's failure to arouse wider support among the Irish in England is seen as being one more indication of the movement's profound weakness. At its peak, just before Parnell's fall in 1890, the INL could only claim a national membership of 40,985. Moreover, given that some branches purchased more membership cards than they had members, even this was probably an inflated figure. Membership fell after the acrimonious departure of Parnell and the consequent bitter struggle between dissident Parnellites and the new Westminster leadership. After the return of some semblance of unity, marked by the creation of the UIL, the movement grew to its previous extent. By 1914, with the Liberals committed to a new Home Rule Bill and optimism at its peak, membership had increased to more than 46,000.[16]

In Manchester and district alone the UIL claimed 1,500 members in 1910.[17] Impressionistic evidence suggests that members in the city were, as elsewhere, mainly drawn from the upper reaches of the immigrant population. Professionals, merchants, shopkeepers, teachers, skilled workers and publicans of Irish birth and descent were all prominent. Doctors seem to have been especially important as branch leaders. As with their counterparts in the United States, many of those in a position of leadership were also active in the Catholic Church.[18] Unlike most other political organizations women were conspicuously absent, even to the extent that there was no female auxiliary Nationalist body. This may be one more expression of the wider Irish Catholic bias against women, which was noted earlier. The position of women apart, Nationalism drew members from a social constituency broadly similar to that of other English-based political organizations: it was male, relatively affluent and more than simply literate. If Nationalist membership was low, then it was probably only because Irish Catholics were disproportionately unskilled and this was a group not noted for their habit of joining even allegedly working-class socialist parties.[19] A brief biographical summary of the lives of Dan Boyle and Dan McCabe, who led Manchester's Nationalists before 1914, is indicative of the movement's character. Boyle was born in 1857 to a family of Fermanagh farmers; he trained as a teacher in Ireland but after moving to Manchester in 1877 took a job as a railway clerk, eventually becoming registrar of births, deaths and marriages. He quickly became an INL organizer for Lancashire and Cheshire as well as a correspondent for the Dublin-based *Freeman's Journal.* During the 1880s Boyle also took a leading role in the Irish National Foresters, a friendly society, for which he was district secretary and twice elected Grand High Chief Ranger. In 1910 he was elected MP for North Mayo. McCabe, in contrast, was born in 1853 to Irish-born parents who were resident in Stockport at the time. They eventually moved to Manchester, where he was raised in St

Patrick's parish and eventually became active in parochial confraternities, the Old Boys' Association and Sunday School. A graduate of a Mechanics' Institute, Boyle eventually came to own a small clothing company in Ancoats.[20]

Nationalism in Manchester was effectively controlled by a group of 'notables', mainly provisions merchants who belonged to the Thomas Davis branch of the UIL, which was located in the city's commercial centre. This was by far the richest of branches, raising one-third of the district's donation to the national UIL in 1910. Between fifty and one hundred such gentlemen Nationalists dined together the Friday prior to the annual St Patrick's Day Free Trade Hall rally. This was clearly as much a social as a political event and continued even after the creation of the Free State in 1921.[21] Elsewhere in the city a more humble form of club life was enjoyed by working-class members, who were content to play inter-branch billiard matches and conclude their evening's entertainment with a rendition of 'God Save Ireland'. Such activities were clearly an integral part of binding members to the Nationalist cause. Furthermore, it was only in the social sphere that women were allowed a public role within the movement – even if it was just to play the piano to entertain audiences before meetings.[22]

The real significance of Nationalism lay not in its formal structure and membership, but in its ability to appeal to the immigrant population as a whole, many of whom did not possess a vote. With them, Nationalism found a vibrant echo, for it provided a point of contact with a homeland many barely remembered or had never seen. It also gave them the opportunity to proudly affirm their nationality in a society in which it was considered to be little more than a quaint joke or, sometimes, a danger to the state. St Patrick's Day was the most important of such occasions, but any and every political contest was transformed into an expression of national identity.

Nationalism was, therefore, a socially stratified movement. To a greater or lesser extent it embraced the majority of those who considered themselves to be Irish, from teetotal professionals to unskilled market porters who took pleasure in drinking themselves into oblivion on St Patrick's night. Despite such social and cultural differences, they were all united in one object: Home Rule for Ireland. Yet, it would be wrong to assert that all Irish-born Catholics were keen to promote the cause of Home Rule in England. One Bolton miner greatly respected the English and was particularly pleased when a nephew became the first member of his family to be born in the country. He had a particular regard for the English landed class, who he trusted to do the right thing. However, such people were small in number and their ideas were firmly refuted by the majority of fellow immigrants.[23]

Nationalism was not a creed imposed from across the water: events in Ireland had a habit of being reflected on the mainland. Manchester's Irish population could even claim their very own patriotic saints – the three Fenian 'Manchester Martyrs' executed in 1867 after an attempted escape from custody resulted in the death of a policeman. Their deaths were commemorated each November by a march and political meeting. There were other means of keeping the memory alive: the Michael Davitt UIL branch kept what purported to be a Martyr's hat in a glass case; St Patrick's also held the last letter written by one of their number; their portraits hung in a number of parlours; they also lived on in community myths.[24] Thus, even on their doorsteps Irish residents were reminded of England's injustice to their homeland.

Although in social composition broadly similar to other political groups, Nationalism nevertheless possessed – national origin aside – its own cultural character. To English radicals, publicans were among the most hated of figures due to their support for the Conservative enemy. This was the case across all of urban England, but especially so in Lancashire, where it was widely assumed that, 'Slumdom to a man and woman is on the side of drink and therefore on the side of Toryism.' In Manchester, the connection between the pub and Conservatism was particularly close.[25] Yet, as one Irish landlord declared, 'it was in the Catholic public house that the National League was cradled.' Those branches too impecunious to rent or own club rooms often held meetings in such pubs. The poor and unskilled also spent much of their leisure time in pubs and drinking clubs run by active Nationalists. These institutions gave the party machine a strategic place within Irish popular culture. Although at times more concerned with drinking, dancing and gambling than directly political matters, they still contributed to party funds, held meetings and mobilized support during election campaigns.[26] Within the Irish Catholic milieu, then, the pub was used to the benefit of Nationalism and, by extension, to that of Liberalism and later Labour. During the 1890s Irish publicans canvassed for the Liberals despite the latter's advocacy of Local Option, which threatened to prohibit their trade.[27] In the face of continued hostility to drink expressed by a vocal minority in both Liberal and Labour parties publicans supported their cause because they, in turn, supported Home Rule.[28] This did not mean that all Nationalists were sanguine about the influence of the brewing lobby within their ranks. One critic went so far as to describe the UIL as entirely composed of drinking clubs, with little interest in politics. Despite such opposition, however, the close connection between alcohol and Irish Catholic politics remained one of its more distinctive and abiding characteristics. Even after 1918 Manchester's strongly Irish Catholic ward of St Michael's returned the only two publicans ever to be elected as Labour councillors in the city.[29]

Before the events of 1916 Nationalism's principal object was the achievement of Home Rule through strictly constitutional means. The potential results of success were deemed considerable: it was assumed, in fact, that political action would cure all Ireland's economic ills. T.P. O'Connor, for example, blamed the Act of Union for causing three Irish famines and the deaths of one and a half million peasants.[30] Thus, Home

Rule was seen as not only bringing political justice to the country but also economic prosperity.

The formal aim of the movement was essentially procedural and the main job of local Nationalists was to locate Irish voters, place them on the electoral register, ensure they remained on it and finally guarantee they voted for the approved candidate. This was a self-consciously level-headed, 'practical' movement; members might have held sentimental notions about their homeland, but precious few were of the Messianic variety.[31] In any case, the failure of the Fenian 'physical force men' in the 1860s had discredited the violent route to change for at least a generation. The futility of terrorism was etched on the memories of turn-of-the-century Nationalists in England, as many of their fathers had been active Fenians. James Sexton's had recruited men into the Irish Republican Brotherhood and concealed guns under floorboards; Sexton himself was a convinced constitutionalist.[32] The movement was also largely antipathetic to the revival of Gaelic culture. Such a project was associated with advocates of more extreme Nationalist politics in Ireland and, more importantly, it was seen by those in England as a diversion from the 'real' task of making the case for Home Rule. As a consequence, only one UIL branch in Manchester held language classes and few members were active in the city's Gaelic League.[33] There was also little support for factionalism within the local Nationalist movement. The Irish in England were loyal not to one man, but the cause of Ireland, something that erstwhile leaders, most famously Charles Parnell, discovered to their cost.

The moderation of local Nationalists was in part a reflection of that of the Dublin leadership. There was an additional reason: they wished to avoid alienating their English neighbours. As one Nationalist in Manchester advised, they:

> . . . should seek by temperance in conduct and in speech to win the goodwill of their fellow subjects in England, for they knew that it was impossible for a small people like the Irish ever to obtain their liberty except by the favour of the people among whom they lived.[34]

It was obviously in their best interests to promote a peaceful form of Nationalist politics. They were, after all, the ones who felt the full force of English anger when outrages were perpetrated in Ireland. The Fenian bombings of the 1860s had led to redundancies in England and, in the case of one unfortunate Bradford Irishman, a 'mock' lynching. The murder of the Irish Secretary and his assistant in Dublin's Phoenix Park in 1882 also provoked a number of anti-Irish riots across the country.[35] It was no surprise that before 1916, the Irish in England were among the first to condemn any bomb outrage committed by their compatriots. This desire for self-preservation, reinforced by the need to win the support of English voters, meant that local Nationalists espoused a moderate vision of Home Rule, one that left Ireland within the United Kingdom. Some even argued that independence would make Ireland a source of greater strength for the empire.[36] In 1897 the INL asked the Irish in England to abstain from celebrating Queen Victoria's Diamond Jubilee. Even so, they still sought to reassure her majesty that this was not intended as a personal insult. It was, they explained, merely meant to indicate that without Home Rule the Irish had no cause to be festive. Moreover, although Victoria's visit to Dublin in 1900 was opposed by many in Ireland, in Manchester Nationalists described her as 'the most illustrious lady in the world.' It was, in fact, a constant Nationalist theme that the Irish were loyal to the Crown. When the chairman of the INL South Manchester branch suggested that the Irish were a 'loyal race of people' his audience applauded the sentiment.[37]

The constitutional road had been developed by Parnell in the 1880s to exploit the potential influence of the eighty or so Nationalist MPs in the Commons. Parnell hoped for a hung Parliament in which he would hold the balance of power between Conservatives and Liberals. In such a position of power he aimed to force one of the parties to concede Home Rule in exchange for power. Unfortunately, for most of the time either the Liberals or Conservatives achieved outright Commons majorities. Their political impotence led to Nationalist impatience and frustration in Ireland, which was often expressed in factional in-fighting. In England, rank-and-file spirits were maintained by two firmly held beliefs, which achieved the status of necessary myths. The first was that Home Rule was always on the verge of being accomplished: if Nationalist rhetoric was to be believed, the Irish were perennially involved in the last round of the final struggle. The second, and most important myth, was the assertion that the agencies of English democracy would ensure the eventual success of Home Rule. These beliefs were most freely aired at the St Patrick's Sunday rally. Buoyed up by patriotic songs and extravagant speeches, delivered by visiting stars of the movement the 5,000-strong audience was told a familiar and stereotyped message. English opposition to Home Rule was essentially based on ignorance; workers were simply misled by malicious Conservatives. The only people who really stood in the way of Home Rule were self-interested land-owners and their self-seeking political representatives. Once in possession of the facts of the matter English workers would quickly rally to the cause.[38] Moreover, Nationalists comforted themselves that they shared with English workers a common enemy and that ultimately they would also realize this. As John Denvir stated, the Irish had no quarrel with the working class, only with 'the class which misgoverned us, just as it, to a lesser extent misgoverned them.'[39] This language was also used in the late 1930s to justify an IRA bombing campaign in England. A leading Sinn Feiner addressed 'the real people of England', the working people, and informed them that, 'in the last analysis, what is right and good for Ireland is also right and good for England.'[40] Thus, far from giving vent to anti-English feelings, Nationalists instead emphasized the possibility, if not the inevitability, of the Irish people winning freedom through the English constitution with the help of their English neighbours.

Irish Liberals

After Gladstone finally embraced Home Rule in 1886 a Nationalist–Liberal alliance was inevitable. This was never an association of equals and the O'Shea scandal merely confirmed the subordinate place of the Irish. Gladstone had given Irish MPs a stark choice after his refusal to deal with the disgraced Parnell: they could either follow their leader into the wilderness or abandon him and trust the Liberals to deliver Home Rule. Despite the factionalism that followed, there was no real choice – Parnell was dispensed with. From that point until the First World War the Liberal connection remained the essential basis for Irish strategy. Despite the passing of Gladstone in 1894, the leadership of the hostile imperialist Lord Rosebery, the prevarication of Campbell-Bannerman and later Asquith, the Irish had no realistic alternative so long as they followed the constitutional path.[41]

This has been seen as an essentially tactical, instrumental relationship: the Irish were not 'real' Liberals and only supported the party because it offered the prospect of Home Rule.[42] If this was so, it can equally be argued that many Liberals were not 'real' Home Rulers. Even Gladstone had not taken up the issue simply because of its intrinsic merits. He had hoped that by rallying the party behind an all-embracing single issue he would obscure the lack of coherence within Liberalism. It was intended that Home Rule would restore Liberal unity of action and confirm his position as leader. The defection of many Whigs and some radicals to the Conservatives in response to his taking up the issue was a price Gladstone was willing to pay. Thus, Home Rule was embraced by the Liberals in a spirit of despair as much as hope. After Gladstone's retirement, the party's support for Home Rule waned and, by the early 1900s, the Liberal Irish policy was in practice largely indistinguishable from that of the Conservatives.[43]

It is, therefore, possibly true that instrumentalism determined the Liberal–Nationalist alliance in Westminster. However, in the country as a whole the inter-dependence of local Nationalists and Liberals was more organically developed. There they collaborated not just in Parliamentary elections, when Home Rule was at stake, but in municipal contests when it was not. Although Nationalists in Dublin looked unfavourably on such developments, because they wished to preserve their movement's independence, they could not prevent it. In Manchester, especially, Liberal and Nationalist unity was advanced with joint selection of candidates and registration work in certain wards. As a consequence of this co-operation many of the Irish in England came to think of themselves as Liberals as much as Nationalists. This had been revealed as early as 1885 when Parnell instructed Irish voters to support Conservative candidates in the general election of that year. Such a tactic was questioned by many INL members across the country, despite the possibility that in so doing they risked expulsion.[44]

By the early 1890s Gladstone was as much a hero of the Nationalist as Liberal rank-and-file: his portrait quickly replaced that of Parnell's above Irish hearths. In fact, as Parnell fell in the estimation of his former followers, Gladstone's star rose. In Manchester during the winter of 1890–1 Nationalists swiftly and almost unanimously turned their backs on the disgraced ex-leader. The Archbishop Walsh branch of the UIL in the South Manchester division, for example, voted forty-one to five against Parnell. North Manchester's Michael Davitt branch held elections for officers which saw Parnellites face supporters of the new leadership: the latter swept the board. The final index of the collapse of Parnell's support came during the 1891 St Patrick's Day rally, in which only two voices were raised in opposition to those who had displaced the former hero.[45] Thus, despite his manipulation of events to rid himself of the awkward, independent, Parnell, Gladstone became the principal object of Irish loyalty and affection. For the remainder of the decade simple mention of the name of 'our benefactor' and 'the world's greatest statesman' was enough to raise a hearty Irish cheer.[46]

Irish affiliation to Liberalism was also given a more practical expression during the 1890s when Nationalists won prominent positions in many ward and divisional parties. Liverpool, however, stands out in stark contrast to these general developments. Principally due to the large size of the Irish population, the city's Nationalists operated autonomously.[47] Manchester was more typical of those towns and cities where the Irish settled in significant, but not overwhelming, numbers. In such places independence would have been counter-productive. The distribution of population also meant that although the Irish were powerful in a number of Liberal ward parties, they were much weaker at the broader divisional level. Thus, in the North-east Manchester divisional party thirteen out of twenty-six members of New Cross ward executive council had Irish surnames; there were only two out of eleven in Miles Platting and none at all in Newton Heath. When the division subsequently selected eight representatives to sit on the city's Liberal Union, Dan Boyle was the only Irish representative.[48]

Although enthusiastic Liberals, differences of nationality, religion and class meant that Irish members retained their distinctive identity. Irish support for Catholic voluntary education put them in conflict with Liberal Non-conformists, as did their reluctance to endorse temperance campaigns.[49] The fact that some Liberals employed Irish labour also raised occasional difficulties. When president of his local INL branch James Sexton was asked to stand against a Liberal in a Bootle municipal election. Initially reluctant due to the support Liberals gave to Home Rule, he allowed his name to be put forward when he realized that the local Liberals were some of the worst of dockside employers.[50] In any case, Nationalists were not treated as ordinary Liberals by other party members. Individual Liberals could be as bigoted as any Conservative. Manchester's Protestant Thousand, established in 1898, united influential Conservative and Liberal figures to co-ordinate their opposition to the influence of

Catholics in local politics. Mixed marriages were also disparaged by some Protestant Liberals.[51] Moreover, many English Liberals were as hostile to Home Rule as their Conservative opponents. In this they only reflected the private attitude of most of their leaders. During the early 1880s the party did not bother to obscure its contempt for the issue: during the 1885 general election Manchester Liberals were even accused of deliberately offending Irish sensibilities. T.P. O'Connor speculated that they, 'had gone up and down the country in search of the very worst and most objectionable candidates they could possibly have.' In East Manchester the Liberal was a known Unionist; in the North-east he was an Irish landowner. Even in the early 1890s Liberal Unionists remained members of Manchester's Liberal Reform club, five years after they had defected to the Conservatives because of their opposition to Home Rule.[52] The antipathy of many Liberals in Manchester for Home Rule was never resolved. In 1912 Sir George Kemp, MP for the North-west division, absented himself from the second reading of the Home Rule Bill. Despite this breach of discipline his divisional association, on which sat few if any Irish, refrained from comment.[53] By this time most Liberals, while not explicitly hostile to Home Rule, felt that other issues deserved priority. They saw it as more of a nuisance to be rid of rather than a principled policy to be honoured. The empty, ritualistic manner in which Liberal leaders advocated Home Rule probably accounts for why even in the party's heartland of north-east England working-class voters were, at best, apathetic about the issue.[54]

Despite these difficulties, some Nationalists did establish a prominent place for themselves within Liberalism. This is illustrated by the careers of Boyle and McCabe, who respectively represented New Cross and St Michael's wards between the early 1890s and the end of the First World War. They also demonstrate the extent to which Irish politicians were not simply obsessed with Home Rule but in fact gestured towards wider radical policies and embraced the emergent labour movement. Both men were leading Liberals in the city and each became vice-president of their respective divisional associations. During the 1900 general election Boyle even served as Liberal campaign manager in North-east Manchester. However, they each owed their electoral success to the support of Irish voters – often in the face of bitter English opposition. In New Cross, which returned two councillors before 1914, Boyle always polled considerably more than his English Liberal running mate. When McCabe became Manchester's first Catholic Lord Mayor in 1913 one Irish tram guard was so impressed he excitedly telegraphed the news to his wife on holiday in Ireland. On McCabe's death in 1919 his procession to Moston Catholic cemetery was a mile long and the route lined by thousands of spectators.[55]

Both men were keen advocates of the municipalization of the gas supply and tramways. These were policies that put them on the radical wing of the city's Liberal Party, which had adopted the reforming Municipal Programme only with the greatest degree of reluctance. Boyle and McCabe saw municipalization as a means by which the Corporation could 'set the tone' in hours and conditions for workers. For this same reason they also supported the introduction of an eight hour day for municipal employees. Boyle envisaged the role of the Corporation as that of a 'kind parent' acting in support of the poorer sections of society. These were policies consistently rejected by the council.

Both men were consequently enthusiastically endorsed by local trade unionists for their efforts. In 1895 McCabe received this message of support from the United Operative Street Masons Society:

> The members had always been pleased to note that whenever the workman's welfare had been under consideration Mr McCabe had taken a very prominent part in their favour.

In 1894 Boyle was unsuccessfully challenged by the secretary of the Bargeman's Union, who stood for the ILP. Three years later this former opponent described him as, 'the most stalwart champion in the Council that the Labour cause has ever had.' Both men were also advanced Liberals in other respects. During the 1890s they proposed that the party adopt more working-class candidates and came to endorse Independent Labour representatives in the early 1900s. In alliance with trade unionists, socialists and other radicals they were also prominent – and unusual as Liberals – in supporting the ILP's attempt to defend its right to hold political meetings on municipally owned land.[56]

The structure of English municipal government meant that neither Boyle nor McCabe were able to emulate their counterparts in the United States. In that country patronage, not to say corruption, was an important means of cementing political loyalties.[57] Even so, both still established their own administrative fiefdoms within the Corporation, such that each held at least some personal influence over the livelihood of many of their electors. McCabe was chair of the Smithfield market sub-committee, which set stall rents and negotiated contracts with suppliers. Thus, the fortunes of the market and McCabe were often linked: in 1907 he was attacked for increasing stall rents but won round critics when he announced that he had recently signed a contract to import American cattle.[58] Boyle's position was even more important. He chaired the tramways committee during the first few years of municipalization: as a consequence the trams came to be known as 'Dan Boyle's light railway'. His was a more delicate position than McCabe's and Boyle had initially refused the chair, thinking that his religion and nationality made him uniquely vulnerable to Conservative criticism. This was a well-founded fear: opponents exploited his background as a means of undermining municipalization. Conservatives pointed to the large number of Irish tram workers and accused Boyle of only employing his countrymen. Those who made such claims were brave indeed, for they aroused the anger of Boyle's Irish supporters who were apt to disrupt meetings where such allegations were aired. When a Conservative candidate had the temerity to suggest that Boyle's trams actually lost money Irish members of the audience abruptly terminated the discussion. Yet, although publicly disputing the claim, some Irish workers believed that Boyle demonstrated a preference for his own kind. As has been suggested earlier the preponderance of Irish tram workers had other causes than Boyle's alleged patronage.[59]

Thus, Boyle and McCabe were at once ethnic leaders and Liberal radicals who took an active interest in local government. Both the politics of Home Rule and the fact that they represented two poor working-class wards pushed them towards the left of their party. The former caused them to mistrust the Liberal establishment, which saw Home Rule less as a matter of principle and more an inconvenient Gladstonian inheritance. The latter made them amenable to the creation of an interventionist local authority and a strong trade union movement in the hope that these would improve their constituents' lot. If such measures appealed to English working-class voters, it was more than fortuitous, for their votes were desperately needed in order to achieve Home Rule. Boyle and McCabe were, then, living embodiments of the Nationalist claim that English and Irish workers enjoyed a common interest. However, the tribalistic nature of popular politics militated against this endeavour, for the assertion of an Irish political identity alienated many English voters. The Conservatives deliberately played on this and constructed a notion of Englishness to which Home Rule was the diabolic antithesis. Therefore, while Nationalists succeeded in taking many of their Irish constituents on a radical political journey they were unable to take many English voters with them.

Catholic education

One of the most compelling characteristics of Nationalist politics was its need to ameliorate the Catholic Church. Formally at least, Home Rule was a national and not a religious cause: as John Redmond told the 1906 UIL convention, 'this National movement is not a Catholic movement'. Nationalists in Manchester continually emphasized this point and a suspiciously large number of Protestant Nationalists made speeches in the city to ram the message home to English voters.[60] However, few Nationalists in England were not Catholic and, in public at least, the Catholic faith was regarded with reverence. UIL meetings invariably concluded with a vote of thanks to 'The Clergy'. In 1898 one Manchester Nationalist remarked that:

> If there was an Irish nation existing today, after the tyranny of three centuries, it was due, more than to anybody else, to the sterling patriotism of the Irish clergy in the past.

After 1916, even members of the Sinn Fein-inspired Irish Self-Determination League organized trips to Holywell and learnt how to answer the rosary in Gaelic.[61] Irish priests were, in turn, often in the forefront of the Home

Rule campaign: during the 1891 North-east Manchester by-election all but one of those working in the constituency was a Nationalist. Such men, as Booth noted in London, 'in sentiment are even more Irish than they are Catholics.' They were also willing to demonstrate their support for the movement in fairly direct terms. During one particularly rowdy Nationalist meeting in Angel Meadow Father O'Callaghan stood up and announced to his audience that, 'He wished he had a dozen of them, one after another, and he would not only show them that he was a priest and a Catholic, but also an Irishman.'[62]

If Nationalists found eager allies among the priesthood they were also confronted by an English Catholic Hierarchy, most of whose members were actively hostile to Home Rule. In 1892 the *Tablet*, owned by Bishop Vaughan of Salford, went so far as to call for the disenfranchisement of Irish voters in England. Whilst Vaughan was Archbishop of Westminster it was alleged that priests afraid of antagonizing the Bishops were reluctant to allow Nationalists use of school rooms for political meetings. Many Nationalists would have agreed with Redmond's comment that English Catholics were more of a menace to Home Rule than most Belfast Orangemen.[63] For practical reasons both sides tried to maintain a truce on the matter: Nationalists needed local clerical support while the English Church could not afford to gratuitously offend Irish adherents. None the less, a latent mutual mistrust remained, and could be exposed by the most trivial incident. For example, when a priest was transferred from St James' parish in Pendleton local Nationalists protested to the Bishop of Salford. They felt that he was being punished for blessing the Manchester Martyrs' memorial at Moston cemetery.[64]

The defence of Catholic schools was the most important issue to bedevil relations between the Church and Nationalists throughout the Irish diaspora.[65] In England the issue forced Irish Catholics to confront a grim choice: should they defend the schools and vote Conservative or advance the cause of Home Rule and choose the Liberals? This dilemma was most clearly evident after the election of a Liberal government in 1906. Non-conformists wished to reverse Conservative legislation, passed in 1902, which allowed denominational schools to be funded through the rates. This measure was, not surprisingly, universally welcomed by Catholics. However, due to Non-conformist pressure, the Liberals were committed to linking increased control of denominational schools to their funding.[66] Catholics angrily rejected the prospect of outside interference in their affairs. Even before the election an impressive number of adherents had been mobilized across the Salford diocese. This culminated in a massive demonstration held at Belle Vue in October 1906. The political reper-cussions of this dispute were almost immediately evident. In the Irish wards of St Michael's and New Cross, Liberal bastions during the 1880s and 1890s, the Conservatives made impressive gains. During this conflict of loyalties some Nationalists gave priority to Catholic schools whereas a number of parish priests continued to place Home Rule before all other considerations. Matters were all the more bitter for the unpredictability of these choices.[67]

Initially at least, most local Nationalists had supported the Catholic protest. This was not least because the newly-installed Liberal cabinet was proving to be barely more willing to support Home Rule than their Conservative predecessors. To their eyes Liberal inaction deserved to be punished. Even Dan Boyle declared that after the Non-conformists had 'nobbled Liberalism' he was being 'driven from Liberalism', but not towards the Conservatives. Hostility to education reform was also evident from within the ranks of local Liberal Anglicans. In 1907 the mainly Anglican East Manchester Liberal association refused to approve a motion that supported the government's education policy.[68]

The tacit alliance between Nationalists and Catholics came to an abrupt end during the 1908 by-election in North-west Manchester. It was, in fact, one of a number of contests used by Westminster Nationalists during the 1906 Parliament to force their Liberal allies to pursue Home Rule more actively. Despite being fought in a middle-class division with few Irish Catholics the by-election was an important test of Nationalist political loyalties. This was not least because the one UIL branch in the division was Thomas Davis, to which most of the movement's notables belonged. At the outset of the campaign John Redmond had suggested that he would not ask Irish voters to support the Liberal candidate. After this announcement, members from Thomas Davis held talks with the Catholic Federation to agree a joint message to the electorate. Presumably this would not have advised them to vote Liberal without certain guarantees on Home Rule and education.[69] The outcome of these discussions was pre-empted by a declaration issued by local clergy, which called on adherents to oppose the Liberals. The Federation quickly complied with this position and issued a similarly worded statement, apparently under the impression that the UIL would eventually follow suit; it did not. At Westminster, Nationalists, having made their point, came out in favour of the Liberal candidate who, they declared, had made concessions on Ireland and the schools. Manchester Nationalists obediently followed this change of policy despite the fact that it came so late they were left with only two days to campaign.[70] In spite of their efforts the Liberals suffered a defeat that was widely assumed to have been the result of the defection of Irish Catholic voters. Yet, such voters were too small in number and too divided amongst themselves to have made much of a difference.[71] Even so, the by-election's aftermath saw Irish Catholics come to blows: five members of Poland Street UIL branch committee were suspended for canvassing for the Conservatives and a Liberal-supporting Sunday school teacher was ostracized by fellow adherents who refused to associate with a 'milk-and-water Catholic.'[72]

The January 1910 general election further exacerbated tensions within the Irish Catholic electorate. With the Liberals more firmly committed to Home Rule than in the previous twenty years it was vital that Nationalists ensured their victory. In spite of this, the Catholic Hierarchy issued a test question on denominational education, which reminded voters of their divided allegiances and aroused further resentment.[73] As a result of supporting Liberal and Labour candidates during the campaign Dan McCabe was attacked by Father Sassen of St Brigid's in east Manchester. During a confrontation, which took place before a meeting of the St Joseph's missionary society, of which McCabe was vice-president, the priest said that it was, 'very anomalous on your part to come and speak on behalf of foreign missions when you can't be obedient to your own Bishops in your own country.' During the ensuing uproar Sassen was informed that by attacking McCabe he had insulted all Irishmen. Although the priest was even disavowed by Nationalists in his own parish he was not alone among clergymen in holding such views.[74] From this nadir, however, relations between Nationalists and the Church quickly improved. The Hierarchy did not issue a test question for the December election as denominational education had slipped far down the Liberal agenda. Furthermore, in the municipal elections of that year the Liberal Nationalist in St Michael's for the first time since 1906 enjoyed the support of a full complement of priests from St Patrick's and St William's. Such was the improvement in relations that Catholics from St Wilfrid's and local Liberals jointly sponsored a candidate under the Progressive banner in the following year's Board of Guardian elections.[75]

The progressive alliance

The emergence of the Labour Party and its precursors seemed to undermine the rationale behind the Liberal–Nationalist alliance. Such parties claimed to be the only organizations which could represent working-class interests and achieve Home Rule. Thus, there was little apparent reason for Irish workers to continue their association with the Liberals. However, despite the avowed aim of many socialists to destroy Liberalism, prior to the First World War the Liberal Party remained the predominant anti-Conservative force in the country. Moreover, during this period Labour acted more as a grouping within advanced Liberalism rather than as a distinct and hostile force. In fact, many in the SDF, ILP and Labour Party were former Liberals who remained trapped by their old party's vocabulary.[76] Thus, the general elections of 1906 and 1910 were all fought under the assumption that Labour, Liberals and Nationalists shared a common interest, even if it was only that of keeping the Conservatives out of power.

In 1892 the Catholic *Manchester Citizen* predicted that once Home Rule had been won those who appealed to workers' economic self-interest 'might annex almost wholly' the Irish vote.[77] Until that time, it was assumed that the Irish in England would vote Liberal as the only realistic means of attaining their desired end. However, this did not prevent Irish Liberals agreeing with many of the policies proposed by those to the left of their party. This was clearly the case during an 1894 by-election in Manchester's New Cross ward where the ILP accused the Liberal–Nationalist of stealing their programme.[78] Home Rule apart, then, there were few reasons for not abandoning the Liberal alliance in favour of a more radical alternative. In fact, many extreme socialists were keen supporters of Ireland's cause even at the height of its unpopularity. One of the few organizations to publicly oppose coercion in Ireland after the Phoenix Park murders was the secularist and socialist Stratford Dialectical and Radical club in London's East End.[79] However, before 1914 only the Liberals were in a position to form a non-Conservative administration: only they could deliver Home Rule. Despite their reservations about many in the party, and enthusiasm for what socialists offered, Nationalists in England had to accept this electoral fact. During the 1895 general election Dan McCabe had to remind a meeting of Irish electors in Ancoats of these realities. He told them that the INL wanted, 'to bring about, as speedily as possible, the freedom of Ireland. They believed they would best do this by the continuation of their alliance with the Liberal Party.' However, he recognized that there were:

> . . . many men at that meeting who were favourable to the Labour movement. He above all others had not one word to say against the Labour Party, and he believed that, above all other men, the Irishmen in this country had nothing to say against any party that went for the improvement of the condition of the labouring classes. The Irishmen in this country had to earn their bread from the sweat of their brows, and whatever was good for the working people and for the bettering of their condition would be to the advantage of the Irish masses in England. But he for one believed that the Irish alliance with the Liberal Party would more certainly bring about the improvement in the condition of labour than by following the Labour Party at the present moment. [. . .] The Labour Party was still young, and all it could do at present was to transfer Liberal seats to the Tories. – (Hear, hear).[80]

This was an argument only an ILP zealot could have refuted.

Despite their many local similarities, impatient socialists looked on Nationalists in Parliament as an irritant. Irish support for the Liberals was seen as impeding the advance of socialism. Moreover, the Liberal espousal of Home Rule was generally seen on the left as a hypocritical manoeuvre intended to obscure more fundamental class issues. Thus, during 1895 the ILP *Labour Leader* accused Parliamentary Nationalists of corruption, while Keir Hardie was moved to declare that he would on no account co-operate with T.P. O'Connor. On other occasions, however, attitudes were rather more friendly, such as when Westminster Nationalists came out in opposition to the Boer war.[81] In Manchester, however, there was little room for ambiguity in relations between the ILP and Nationalists. There, the ILP was notoriously hostile to the Liberals and their allies due to its deep-seated antagonism to reformism. The Manchester ILP even took the unique step of including a clause in its constitution that forbad members from voting for another party.[82] Therefore, despite their advanced position within local Liberalism, Manchester Nationalists were found guilty by association.

Socialist impatience with Home Rule was especially acute in Lancashire, where the issue was put to the fore by Nationalists intent on winning Irish votes and Conservatives courting the English. So far as the ILP was concerned, although a correct policy Home Rule was an issue which only divided the working class along irrelevant sectarian lines. One activist stated in 1893 that:

> The greatest obstacle we shall have to fight is the Home Rule question. If the candidate does not promise to vote for it, he will lose the Nationalist vote. [. . .] If he does, the Conservative working-man will look upon it as a Radical dodge . . .[83]

Leonard Hall, who campaigned in North-east Manchester for the ILP a year later argued that:

> To win this seat it is absolutely necessary to convert at least a percentage of Tory workmen and indifferent voters to Labour and progressive principles. Will that be done by talking about nothing but good old Ireland and Home Rule? Will it be done by putting Home Rule and Ireland in the forefront of the fight and at the head of the programme? No, sir.[84]

After losing the endorsement of the INL in South West Ham, and under attack from local priests, Hardie let his irritation with Irish politics get the better of him:

> The English workman when roused can be as strong and determined as the Irishman. The Englishman is in a majority, and can make and unmake Parliaments, and if the Irishman or their leaders are foolish enough to rake up the dying embers of the old hatred, then on them and not us be the responsibility. – (Cheers) – Do you say that it is a question of Home Rule first? I can understand an Irishman in Conemara saying that, but here in South West Ham it is Labour first. – (Loud cheers).[85]

Such an outburst won Hardie few friends among the division's Irish voters.

Relations between Nationalists and those to the left of the Liberals became more amicable after the turn of the century. This was largely a result of the fundamental shift in labour politics after the 1901 Taff Vale judgment, which seriously hampered the ability of trade unions to pursue industrial disputes. This led to more trade unions supporting the LRC as a means of winning Parliamentary representation in order to reverse the judgment through legislation. Such unionists were not socialists, many were Liberals and few trusted the ILP. Their influence forced the ILP, which also formed part of the LRC, to tone down its socialist rhetoric, for

Hardie needed trade union money and votes. Manchester's LRC was especially moderate and had an especially large contingent of Lib–Labs.
It was a natural consequence of this turn of events that the LRC and
Liberals reached an agreement in 1903 to reduce the number of seats
which both contested, thereby maximizing the anti-Conservative vote. The
1906 general election saw this alliance bear fruit. In Manchester, Labour
candidates J.R. Clynes and G.D. Kelley both spoke a language largely
indistinguishable from Liberalism: the word 'socialism' was almost
completely absent from their speeches. As a means of signifying this
progressive alliance, the city's UIL branches decked themselves out in
Liberal red, Nationalist green and Labour yellow during the campaign. At
the St Patrick's rally that year John Redmond anticipated a time when
Labour was a party of government and congratulated Irishmen on their
part in Labour's triumph. He concluded: 'the Labour representatives . . . are
our best friends.' After this time it was hard to see Labour as anything
other than a more radical form of Liberalism.[86] So far as the Irish were
concerned, the dividing line between the two parties became increasingly
irrelevant and hard to determine. Before 1914 some Nationalists looked
forward to Liberalism's supersession by Labour with enthusiasm.[87] Yet, after
the collapse of Liberalism after 1918, even those Irish who enthusiastically
voted Labour still hung a portrait of Gladstone in their parlours.[88]

The two general elections of 1910 marked the summit of this progressive
alliance. It was underpinned by the Lords' decision to veto Liberal social
legislation, an act that placed a large question mark over the fate of
Asquith's newly-proposed Home Rule Bill. The Lords, for many years
considered 'the real enemies of progress' by Liberals, Nationalists and
socialists was seen as standing between the people and reform. The upper
chamber also held a special place within Nationalist demonology, being
seen as the almost exclusive cause of Ireland's troubles. As Dan McCabe
declared, they were responsible for, 'all the sorrow, all the emigration
from Ireland during the last hundred years . . .'[89] In 1910 the question
was conveniently simple and dichotomous for those on the left: it was 'the
Lords versus the people'.[90] By their intractability the Lords made real the
Nationalist claim that Home Rule for Ireland and reform in England were
intertwined. Both social reformers and Nationalists united behind the
proposal to remove their obstructive veto over legislation.[91] In Blackburn
opposition to the aristocratic enemy even drew together on one platform
an unlikely rainbow coalition of Liberals, Nationalists, SDF, the Band of
Hope and the Free Church.[92]

Behind this animus to the Lords was a widespread antipathy for
landlordism. Hostility to landlords and the upper classes had been endemic
in rural Ireland for many decades.[93] In 1910 a fundamental transformation
in the nature of land ownership was also anticipated by most members of
the progressive alliance. It was on this basic question that socialist and
Liberals, Nationalists and English, town dweller and villager found common
ground. The 1892 Liberal candidate in East Manchester had tried to

construct an alliance between English and Irish voters on their common hostility to landlords. Labour candidates in the city in 1900, 1906 and 1910 had each presented 'crushing landlordism' as the main impediment to social progress. The New Liberals also thought the land question of fundamental importance. Therefore, it was with no small degree of conviction that McCabe announced that, in attacking the Lords, 'for the first time the interests of the English working-class and the interests of the Irish people are identical.'[94] The moment was ripe with future promise and fragrant with well-developed rhetoric. As the Nationalist MP Willie Redmond declared to those present in Ancoats' St Patrick's Church Hall:

> ... the present alliance of the Liberals, Labour and Irish parties was going to continue until every reform dear to the hearts of the Liberal and Labour parties was carried into law despite the powers of privilege and class. – (Loud cheers).[95]

The *Labour Leader* echoed this claim, declaring that:

> ... the greatest argument of all for political unity is that economic circumstances have long since united us in bonds that are indissoluble. The landlord and capitalist class captured the Parliament of Ireland, seized the land of Ireland, controlled the judicial system, instituted a police system that has cursed the country; they drove the people abroad. [...] And yet all they did to you they did to us likewise ...[96]

Such was the unpopularity of the Lords in Manchester that the Conservative candidate for North Manchester was forced to announce that, 'You can hang 'em, drown 'em, do anything you like with 'em. I don't like lords.'[97]

Despite this unity there were still problems within the alliance. The UIL manifesto gave no automatic priority to Liberal candidates over those from the Labour Party in seats where they stood against one another. However, in practice, Parliamentary Nationalists favoured their old allies and tried to impose this preference on their English subordinates. Such a position angered Irish supporters of Labour who argued, with some justice, that their party was more firmly committed to Home Rule than many Liberals: whereas only 30 per cent of Liberal candidates mentioned Home Rule favourably 70 per cent of Labour's did so. Local branches challenged the central body's original decision to endorse the Liberal, but with little success.[98]

In Manchester only one contest strained Irish loyalties. This was in the South-west division in January where the ILP sought to replace the retiring Labour MP. The Liberals had, however, staked an early claim for what was historically a Liberal division. After both sides had refused to compromise, Dan McCabe was given the difficult task of convincing Irish voters that it was their duty to follow the UIL directive and vote Liberal. His appeal reflected the delicate nature of the Nationalist position, verging as he continually did on the apologetic. McCabe reminded the meeting that the UIL:

... did not support Mr Needham because he was Mr Needham, nor because he was a Liberal, nor did they oppose Mr McLachlan because he was a Labour man. They simply acted as a united organization which existed for the specific purpose of winning self-government for Ireland and those responsible for the management of the organization – and they had no reason to doubt their capacity – had asked them to support the Liberal on this occasion. They had no personal fault to find with Mr McLachlan whatsoever...

It was apparently only with great reluctance that Irish voters followed his advice. Yet, this was enough to end McLachlan's hopes of winning the seat. Even so, with the progressive vote split, the Liberal had to wait for December before becoming an MP.[99]

By the turn of the century, Nationalists in England had come to embrace a political position that had long been advocated by Michael Davitt. Davitt, a Lancashire-born Fenian, came to think that Home Rule could only be won with the support of the English working class. Therefore, he felt that a strong labour movement was a good in itself as well as a prerequisite for Home Rule. His social programme was radical rather than socialist and his political position that of a Lib–Lab: he viewed the ILP's anti-Liberalism as indulgent and counter-productive.[100] If, in 1910, Irish voters could be prevailed upon to vote Liberal rather than Labour this was accomplished only after a great deal of pressure and persuasion. They were warned that any other course endangered Home Rule. This rationale was, however, weakening, especially given the generally close ties between Liberal and Labour. Moreover, in certain districts where Labour had come to be the automatic anti-Conservative party the argument actually went against the Liberals. In Manchester as a whole Labour had established a well-entrenched municipal and Parliamentary position.[101] Before 1914 Labour had held North-east Manchester and neighbouring Gorton divisions through three general elections. In 1911 the New Cross Liberal Party closed down; by 1913 the party's position throughout the entire North-east division was in danger of collapse.[102] If for no other reason, Irish voters increasingly turned to Labour in Manchester and elsewhere because the Liberals had vacated the field.

Towards independence

The shift of Irish political allegiance from Liberal to Labour was a slow process, which was rapidly accelerated by events in Ireland after 1916. During August and September 1914 Nationalist leaders had exhorted followers to join the British army to defend their country against the alleged threat of German aggression. Home Rule had been placed on the Statute Book, but it had not been enacted due to Ulster Protestant opposition. Nationalists were urged to demonstrate their loyalty to the

Crown and thereby show themselves worthy of Home Rule. T.P. O'Connor became one of England's most vocal Hun-bashers and the Manchester Martyr's procession became an expression of Irish support for the Allied cause. By October 1914 it was estimated that 8,000 Irish men in the city had answered the call to arms.[103] In Newcastle immigrants even formed their own brigade. As one Tyneside Irish Nationalist declared:

> When King George put his signature to Home Rule, the Irish chaps from the yards and the collieries about the place came rushing to join the Army, and no power on earth could stop them.[104]

In Ireland, in contrast, such fervour was in short supply.

Despite these demonstrations of loyalty and the consequent sacrifice of thousands of Irish lives in France, Nationalists in Westminster were still unable to persuade the Liberal government to implement Home Rule after the war. Under pressure from Orange militants and their Conservative supporters Asquith was unwilling to make such a commitment. The failure of constitutionalist Nationalists at the final hurdle slowly corroded their support in England: the events that followed the 1916 Dublin Easter Rising accelerated this process. This was not because many followers in England had supported the Rising: at the time James Connolly and his colleagues were widely denounced as traitors. Irish people were, nevertheless, united in their opposition to the execution of the rebels. It was Asquith's stubborn decision to order their deaths that completely transformed matters and marked a decisive change in attitudes.[105] After facing the firing squad the rebels were quickly transformed into Nationalist martyrs and the Rising elevated into a holy act. In Manchester, St Anne's in Fairfield held a mass for the souls of Connolly's comrades, during which the parish priest praised their 'high character and stainless lives.' After being urged to defend their King and Empire in 1914, the Irish in England were beginning to appreciate the nature of their reward. They could only with some effort conceal their new feelings about the monarchy. As Bill Naughton recalled of the period:

> Any time when in school we were gathered to sing 'God save the King', I would sing 'God save Ireland' to myself, and the big picture of King George and Queen Mary in all their regalia were to me but the images of two figures in a waxwork show, and I would try to imagine Robert Emmett or Patrick Pearse, or think of James Connolly being carried out on a chair to be shot – these were my heroes.[106]

As a result of events after 1916 and their inability to stop them, the UIL lost support in England almost as rapidly as it did in Ireland. While Connolly and his like were praised for their heroic failure, the UIL was castigated for its cowardly ineffectiveness. From being on the verge of success in 1914, the UIL had helplessly seen victory slip from its grasp during the War. The whole foundations for the constitutionalist strategy lay in ruins in the face of their inability to cajole their Liberal allies to implement the long-awaited Home Rule Act. Although formally disbanded in 1923 the organization had long since lost the respect and leadership of the Irish in England. It had been supplanted by the Irish Self-Determination League (ISDL), formed by members of Manchester's Sinn Fein in 1919, which attracted younger members of the community.[107] For those in Manchester's UIL branches, this was a painful period of transition. Some joined the League, a number remained loyal to the old movement, whereas others turned their backs on Nationalism completely and transformed their branches into non-political Irish clubs.[108]

During the ISDL's short but eventful life its fortunes were closely tied to events in Ireland: while the number of Black and Tan outrages increased, so did membership. Manchester was the League's most important centre of activity, claiming 7,465 members out of a national total of nearly 39,000 in 1921. Moreover, unlike the UIL, League branches actively promoted Gaelic culture: one even had its own Gaelic football team. During the period 1919–22 the Irish in England identified with the plight of their compatriots across the water as they had never done before, nor were to do so again. They took to the streets and greeted Republican prisoners released from Strangeways prison as if they were heroes. Some expressed their patriotism in a fairly harmless way: one painted his house in the colours of the republican tricolour.[109] During the late summer and early autumn of 1920 the attention of many Irish households was focused on the fate of Terence MacSwiney, the Mayor of Cork, on hunger strike in Brixton jail. His death caused widespread anger and distress and Irish communities across the country organized their own protests. In Manchester, every element of the population was represented, from the Catholic Church to Sinn Fein. Their public expression of support for the dead mayor provoked a counter-demonstration when marches made their way through Collyhurst. Small gangs of Protestants waved Union Jacks and sang *Rule Britannia*; fights inevitably followed.[110]

During these years, the battle for independence was fought with more than words. However, some Irish remained cautious because of the danger of an English backlash. The *Manchester Catholic Herald* condoned violence so long as it was in self-defence and confined to Ireland. However, evidence of British atrocities led even Manchester's Liberal councillor and provisions merchant Hugh Lee to observe that:

> For many years the Irish people had worked constitutionally, but the only answer from the Government was shattered hope and coercion. Finally, Irishmen were driven to hitting back with the same weapons with which they were attacked.[111]

By the winter of 1920–1 a few of the Irish in England decided that it was time to take more direct action and began the first campaign of organized violence on the mainland since the collapse of Fenianism.[112] As a result of arousing English paranoia, the entire Irish population fell under suspicion and relations between the two national groups became strained. In

Oswaldtwistle, Lancashire, Mary McCarthy, daughter of an English mother and Irish father became, 'the focal point of the reaction of the English children to the troubles' after 1916; school chums were, 'transformed from familiars and friends into dangerous, sadistic little hooligans.' In the aftermath of 1916 Lancashire farmers had refused jobs to Irish labourers; after Sinn Fein's assassination of Sir Henry Wilson in 1920 Irish workers in many trades were made redundant.[113]

In Manchester, this brief period of violence culminated in a shooting incident and the death of a Sinn Feiner during a raid by one hundred police officers on an Irish club in Hulme. Guns, petrol and explosives were found: Sinn Fein's Lancashire campaign had been co-ordinated from the club's back room while whist drives and dances were held in the main hall. This was, however, a rather modest operation, which involved no more than thirty men who performed drill after Sunday mass, despite having only four rifles between them. Of those subsequently convicted of conspiracy most were well-established members of the population, among them being a grocer, clerk, plumber and even a prominent member of the local Labour party. By no means all had been born in Ireland: Sean Morgan, who died during the raid, had been raised in St Patrick's parish and even fought in the war.[114] Despite English hostility there seems to have a been a widespread acceptance of the legitimacy of the bombers among the Irish: events in Ireland made it difficult for them to condemn such actions. Morgan even assumed the mantle of a hero, for a time being compared with the Manchester Martyrs. His funeral attracted a large number of well-wishers; as did the unveiling of a memorial on the ninth anniversary of his death.[115]

During this period of turmoil Labour increased its strength within the city's Irish population, appealing to pre-war Liberals hostile to the ISDL as well as to advocates of the League. This was largely because, after 1916, Labour was the only 'friend of Ireland' left: the Conservatives were further tainted by unquestioning support for Ulster Protestants, while both the Lloyd George and Asquith wings of the Liberal Party were stained by Irish blood. The Liberal connection had by this date become well-nigh defunct. Despite this, during the 1919 municipal elections Liberals in Miles Platting assumed they could still call on Irish loyalties. They were soon disabused of this view when Labour won the ward with over two-thirds of the ward vote, a result in which Irish voters were said to have played a decisive part.[116]

In Manchester, local Labour parties organized meetings and demonstrations in support of Irish independence and called for a strike to halt arms shipments to Ireland. Nationally, however, Labour was suspected of fighting shy of the issue and ignoring it whenever possible. This was indeed the case, for Labour leaders realized the risk they ran of alienating English voters.[117] Irish party members were unhappy with such prevarication. Thomas Neafsey, a resident in England since 1900 and Labour member since 1916 told a meeting in South Salford that:

104 Class and ethnicity

> ... though a member of the Labour Party he was not going to sell himself, body and soul, to that party, for his first thoughts were for justice to the land that gave him birth.[118]

J.R. Clynes, at once a local MP and national party figure, felt the full force of Irish frustrations. In 1918 he was accused of supporting the introduction of conscription to Ireland and opposing Home Rule while a member of the cabinet. Only by publicly denying both these charges did he avoid facing Dan Boyle in his constituency during the general election of that year.[119] An Independent Irish candidate actually stood in the Stockport by-election of 1920 because Labour's commitment to Irish independence was felt to be too weak and vague. However, despite misgivings the Irish vote remained solidly behind the party after 1918.[120]

During 1921 the ISDL lost half its members. Many had become disenchanted with the Nationalist cause during the civil war between Irish Free Staters and Republicans: by July 1922 the League in Manchester was virtually defunct.[121] By the time of the 1923 general election T.P. O'Connor announced that Ireland would play no part in deciding the loyalties of Irish voters.[122] Despite this, the ISDL staggered on: in 1924 it was rumoured to be considering standing a candidate against Clynes, although nothing came of this.[123] In fact, the creation of the Free State and the bloody divisions that tore the Nationalist movement in Ireland apart caused a widespread disillusion among the Irish in England. Community events were quickly depoliticized: the Nationalist St Patrick's rally was replaced by a night of song and dance; the Manchester Martyr's march dispensed with its political meeting.[124] In Scotland, both Sinn Fein and the Gaelic League also lost members as a result of this turning away from Ireland.[125] However, this did not mean that the Irish had been politically assimilated into English politics and that ethnic influences had evaporated. If nationality lost its immediate impact, it remained an important foundation for Irish support for Labour throughout the inter-war period. Moreover, the – albeit imperfect – solution of the Home Rule question left the field open for the Catholic Church to pursue its own interests unmolested by national considerations. This will be the major theme of the next chapter.

six

Labour and the Church

Annexing the Catholic vote

After the Irish issue effectively fell into abeyance in the early 1920s, the political allegiance of Irish Catholic voters in England became the subject of renewed speculation. Labour leaders had long assumed that, as a consequence of their working-class identity, most voters of Irish descent would support them. In 1912 Ramsay MacDonald had anticipated that, once they had been 'released' from their obligation to support Home Rule, Irish labourers would vote to improve their own lives in England. Thus, he felt it was inevitable that they would eventually turn to Labour.[1] The immediate post-war period seemed to vindicate such confidence: both for reasons of class and nationality, most Irish voters felt they had no option other than to support Labour. In fact, throughout the inter-war period the Irish were one of the most consistently pro-Labour elements within the working class.[2] However, if national considerations propelled Irish voters towards Labour, their continued allegiance to the Catholic Church meant that this affiliation was qualified. A number of active working-class adherents even hoped that after the creation of the Free State fellow Catholics would follow their Church's political lead.[3] If these expectations were largely frustrated, Labour was nevertheless unable to win complete political ascendancy over the Irish Catholic electorate. Potentially, therefore, Irish political allegiances were just as divided as they had been before 1914. This fact was usually obscured because both party and Church reluctantly accepted each other's existence. However, this uneasy peace

occasionally gave way to open conflict. Such tensions traced their origin
to a single root: the mutual mistrust of Irish Catholics and the rest of their
Labour colleagues. In Liverpool, for example, the dividing line between
Irish members and the rest was so stark they did not even sit next to one
another at meetings.[4] The former suspected that many within the party
sought the abolition of their Church and consequently their distinctive
way of life. Many of the latter imagined that, as one Manchester activist
suggested, 'Catholics entered the Labour Party for their own ends'. They
were irritated by Irish adherents who remained loyal to Church and nation:
because of this they were not considered to be 'proper' Labour Party
members. As a former secretary of Manchester Trades Council declared in
1935, 'The man who was a Catholic first, an Irishman second and a Labour
man last ought to be given his marching orders.'[5,6]

The main focus of many of these internal party conflicts was the issue
of denominational schooling. Many Labour members opposed the control
of education by religious bodies with a fervour more intense than even
that of most Liberal Non-conformists. So far as such activists were concerned, secular education was one of the crucial means of sweeping away
popular ignorance and clearing the path for socialist enlightenment. Others
were also critical of all forms of organized religion, which they saw as
buttressing the existing social order. Catholic schools were particularly
criticized due to the Church's anti-socialist and anti-Communist pro-
nouncements, which were issued with ever greater frequency after 1917.
As a consequence, Catholic education was seen as an impediment to 'real
reform', while the Church as a whole was thought to be an 'instrument of
capitalism', which had to be destroyed.[7] Those most hostile to the Church
were on the left of the party, and were especially numerous in the ILP. As
early as 1910 the *Labour Leader* had attacked the Catholic Church for as-
sociating with, 'drink merchants, land thieves, war-mongers, and tariff
jugglers.'[8] Moreover, Labour activists were also concerned with other
issues that brought them into conflict with the Church. Feminists and
others sought to encourage birth control among the working class to
raise living standards and free mothers from unnecessary drudgery. They
were attacked by clerics who drew the line at 'unnatural' methods of
limiting family size. Cardinal Bourne deprecated families with fewer than
three children because he feared that contraception would lead to a fall
in the size of the Catholic population.[9] Compounding these problems was
a vocal minority within the party who sympathized with Marxism, the
Communist Party and the Russian revolution, all of which Catholics saw in
diabolic terms.[10] Yet, if there were aspects of the Labour Party that per-
turbed Catholics, there was also much that they supported. Labour's economic and welfare reforms were just as welcome to Irish workers as they
were to an increasing number of their English counterparts. However, the
key issues of education and birth control emphasized the extent to which
many in the party were out of sympathy with Labour's Irish Catholic
supporters.

For prudent, tactical reasons Labour leaders sought to conceal any differences between party activists and Catholic voters. However, most Church leaders were unwilling to seek a middle ground. Catholic intransigence actually increased in the 1920s and 1930s: a Papal Encyclical on education issued in 1930 re-emphasized that the state should not interfere in parental choice; another had earlier condemned any form of artificial contraception.[11] Catholics did not support their Church on these issues because they had become ideological anti-socialists – only a minority of working-class Catholics were ever that. Instead, they saw these two matters, education in particular, as vital to their cultural identity. Labour was vulnerable to insurrections on such issues because it had been on the level of culture, rather than explicit ideology, that the party had made its most powerful appeal to Irish Catholic loyalties. Labour considered all religions equally useful, to be praised and manipulated as occasion demanded.[12] Thus, Catholicism, Irishness and Labourism were presented as being compatible creeds. Labour was not willing or, more to the point, able to promote its own distinctive ethical vision within the electorate, despite the fact that it was this that motivated many of its activists. Instead, the party claimed that it was purely and simply appealing to the economic self-interest of workers. All else was irrelevant and could be left to the individual's moral sensibility. As J.R. Clynes told an Ancoats audience in 1907:

> As a party they had nothing whatever to do with a man's conscience or faith. He hoped they would always be defenders and protectors of freedom of faith and conscience. He desired to say to Christian and Agnostic alike that their proposals were industrial and economic proposals, and they dealt with man's relationship to man, and not his relationship to the Almighty Power.[13]

This claim was superficially borne out by Joe Toole's campaigns in the South Salford constituency, which he contested five times between 1923 and 1935, twice coming out the victor. Toole's Conservative opponents appealed to the English virtues of patriotism, deference and Anglicanism. In contrast, the main thrust of his campaign speeches was that Labour was the only party that would defend working-class economic interests. According to Toole, there were only two sides: the working class and their oppressors. Those workers who dared to vote Conservative were, in his eyes, class traitors.[14] Even so, subsumed within this class-based economistic rhetoric was a specific call to the communal loyalties of Irish Catholics. Catholics comprised about 10 per cent of South Salford's electorate, a vital proportion given the finely balanced nature of the constituency. Moreover, as a third generation Irish Catholic raised in the locality Toole was particularly well-placed to make such an appeal. During 1923 he held a meeting in Mount Carmel school, Ordsall, where he reminded his audience that he had been taught there. In 1929 he circulated a leaflet, printed in green ink, which contained endorsements from T.P. O'Connor and a Catholic priest.[15] Toole therefore employed the language of class but underpinned it with an appeal to ethnicity. Irish Catholics were addressed principally as workers but were reminded that their religious and national differences also meant they should support Labour. Thus, Toole's rhetoric made the integration of Irish Catholic working-class voters seem more real than it actually was. Such an approach was often successful in garnering votes at election time, but it left Labour vulnerable when the constituent elements of the Irish Catholic identity were no longer in harmony with party policy. Labour discovered that when ethnicity was employed against class loyalty the latter buckled under the strain.

For much of the time, however, any conflict between Labour and Catholic loyalties remained dormant. Most Catholics advocating 'socialism', whether in the form of joining or simply supporting Labour, or indeed any of the parties to its left, did so with little sense of personal discord. Although secretary of the ILP in Miles Platting prior to 1914 one Irish Catholic did not feel it necessary to stop attending mass.[16] The socialism of such Catholics took the shape of pragmatic reformism. As one Openshaw adherent wrote in 1907:

> I contend that if the Socialists only remove the terrible nightmare from poor peoples' minds of having to end their days in the work-house, they will have done a great deal in following the advice of Our Lord to His disciples when he said, 'Feed My lambs; Feed My sheep.'[17]

The most famous Catholic who attempted to reconcile any alleged contradiction between socialism and Catholicism was Glasgow's John Wheatley. He also saw socialism as the peaceful implementation of Christian principles, which involved the abolition of poverty but not of all private property.[18] In seeing socialism as the continuation of Catholic principles Wheatley was by no means alone. During a Parliamentary by-election in 1903 the *Preston Catholic News* advised readers who 'endorse the Holy Father's views on labour' to vote for the ILP candidate.[19] Despite warnings from the pulpit those Catholics who supported Communism still reconciled this aggressively atheistic creed with their faith. During his sermon on 'The menace of Communism', a St Wilfrid's priest reported that at a Communist procession in Liverpool half the demonstrators raised their hats as they passed a Catholic church.[20] On being asked which way he was voting in a municipal election in St Helens, a member of the Unemployed Workers' Union told his priest that he was voting Communist. 'Nobody can be a Catholic and vote Communist, Patrick' said the priest, to which came the reply: 'I'll see you at mass on Sunday, Father, but I'll vote Communist on Thursday.'[21]

Thus, despite their support for Labour, it is likely that proportionately fewer working-class Catholics became socialists in its strict ideological form than did non-Catholics. Yet, a minority raised in Irish Catholic families did come to believe in a form of socialism that led them out of the Church. During the 1870s and early 1880s the old Chartist and lapsed Catholic

Myles McSweeney was a leading secularist lecturer in London's proletarian clubland.[22] In turn-of-the-century Manchester the son of a former Irish army sergeant also embraced secularism and sent his children to a socialist Sunday school.[23] Yet, the price paid by such people was that they were treated like renegades by those communities in which they had been raised. On joining the SDF in the 1890s the young Joe Toole was called a traitor, an atheist and free-lover by old school friends, while his father refused to allow him in the family home. By standing against a Catholic candidate in a Board of Guardians election Toole aroused so much hostility he felt it wise to leave Ordsall.[24] When James Connolly visited Manchester in the early 1900s he was only able to form a branch of his Irish Socialist Republican Party in the distant township of Pendleton, where miners faced particularly hazardous working conditions.[25] After 1917 the Church's insistent anti-Communist rhetoric seems to have further reinforced such antipathy: Catholics were probably the staunchest of working-class anti-Communists. In St Helens they emptied chamber pots over the heads of speakers at a Communist meeting in a Catholic neighbourhood. During another incident in the town a Communist demagogue was disrupted by a group of two hundred Catholics who fell on their knees and sang *Faith of our Fathers*, eventually chasing him down the street. Bill Naughton's father's view of Communists in early 1920s was perhaps typical:

> '. . . an' though they're right in many ways, the first thing they'd do if ever they came to power would be to go round to all the Catholic churches, take out the priests, line them up against the wall, an' – ' he went silent and raised his hands in the gesture of a man firing a gun.[26]

Such attitudes were undoubtedly entrenched during the Spanish Civil War in the late 1930s, when alleged Communist atrocities against the Church were splashed across the pages of the Catholic press. As a result of such hostility Communists arrogantly dismissed Catholics as the least politically conscious portion of the working class.[27]

The politics of Catholicism

Much to the despair of those closest to the Church, few Catholics took their anti-socialist strictures seriously. This was because, so far as most adherents were concerned, Catholicism was not an ethical religious doctrine to the same extent that, for example, Non-conformity was. The vast majority of Catholics did not choose to become members of the Church, but were simply born into the Faith. Thus, so far as many were concerned, membership did not depend upon qualities such as sobriety or thrift but upon simple attendance at mass – and sometimes not even that. Popular Catholicism sprang less from an acceptance of a set of ideas and principles and more from socially-grounded loyalties. These were primarily centred in the family, where issues relating to education and birth control were obviously most relevant. Popular Catholicism was pragmatic and, as a consequence, so far as any adherent's party affiliation was influenced by their faith, it gave rise to a pragmatic politics. This was why those Catholics who became Labour activists did so for practical rather than ideological reasons. They were usually trade unionists and Labour was the party of the labour movement as well as the party most favourably inclined towards Ireland. In contrast, Non-conformity's emphasis on individual morality engendered an ethical Labour politics amongst many chapel-goers.[28]

Working-class Catholics motivated by explicitly ideological motives might have been a small minority, but they were none the less vocal and played a disproportionate role in colouring the Church's relationship with Labour. Their world-view was largely prompted by the Catholic social gospel which, despite the view of its socialist critics, expressed genuine hostility to capitalist excess. In fact, the English Catholic Church considered the rise of capitalism to have been predicated on its own destruction in the sixteenth century. During the early nineteenth century, priests had also been prominent in criticizing the emergent factory system.[29] Later, numerous parochial lecture series were devoted to outlining 'The evils of Capitalism'.[30] Capitalism, or at least that system in which self-interest held exclusive sway and the gulf between rich and poor grew ever-wider, was severely criticized.[31] In contrast, the Church sought to promote social harmony, which it felt was impossible under capitalism. It wished to draw the classes together in the way medieval trade guilds were thought to have unified employer with worker. As the Bishop of Salford reminded members of the Co-operative society in 1897, the guilds brought:

> . . . not only temporal but spiritual blessings; they joined all classes together in the practice of justice; morality and religion – for, that was possible at a time when the whole people of this empire were knit together in the profession of one faith. There could be no doubt that if those guilds and kindred benevolent societies which then existed in what was called Merry England had not been broken up by royal cupidity, we would not have required workhouses for the poor, we would not have had employers engaged in bitter strife, we would neither have had strikes, not their calamitous consequences to our national industries; for from the highest to the lowest all were locked together in the bonds of natural fellowship.[32]

As Canon Sharrock suggested in 1913, 'The only power which could heal the diseased condition of working-class life was the power of holy religion, backed in the right measure by the interference of the state.'[33]

Therefore, the Church sought to reform, if not abolish, capitalism. In the 1890s Cardinal Vaughan called for better housing for the poor and a ten shilling state pension for all those in need.[34] This could be interpreted as the Church's own brand of Tory paternalism. Although protests were made over class inequality – workers were described as 'paid slaves' – it was done in a manner that would have offended only the most dogmatic of economic liberals. Moreover, improvement was generally seen as coming through individual, moral transformation rather than structural change. Employers were urged to look to their consciences: they were exhorted to pay workers more so they could enjoy a better standard of life.[35] In a working-class context, however, such views assumed slightly more radical connotations. Importantly for working-class adherents, the Catholic world view conceded to trade unions a central role as one of the few means workers had of creating a more equitable relationship with employers. This had been the case since the 1830s, once trade unions had ceased to act like secret societies.[36] However, the Church only supported what it took to be 'responsible' trade unionism, which sought arbitration in favour of unnecessary conflict. It was in this spirit that Cardinal Manning had successfully intervened in the London dock strike of 1889. Strikes were conceived as the weapon of last resort, which could only be used in the furtherance of economic disputes. It was because he mistakenly saw the 1926 general strike as an attempt to overthrow the Conservative government that Cardinal Bourne condemned it as 'immoral'. He was not expressing hostility to the labour movement as a whole and even called for no re-crimination after the strike's end. In fact, in his Pastoral of 1918 Bourne had detected in the labour movement 'the true lineaments of the Christian spirit'.[37]

If the Church was hostile to certain aspects of capitalism it was also antipathetic to what it saw as extreme forms of socialism. Given the social group from which most of the Hierarchy and many of the clergy was recruited, it is hardly surprising that emphasis was given to the latter rather than the former threat. In 1910 the 'general intention' for March in the Holy Name parish was 'the war against socialism'.[38] If the Church hoped to reform capitalism, it wanted to destroy socialism. In fact, some clerics saw the Church as the only force standing between working-class Catholics and the alleged menace of extreme socialism.[39] Formally, however, both were seen as threatening individual freedom and were, in their different ways, enemies of the Faith. Whereas capitalism concentrated property among a tiny handful of individuals, socialism was perceived as proposing to concentrate ownership in the hands of an all-powerful state. As a consequence of this, the Church presented itself as standing between these two economic systems, advocating 'a controlled Individualism and a modified Collectivism.'[40] It was felt that individual freedom could only be safeguarded by a more widely dispersed ownership of property, which neither rampant capitalism nor extreme socialism would allow. This idea was developed in a more systemized form by Hilaire Belloc and G.K. Chesterton under the name Distributism. This theory won a limited, if devoted number of adherents, mainly among Catholic university students and a small handful of priests during the inter-war period.[41] However, such ideas had formed part of a devout Catholic's common-sense notion of political economy well before 1914.

In principle, Catholic ideology was not inherently hostile to the kind of policies propounded by Labour. Nevertheless, relations between party and Church were punctuated by numerous debilitating misconceptions, most of which traced their origin to Pope Leo XIII's 1891 Rerum Novarum. In this, Leo had attacked the influence of 'socialism', by which he meant a creed that sought the state monopoly of economic life, complete control of civil society, abolition of private property and the suppression of religious belief.[42] This was primarily directed against the growing influence of anti-clerical socialist parties in Catholic Europe rather than those less ideologically coherent, religiously-infused parties of the English left. Such confusion was compounded by Labour leaders like Ramsay MacDonald who described their party as 'socialist' yet remained ambiguous about many of the term's implications. On various occasions before 1914 Catholics sought numerous points of clarification but without success.[43] As a consequence, some adherents felt that Labour had to be rejected. After the 1917 Russian revolution and the European upheaval that followed the end of the First World War these feelings were reinforced: it seemed that the continent had become a battle-ground between Communism and the Church. During the early 1920s the *Manchester Catholic Herald* regularly carried stories about Lenin, the 'maniac' Bolshevik and his 'ruthless warfare' against religion. The dangers of 'Godless Communism' were a regular topic of sermons and clerical warnings throughout the 1920s and 1930s.[44] In this struggle Labour was seen as, at best, sitting on the fence. The *Herald* believed that within the Labour movement was a body of, 'unscrupulous revolutionaries who are taking their orders and their incomes in many cases from the Russian Bolshevists' and called on Catholics to counteract their influence. After 1917, therefore, the question of Labour's alleged socialism became much more acute.

The Catholic Federation

Despite their distinct cultural identity, most Catholics did not seek to form their own political organization. Some, like Cardinal Bourne, feared that a Catholic party would only arouse the prejudices of the Protestant majority.[45] Others, however, did support the idea: as early as 1888 the *London Catholic Herald* proposed the formation of such a body.[46] A large number of practical obstacles confronted Catholics with this ambition. Adherents were divided by nationality and class: their Catholicism might have been important, but it did not override other forms of identity. Even if such differences could have been overcome, Catholics were too dispersed and small in number to guarantee the return of representatives to Parliament. If the Irish in England managed to elect only one MP, the chances of Catholics exceeding this achievement were remote. It is possible that a Catholic party might have won a few municipal wards in some of the bigger towns and cities, but it would not have achieved much influence in most council chambers.

In certain areas of local government there was a strong case for independent Catholic activity, which overcame other considerations. Since the late nineteenth century Church-approved candidates had stood in School Board and Board of Guardians elections. Between 1870 and 1902 local School Boards were responsible for the administration of schools and were therefore of obvious interest to Catholics. In Manchester, adherents were the most effectively organized of all the contending parties.[47] There was also a strong case for Catholic representation on local Boards of Guardians because of the way these bodies supervised the religious life of those unfortunate enough to rely on the Poor Law. Few would have disagreed that it was necessary to contest the Protestant Thousand's attempt to deny Catholics in workhouses access to a priest.[48] By the early 1900s, however, Board elections increasingly revolved around purely economic considerations. The amount of benefit paid to Poor Law recipients, rather than their spiritual well-being, exercised voters. Middle-class Catholic representatives were not necessarily more sympathetic to the cause of the poor than Protestant colleagues. When the ILP led a delegation of unemployed people to meet Chorlton Guardians during the winter of 1894 it was a Catholic who 'asserted that the men outside had been compelled to join the procession by force or bribery.'[49]

The failure to establish a national Catholic party should not obscure the existence of a separate Catholic political identity. For, when Catholics were exercised by issues that affected them as members of the Church, they acted within secular parties. Because so many working-class Catholics belonged to, or simply supported, Labour it was within its ranks that they naturally tried to further their religious interests. In practice, working-class Catholics critical of aspects of Labour's character had two options. They could seek to influence the labour movement from within, taking the good and improving the bad, or it was open to them to reject labour out of hand and establish an alternative, thereby risking almost certain isolation. The most important vehicle for such dissident workers, the Catholic Federation, initially took the former road but ended its life attacking a party deemed beyond redemption.

The Federation was formed in the Salford diocese in 1906 by trade unionists who objected to moves within the Trades Union Congress (TUC) and LRC to support secular education. Although the Salford diocese remained the focus of Federation activity, by 1910 branches had been established in other parts of the industrial north such as Bradford, Hull, Leeds, Liverpool, Newcastle and Sheffield. Its original aim was to mobilize Catholic unionists and defeat these proposals; more generally, it hoped to blunt socialist influence within the movement. These ambitions were fully endorsed by Bishop Casartelli, who saw the Federation as the first step towards the creation of a popular national Catholic political party.[50]

The Federation was formed by skilled and white collar workers active in both the labour movement and Church; the Federation was their attempt to reconcile these two interests. Founder Henry Campbell belonged to both the Amalgamated Society of Engineers (ASE) and National Union of Life Assurance Agents and sat on Gorton trades council. Edmund Riley, the Federation's first chair, was a cabinet maker, branch secretary of the National Amalgamated Furnishing Trades Association (NAFTA) and delegate to Manchester trades council. He lived only a few yards from St Patrick's in a house, 'like a wayside chapel breathing true Catholic devotion and prayerful service.' James Berrel, who chaired the Federation's trade union committee, was a long-time ASE branch secretary in Ancoats, Manchester trades council delegate and had nominated J.R. Clynes for North-east Manchester in 1906. Thomas Burns, organizing secretary for most of the Federation's life, belonged to the Railway Clerks' Association (RCA) and was active in numerous Holy Name confraternities.[51] The outlook of such men was that of the skilled in general: they were, for example, deeply hostile to monotonous and repetitive work.[52] They also looked to arbitration rather than strike action and generally sought a more 'Christian' spirit in relations between capital and labour.[53] Despite their religious faith, they did not seek to introduce sectarianism into the labour movement and considered that workers had identical economic interests and so needed to unite against employers. So far as trade union matters were concerned, they were conventional in most of their views and supported the right to strike and picket, advocated the closed shop and detested strike-breakers. There were even advocates within the Federation for a state-imposed minimum wage.[54]

Like other skilled trade unionists, by 1906 Federation leaders looked upon Labour as nothing more than a means of protecting their occupational interests in Parliament. Labour was seen as strengthening a deteriorating bargaining position at the work place as both the ASE and NAFTA faced employers keen to implement de-skilling. Moreover, due to the legal status of the railways, the RCA could only improve working conditions through Parliamentary action.[55] Thus, Labour was seen in instrumental terms: it was a necessary part of a trade union's weaponry and was legitimate so long as it remained subordinate. It had no place, for example, taking political positions outside the industrial domain and was certainly straying beyond its sphere of influence by telling parents how they should educate their children.[56]

From the outset Federation members were fundamentally divided over strategy, between those who sought to influence Labour from within and those who considered it inherently socialist and therefore to be abandoned. This debate was brought to a head in 1908 when Berrell's ASE branch voted to disaffiliate from the LRC as a protest against its continued support for secular education. This measure had been proposed by a Catholic but was passed by a majority mostly composed of Anglicans. This action was opposed by many other Catholic unionists, who felt that it only made their attempt to defeat socialists in the labour movement that much more difficult.[57] Catholic pressure within the labour movement did, indeed, have some positive effect, leading as it did to the defeat of secularism.

Although supported by union leaders such as the self-declared revolutionary Will Thorne, secular education had ironically been seen by many in the labour movement as a way of avoiding sectarian disputes. Thus, when a motion supporting a national system of education 'under full popular control, free and secular' was presented to the 1906 TUC it was presented by a practicing Anglican. Although a socialist, he was no atheist and stated that the measure was not intended to be an attack on any denomination. However, Catholic delegates, prominent among them James Sexton of the Liverpool dockers, felt that it was inappropriate for the TUC to discuss such matters. He claimed to represent Catholics who:

> ...joined the Labour movement for Labour purposes. Had they been asked to join it with the idea of introducing secularism into the schools they would have kept out of the movement altogether.

In his view the Labour movement needed to help the unemployed rather than spend time debating irrelevant motions on education. Other Catholics echoed the Church's teaching by stating that parents had the right to bring their children up in their own way. This right was keenly contested by other delegates, who felt that children had to be allowed to make up their own minds about religion when they were old enough to do so free of parental pressure. Notwithstanding Catholic protests, between 1906 and 1912 secularism was approved by large majorities at the TUC. Yet it had also become by 1910, in the words of one delegate, 'a hardy annual that has done more to cause dissent within the ranks of Labour than any other question.' This culminated in scenes of violent disorder at the 1911 Congress, when Sexton's attempt to speak was met by attempts at physical intimidation. After such scenes, the next Congress took the unprecedented step of passing a motion forbidding future discussion of secularism. The issue had aroused so much ill-feeling the movement could not risk further mention of it.[58]

Even after this Catholic victory, there were still some Federationists who felt that there was need for a Catholic party. This would become clear not immediately, but:

> ... the day after tomorrow when minor differences shall be sunk before the inevitable struggle between the forces of Christianity and the pent-up forces of Secularism, Socialism and Materialism.[59]

To those who continued to see Labour as intrinsically socialist the party's 1918 constitution confirmed what they had always suspected. In their view, it was even more vital for Catholics to abandon the party. Labour's commitment to, 'the reconstruction of society upon the basis of common ownership of the means of production' was taken to be conclusive proof. The National Council of Catholic Trade Unionists (NCCTU) called on the TUC to form a Christian Democrat party with a programme similar to that of the, 'late

Labour Party, but excluding the Collectivist or Socialist formula.'[60] That the TUC chose to ignore this proposal is not surprising. However, it was also rejected by both the Hierarchy and vast majority of working-class adherents. Moreover, when Federation members in the Salford diocese were balloted as to whether they were prepared to cease paying their union levy to Labour in protest at the new constitution few even bothered to vote. Of those who took the time to express their opinion on the matter, an overwhelming majority felt that Labour was not socialist and that even if it was, this was not very important.[61]

Despite this lack of support, Thomas Burns formed the Centre Labour Party (CLP) in September 1918. The imprint of Catholic ideology on the CLP programme was obvious: it was announced that the new party would be the, 'political expression of the needs of the Workers' positioned as they were between Capitalism and Socialistic excesses'. The dispersal of the means of production to as many people as possible was advocated, as was 'expedient' nationalization. Even less surprisingly, religious liberty and denominational education were both endorsed. Burns's party did not prosper and established only two branches, one in Manchester and the other in Blackburn. The CLP also only managed to stand in one municipal ward election, Gorton North, where its candidate was easily defeated by Labour.[62] Although Bishop Casartelli had supported the formation of the CLP the rest of the Hierarchy was less convinced. Cardinal Bourne was especially worried about its implications and wrote to Casartelli informing him of his disquiet. Thus, Burns and his Bishop found themselves isolated within the Catholic leadership. If few looked on Labour with much enthusiasm, then most saw that it was impossible to destroy it. In any case, MacDonald's moderation was increasingly apparent to some.[63] The Federation, however, never reconciled itself to Labour after 1918 and ended its days stubbornly referring to it as the 'Socialist Party'. In so doing, it cut itself off from the possibility of influencing matters within the party's ranks: until disbanded in 1928 the Federation could only criticize from the sidelines.

From the outset, the Federation had been beset by a number of potentially fatal weaknesses. Initially formed in defence of Church schools it was associated with an issue that all Catholics could enthusiastically support. However, its eventual pursuit of a purely ideological campaign against the chimera of socialism left most working-class adherents cold. Moreover, the Federation's neutrality on Home Rule was inspired by the vain hope that this would allow both Irish and English Catholics to support it. Although Federation members were said to have favoured Home Rule because of their Irish origins, Irish Nationalists interpreted neutrality as hostility under another name.[64] Some priests also resented the Federation's attempt to introduce democracy within parochial affairs, seeing this as undermining their own influence. Mistrust among most other Bishops also seems to explain the failure to establish a vigorous presence in dioceses other than Salford. There were also too few skilled Catholic trade unionists to sustain the movement. Membership was never more than 6,000 in Manchester and many of these seem to have been paper members only. By 1914 the Federation's leadership had fallen completely into the hands of lower middle-class members who were clearly not overly fond of the idea of a Labour party. Thus, when it came to finally breaking with Labour Federation leaders were quite prepared to make the sacrifice.[65]

Above all the other problems faced by the Federation was the reluctance of most adherents to place their Catholic identity before any other. This was something appreciated by the Hierarchy and explains why the response of most Church leaders to Labour's 1918 constitution was far more circumspect than that of Burns. After much deliberation Cardinal Bourne eventually decided that although some party members were clearly opposed to the Church's interests Labour was not intrinsically socialist in the sense meant by Pope Leo.[66] Yet, such a formula did little to dispel Catholic reservations about Labour – it was still possible, for example, to argue that the party was being taken over by extremists. Thus, the 1920s still saw adherents continue pre-war arguments about whether true Catholics could belong to the party.[67]

The failure and eventual demise of the Federation did not mean that Catholic doubts about Labour had been reconciled. Irish Catholic members of the party remained mistrustful of many of their colleagues. A meeting in Manchester during 1925 exposed the extent to which this remained the case. Leading Irish Catholics in the city gathered in the club room of a former UIL branch to discuss the formation of the Irish Democratic League. The League had been established two years earlier on the ruins of the UIL by T.P. O'Connor in an attempt to keep his own political voice alive. It was, in fact, one of a number of 'Irish Labour' parties that affiliated to local Labour parties after 1916.[68] Members gathered in Manchester were principally concerned with the continued growth of what they described as 'atheistic Socialism and Communism' within Labour's ranks. Particular criticism was reserved for Labour clubs, to which many young Irish Catholics belonged. They felt that:

> The atmosphere of some of these establishments is proving to be inimical to their religious and moral welfare. Discussions take place, in which such proposals as easy divorce and state guardianship of children are strongly supported by extremists who frankly admit that they regard the Scriptures as a fairy tale. Birth control is also lauded, and pamphlets dealing with this distasteful subject as well as sexual matters are openly sold.

In contrast the League was, 'a body Catholic in tone, that would be affiliated to the Labour Party and prepared to cooperate with it on all matters prejudicial to religion or Irish nationality.'[69] This was a clear attempt to defend the unique nature of Catholic identity and yet remain tied to the labour movement. Labour did not welcome the creation of this new body in the city and relations were anything but harmonious. In 1925 the League opposed the Labour candidate in St Michael's ward, despite his Irish birth, with a beer retailer: the League came third with 22 per cent of votes cast. This was not an especially impressive performance, but it was enough to deny Labour the seat and gave the Conservative a narrow victory. Moreover, this was only one of two defeats suffered by the party in the ward throughout the whole inter-war period.[70]

Separate Catholic organizations either within or on the margins of the labour movement were not very successful, either in influencing policy or in mobilizing Catholics on a permanent footing. The strength of Catholic politics did not lie in such activity but in *ad hoc* responses to certain issues that threatened to undermine aspects of their culture. Thus, the vast majority of working-class Catholics did not seek to transcend Labour – this was impossible – but, equally, they did not want Labour's socialist elements to transform their way of life either.

Labour's Catholic dissidents

Contraception was a subject about which Catholics and their Church became increasingly concerned after 1918. As the *Glasgow Observer* suggested during this period, 'the mere mention of birth control is enough to set the Catholic electorate on its hind legs.'[71] Apprehension was exacerbated by the activities of Labour members who wished to propagate such measures. In 1923 the Labour Women's Conference passed a resolution calling for contraceptive advice to be provided free to working-class women. Despite mounting pressure from within the party, the National Executive Committee (NEC) was afraid the issue was too controversial and would alienate the electorate. This is why in 1925, the NEC lamely advised the Party Conference to leave the matter to the individual conscience. A Manchester delegate complained that the NEC was afraid of religious organizations that were 'trying to permeate and infect' the labour movement. This was an obvious reference to the Catholic Church, for the Anglicans were gradually modifying their opposition to contraception. Catholics were certainly vocal in attacking the proposal, one delegate even referred to birth control as 'intrinsically evil'. It was James Sexton who warned that Catholics would 'rend the Labour movement from top to bottom' if it was passed. This determined Catholic opposition influenced Conference's decision in 1927 to accept the NEC's motion and avoid further discussion of the matter.[72]

Although nationally Labour leaders succeeded in preventing the Party committing itself to promoting birth control, local members still tried to propagate contraceptive advice. The battle between Catholics and birth control advocates could degenerate into acts of violence: in Bradford Catholics were implicated in an attack on a van used by supporters of contraception.[73] However, the Church usually restricted itself to condemning the measure from parochial pulpits. When Labour-dominated St Helens council approved the establishment of a birth control clinic in 1930 the following Sunday every Catholic service contained an attack on this 'resolution of an undoubtedly immoral nature opposed to the natural law of God.'[74] When Bootle council voted to fund birth control material, in order to limit the size of poor families, a local priest condemned the idea. He declared that, 'Knowing the Catholic women of Bootle as I do, I am perfectly safe in saying that rather than receive that knowledge they prefer even death itself.'[75]

The issue inevitably disrupted relations between local Catholics and Labour. In Dundee it ended what had been friendly co-operation. Prior to 1927 the city's ILP branch had met in a Catholic parochial hall. However, in that year the party held a talk on 'Socialism and Sex Hygiene' in which the speaker declared that contraception 'was a thing not for the politician, nor for the priest but the individual'. This led to the ILP losing the use of the hall after the local priest declared that he had 'no objection to the advocacy of an honest Labour programme' but that, 'blatant propaganda of such subjects as birth control, divorce, secular education, etc' could not be tolerated.[76] Similar tensions were aroused in Nelson when a talk on contraception held by the town's Women's Co-operative Guild was shouted down by Catholics. When a leading local birth-control advocate later contested a council seat in the town a normally pro-Labour Independent Irish councillor refused to support her.[77] A member of South Salford Labour women's section recalled arguments during this period between birth control advocates and Catholic colleagues who, she claimed, 'just followed what the priest said.'[78] Thus, despite the best efforts of Labour's national leadership across the country members and Catholics both inside and outside the party were coming to blows over the issue.

By the end of the 1920s differences over birth control merged into a wider series of disputes within local Labour parties. These arose across industrial England, although Lancashire lay at the heart of these disturbances and Manchester was the 'storm centre' of discontent. The north-east was also riven by similar divisions, which led to resignations and expulsions from parties in Newcastle, Sunderland, Blythe and Wallsend.[79] Each local conflict can be traced back to one of three causes: education, birth control or, after 1936, the Spanish Civil War. The schools question was the focus of discontent in the majority of cases. The arena of conflict was mainly confined to municipal government and local parties, principally because Labour's tenure on national office was only brief and precarious. Moreover, although Catholics were unable to mount a national campaign, their local concentration gave them isolated footholds in the labour movement.[80] Significantly, events in Liverpool took a rather different turn to those evident elsewhere. In that city conflicts over denominational education actually drove Catholics towards Labour, further reinforcing the explicitly sectarian nature of party loyalties. In accordance with provisions in the 1936 Education Act the Church had asked Liverpool's local education committee to finance an increased number of school places in the overcrowded dockside district. This was supported by Labour but rejected by the ruling Conservatives, who were keen to minimize the rates burden and had enthusiastically pared back council expenditure since the 1931 slump. In the 1937 local elections the Conservatives made an effective appeal to both sectarian prejudice and economic self-interest under the slogan of no 'Rome on the rates' and won an extra eleven wards. Despite intense pressure from the Board of Education throughout 1938 the education committee refused to budge, a stance that helped Conservatives to increase their majority at Labour's expense. The municipal elections of that year effectively forced Labour back into a Catholic bridgehead. It took measures verging on blackmail by the Board of Education to force the Conservatives into acceding to the Catholic request in May 1939.[81] Liverpool, however, was not quite on its own: in Gateshead in 1931 Conservatives had opposed a new Catholic elementary school, while Labour supported it.[82]

That Manchester should have taken a leading role in Catholic opposition to Labour was rather surprising. Immediately after the end of the First World War relations between Catholics and the party in the city had been friendly. This was evident in the degree of co-operation between the two sides during Board of Guardians elections. In 1919 the Catholic candidate in Hulme ward enjoyed the endorsement of the local Labour party and Irish club. Until 1926 both sides in Central ward, where Catholics were especially concentrated, enjoyed what was described as an 'entente cordiale'. Relations were soured in 1926, possibly as a result of Bourne's criticism of the general strike and the support of Catholic representatives for the deduction of ten shillings from the amount of relief that could be claimed by the families of strikers.[83]

Degeneration continued apace in 1928 when the city council endorsed the education committee's refusal to fund the construction of a new Catholic school in St Robert's, Longsight. The Church wanted to build a secondary school in the parish so that children would not have to travel across the city to other Catholic establishments. It was also hoped that a new school would maintain loyalty to the parish in later life. However, the committee followed the 1926 Hadow report's recommendation that centralization was the best policy; the maintenance of parochial units was deemed inefficient.[84] In the wake of this decision the Catholic Federation called on electors to vote against those councillors who had supported the education committee.[85] Five 'non-political' meetings were held during the 1928 municipal election campaign to make this case. One such meeting was held in New Cross, where the chair of Manchester Borough Labour Party, and keen opponent of funding Catholic schools, was standing for re-election. He lost, his 1925 majority of 248 being turned into a deficit of 479. This defeat was widely blamed on the defection of Catholic voters, which was, in turn, explained by the role of Richard Lundy a second-generation Irishman and Labour councillor who spoke at the meeting. He was accused of making comments prejudicial to his party's interest and was promptly expelled from the Borough party.[86] Lundy continued to receive the support of members in his own Platting constituency, which was essentially the old division of North-east Manchester and so contained areas of heavy Irish Catholic settlement. The party in Manchester was so split by the issue that the NEC gave Herbert Morrison and George Lansbury the thankless task of trying to solve the dispute.[87]

This was more than a falling-out over the conduct of one particular party member. The St Robert's issue succeeded in revealing a divide between the two camps that, once exposed, was almost impossible to bridge. Some Labour members felt that spending money on the new school would have wasted public funds on something 'scandalously inferior . . . unworthy of Catholics or any other Manchester children'. One seemed genuinely puzzled by the apparent irrationality of the Catholic position. More ominously for Catholics, two others stridently attacked the supposed right of parents to choose their children's school and to 'pollute' their minds with religious 'folk-lore'. In response to this criticism two Labour Catholics from the parish in question defended this very right. Their point of view was endorsed by another adherent, who suggested that all his eight children had benefited from a Church education – whereas council schools seemed to produce godless criminals.[88] It was no shock, therefore, that the NEC's mission failed to bring harmony to the city. While accepting that Lundy had intended to bring about Labour's defeat in New Cross, the NEC supported his re-admittance on condition that he promised not to repeat the misdemeanour. Backed by both the secretary and agent of the Platting ward, Lundy refused the olive branch and persisted in claiming 'the right, as a Catholic, not only to state, but to work for, the point of view which Catholics hold in regard to educational affairs.' The Borough party was also unwilling to compromise and, with a majority larger than the one that had initially voted for Lundy's expulsion, rejected the NEC's formula. With a general election in prospect, the NEC again tried to facilitate a peaceful settlement, but without success.[89]

The issue of Catholic education did not dominate the general election of 1929. In any case, after a painful investigation of the subject, Ramsay MacDonald had instructed candidates to avoid commitments on the issue.[90] The main point of potential contention was the Hadow report's recommendation to raise the school leaving age from fourteen to fifteen years of age. Labour was known to support this measure, but remained ambiguous as to whether it would increase funding to meet the consequent extra costs for schools.[91] Hard-pressed Catholic authorities were afraid that they would have to pay for the extra year. Despite this cultivated ambivalence the *Manchester Catholic Herald* opposed Labour. Adherents in at least the Holy Name parish were also directed, albeit elliptically, to vote Conservative. Despite this pressure, most Catholics were not moved by the issue during the campaign.[92] It seems that even most readers of the *Herald* considered Catholic schools safe in Labour's hands. For some Irish voters, nothing would induce them to abandon the party. One explained that:

I could not vote Tory; I never have done so, and never shall. As an old Home Ruler, I loathe Toryism and all its works. . . . And Liberalism is dead. I consider true Liberalism died with Campbell-Bannerman. I do not forget the 'Black and Tans' and the shooting of the Irish 'rebels' after Easter 1916.

Some, however, persisted in voting Liberal due to their 'consistent advocacy of Home Rule which alienated their closest friends and sent them into the wilderness years.'[93] Such insouciance was due to the fact that, despite MacDonald's injunction on the matter, Labour candidates in Irish Catholic seats pledged to protect the Church's educational interests. It was no accident that Platting's J.R. Clynes was one of that number – much to the disgust of Borough party delegates.[94]

If Labour had not formed a government after the election MacDonald presumably would have continued to assiduously avoid the education issue. However, after being installed as a minority administration reliant on Liberal votes it was soon clear that Labour could not avoid a confrontation with working-class Catholics. When the former Liberal C.P. Trevelyan was appointed President of the Board of Education, Catholics expected the worst, for he had also been a junior member of the Board under Asquith. When Trevelyan refused to increase grant aid, despite proposing to raise the school leaving age, and then linked any extra cash to increased control, they saw a fearful combination of godless Labour and Non-conformist Liberals conspiring to destroy Catholic schools. It seems that Trevelyan was probably more influenced by Treasury-imposed constraints on expenditure than by any personal religious or political prejudice.[95] Nevertheless, outside Parliament ordinary Catholics made their feelings plain. In Manchester 15,000 attended a meeting at the Free Trade Hall to register their feelings and numerous parishes in the city formed Catholic registration associations to mobilize adherents into an anti-Labour voting bloc.[96] In the Commons Labour's Catholic MPs combined with Conservatives around the Scurr amendment to ensure that legislation would not be implemented until financial provisions had been made for voluntary schools.[97]

As the Education Bill made its faltering progress Manchester generated a second, related conflict. It began when George Clancy, former chair of the city's ISDL, became Labour nominee for a municipal ward in Gorton. Before being formally adopted he was asked to agree that:

> Each candidate for municipal and party honours shall abide by the constitution of the Labour Party, even if it conflicts with the Church of the candidate's faith.[98]

This was an obvious attempt to prevent Clancy emulating Lundy's example. It also transgressed the accepted practice of allowing party representatives a free hand on issues of 'conscience'.[99] Unwilling to put party before Church, Clancy resigned. As the Bishop of Salford commented, to have remained a Labour member under such conditions would have meant Clancy abandoning, 'all his convictions as to who was his spiritual leader and take on another leader.' An editorial in the *London Catholic Herald* declared that the Gorton clause meant that Catholics could no longer remain in the Labour party if they also wished to remain loyal to their Church.[100] Even so, by no means had all Labour Catholics opposed the resolution.[101]

Although motivated by antipathy for the Catholic Church the education issue also aroused the anger of some Labour Anglicans, who remained committed to preserving the independence of their schools. When Clancy unsuccessfully stood as an Independent in the 1930 municipal elections for Openshaw – a ward not noted for its Irish Catholic population – he appealed to voters of all denominations and won the support of local Anglican clergymen. A few weeks after this contest a handful of Anglicans resigned in both Manchester and nearby Ashton-under-Lyne in protest against their party's alleged atheism. However, this remained a predominantly Catholic campaign: when a priest was seen leaving a polling booth in Openshaw he was met by cries of 'Down with the Catholic Church'.[102] Openshaw was not the only Manchester ward where Catholics and their party came to blows that year. In Hulme's All Saints ward, the local Labour party chair Patrick Casey and fellow Catholic and party member D.F. McNicholl resigned on the eve of poll after accusing their candidate of being anti-Catholic. When both men subsequently attended a Labour meeting they were set upon by angry members, whose tempers were not assuaged when an Independent Catholic split the Labour vote allowing the Conservatives to win what had been one of the party's safest seats.[103]

Two Parliamentary by-elections in Ardwick and Ashton gave Catholics further opportunities to express their dissatisfaction with Labour. Because the government was rapidly losing support at this time, it would be unwise to blame Labour's bad showing in these contests simply on the defection of Catholic voters, although it would be prudent to suggest that it contributed to them. The failure of Ashton's sitting Labour MP to support the Scurr amendment had led a number of local Catholics to resign from the party. When he died, his successor – a Catholic – was also considered insufficiently committed to Church schools. Labour's 1929 majority of 1,400 was turned into a deficit of 3,400 in a constituency where there were said to be 4,000 Catholic voters.[104] Oswald Mosley's New Party (NP) candidate had won over several ex-Labour Catholics in the division because of his support for the conscience clause. Before it became a fully-fledged Fascist organization support for the NP was probably the ideal compromise for disenchanted Labour members who fought shy of endorsing the Conservatives.[105] In Ardwick, with a reputed 10,000 Catholic electors, local priests came out in force and backed the Conservatives. D.F. McNicholl also worked enthusiastically against his old party; Labour's majority was cut from 7,000 to just 314.[106]

In the wake of these contests there was talk of exiled Catholics forming a Christian Democrat Party. However, this was little more than wishful thinking on the part of some particularly conservative priests and won little support from the émigrés themselves.[107] They tended to view matters as an internal party conflict that had temporarily got out of hand. In contrast, members of the clergy saw the issue as much more fundamental: according to one, Catholics had to ask themselves whether they were to go on taking Labour's 'Lenin's dope' or remain within the Church.[108] Both Lundy and Clancy were wary of this type of rhetoric and criticized talk of establishing a new party. Lundy carefully reiterated that, apart from matters that bore directly on their Church's interests, he supported Labour.[109] Moreover, by no means all Catholics were willing to sacrifice party membership and municipal office for their Church in a dispute they deemed ultimately soluble.

Those clerics who wanted to encourage the formation of a distinctive Catholic political presence looked with hope on the activities of Trade Guilds. These were intended to mobilize adherents against the alleged menace of Communism within the trade union movement during the 1930s. Despite this, even those on the right of the labour movement, such as Ernest Bevin, did not welcome their intervention.[110] A Police Guild was formed in Liverpool, a Tram and Busmens' Guild in Birmingham and a Busmens' Guild and Railway Guild in London.[111] In Manchester, the Catholic Transport Guild was formed at the height of the Clancy controversy. In fact, many of the guild's founder members were Labour exiles, such as Lundy and Clancy, as well as Thomas Burns of the defunct Catholic Federation. George Griffin, incumbent at St Robert's, the parish at the heart of the matter, was guild chaplain; his brother Norbert, a Conservative councillor was also a leading figure.[112] The guild, it was claimed, would be neither a political party nor a trade union, but simply a means of uniting Catholics working in municipal transport. The hope was that members would, 'encourage the spiritual side of their lives.'[113] However, it was also anticipated they would become more conscious that, as Lundy put it, 'religion came before their politics, or trade union, or anything else.' It was consistent with this view for the guild to promote Catholic education and oppose birth control.[114] It was, as Father Ingram of St Edward's, Rusholme, had it, a buttress against the 'pagan doctrines' of Communism and 'extreme' socialism. Despite the grandiose nature of these plans only a few Catholic transport workers joined. Membership never exceeded 400, a figure that was inflated by the inclusion of middle-class car owners.[115] This was also the experience of guilds established elsewhere.

In the immediate wake of Lundy's expulsion the *Manchester Catholic Herald* had suggested that half a dozen councillors had been on the verge of resigning and standing as Independents. The approaching general election apparently made them reconsider their position: they were not willing to make a point on behalf of their Church if this endangered Labour's electoral chances.[116] Labour's crushing defeat of 1931 and its weak recovery in 1935 dampened the ardour of most Catholics to continue the fight. This was not least because the formation of the National Government brought about the demise of the hated Education Bill.[117] Although a few dissidents remained committed, by the early 1930s few Catholics were interested in pursuing their conflict with the party.[118] Moreover, by 1935 both National and Labour education proposals were virtually identical, so far as provision for Catholic schools was concerned.[119]

Although Catholic attitudes to Labour possibly improved with the disaffiliation of the ILP in 1932, Catholic–Labour differences had not been completely reconciled.[120] As the 1930s went on, an increasing number of Labour members were more overt in their enthusiasm for the Soviet Union. This only confirmed the suspicions of Catholics, who were already wary of Labour's close ties to Communism.[121] The Spanish Civil War put further strains on relations. Whereas Labour Catholics saw the Spanish Church under Communist attack, non-Catholic members viewed it as more akin to a battle between democracy and Fascism. Thus, because of its support for the Nationalist cause, the Catholic Church was regularly accused of being Fascist.[122] These differences generated more controversy in Glasgow than elsewhere, despite attempts by both Catholic and Labour leaders to calm tempers. As many as 70,000 adherents participated in masses of reparation for crimes committed against the Church in Spain at a Lanarkshire shrine. In 1937 two Catholic councillors were expelled from the Labour Party for collecting money for the Nationalists, while the Catholic Union withdrew support from two ILP councillors because of their support for the Republicans. Elsewhere, tensions usually remained under the surface. However, the support of some Labour Catholics for Franco seems to have been the last straw for a number of local parties weary of such persistent nuisances.[123]

Mosley's British Union of Fascists (BUF) had hoped to benefit from continued Labour–Catholic tensions when it stood in four of Manchester's most Catholic municipal wards in 1938. In Collyhurst especially, the BUF made a blatant grab for the working-class Catholic vote and made much of Labour's alleged extremism and atheism. It was even suggested that the BUF's 'Labour-cum-Communist' opponent wanted to abolish religion completely. Despite the failure of this campaign some historians have indicated that Catholics across the north of England were drawn disproportionately to Fascism. Such was the number of Catholics in the Leeds BUF for example, that Mosley was known as 'the Pope'. The basis of the party's appeal to Catholics appears to have been its strident anti-Communism and hostility to Jews, both of which had been endorsed in the pages of the Catholic press. It was certainly true that Catholic anti-Communism did sometimes spill over into anti-Semitism. The prominent position of Jews in both the Russian Communist Party and its British counterpart indicated to paranoid adherents that this was an international conspiracy. However, Irish hostility to Jews might also have been due to the jealousy of one immigrant group for another. In Stepney Irish Labour councillors voted down their party's candidate for mayor because he was a Jew. In New York the prominent Jewish presence in the Communist Party made Irish Catholics more reluctant to support its trade union activities.[124] However, it is highly unlikely that Irish Catholics were any more tainted by anti-Semitism than their English Protestant neighbours.

A number of middle-class English Catholic converts certainly noted with approval the superficial similarities between Mussolini's corporate state and Catholic social teaching. However, it has been suggested that the BUF particularly appealed to Irish Catholics because of Mosley's opposition to Black and Tan excesses during the early 1920s. There were certainly contemporaries who claimed that most of Liverpool's Fascists were of Irish Catholic extraction.[125] Yet, the specific appeal of Fascism to Catholics of Irish descent seems rather unlikely due to the aggressively nationalist tenor of BUF campaigns, which encouraged native hostility to all minority groups. In any case, such a view ignores the extent to which some Catholic intellectuals and workers were explicitly anti-Fascist. It also conflates Catholic support for the anti-Communist nature of Fascism with approval of its intrinsic character.[126] As the persecution of the churches in Germany and Italy became more blatant even leading English Catholics reassessed their support for continental Fascism. During September 1938 Cardinal Hinsley described Nazism, Fascism and Communism as opponents of the Church: all three were, 'equally contrary to Catholic doctrine'.[127] John Strachey even suggested in the Communist *Daily Worker* that the Church could become part of an anti-Fascist Popular Front. These overtures were tersely rejected.[128]

The conflicts described in this chapter were not the exclusive concern of Labour Party activists, a small body at the best of times. It is true that the preoccupations of Catholic members did not perfectly reflect those of their less politically engaged co-religionists. It was, in this respect, Labour's misfortune that many of its Catholic rank-and-file were some of their Church's most enthusiastic adherents. They, above all others, were sensitive to moves that appeared to threaten their distinctive religious culture. Yet, such feelings nevertheless reflected, in an exaggerated way perhaps, wider concerns shared by most of those raised within the Church. Thus, Catholics in the Labour Party were caught between clerics, who missed few opportunities to encourage them to break with 'socialism' and dogmatic socialists, who disapproved of ethnic loyalties that allegedly compromised the purity of their class consciousness. It was up to the likes of Clancy and Lundy to reconcile these seemingly incompatible points of view. For the most part they were able to demonstrate that in politics, just as in social life, class and ethnic sentiments were inextricably intertwined. Their occasional failures proved that even by the 1930s there had been no simple and linear transition from ethnic to class politics.

Conclusion

This study is but one step towards a greater understanding of the nature of the experience of Irish Catholics in England before 1939. Such work has hardly begun for the years after 1945. The Irish presence during this latter period has been largely overlooked by historians who consider the numerically less significant influx from the West Indies and Indian sub-continent to be of greater interest.[1] One recent social history of post-war Britain, for example, only briefly mentioned the Irish in relation to Ulster and the activities of the IRA.[2] The Irish in Scotland are, in this respect, rather better served.[3] This concluding chapter looks at some of the most salient features of the decades that followed 1945. Important differences notwithstanding, the experience of most Irish immigrants after the Second World War manifested many of the characteristics of the preceding decades. It therefore confirms this study's basic premise that class and ethnic identities were only resolved in a partial and ultimately inconclusive manner.

The Irish remained England's largest ethnic group after 1945. In numerical terms the Irish-born population increased to levels not seen since the 1860s. By 1971 the Irish-born population resident in Britain totalled 952,760, 74 per cent of whom had come from the Republic, most of these being from the countryside. The reasons for immigration being principally economic remained generally consistent with the earlier period. Irish rural unemployment was still endemic and was, in fact, exacerbated by the mechanization of production. In contrast, the expansion of the economy after 1950 meant that employment opportunities in England had never been so numerous, nor jobs better paid. There were other, less economistic, reasons for leaving Ireland, which were especially applicable to young women tired of the overweening influence of the family and Church. Although hardly granted full equality in England, women enjoyed a greater chance to move into white collar occupations and pursue an independent life than they did in rural Ireland. Contraception was also freely available, while abortion after the mid-1960s was fully legalized.[4]

Although there was a slight improvement in the types of jobs performed by immigrants the building trade in particular still employed a disproportionate number of unskilled Irish workers. To English eyes immigrants also remained associated with 'social problems', in particular with crime. This was partly due to the fact that immigration continued to be the preserve of young single people: their English counterparts were a similar cause for concern. Moreover, new arrivals also faced the potentially disorientating experience of coming to terms with a new culture. The strains of immigrant life possibly explains why, even in the 1980s, 1 per cent of immigrants from Ireland required mental hospital treatment, a proportion three times greater than that of the indigenous population.[5]

Despite an overall increase in immigration since the late 1920s many Irish Catholic communities established during the nineteenth century were under threat of dissolution. One of the most salient reasons for this was that new immigrants sought jobs in the affluent midlands and south-east, areas that, after 1945, became even more attractive. London increased in importance as a place of settlement: by the 1960s one in four of all Irish-born lived in the capital. Yet, even in London new immigrants favoured the prosperous West End over the less economically vibrant but traditionally Irish East End. Thus, as formerly English districts assumed a more Irish character, old Irish areas lost some of their green tinge.[6]

If the importance of nationality was in decline in traditional places of Irish settlement, Catholicism remained a power to be reckoned with. Even so, ominous forces challenged the Church's predominance in such areas before 1939. In places of increasing immigration the Church faced an old threat on a new scale. During the late 1930s the conduct of young immigrants in London was a cause of particular concern. Illegitimate births, excessive drinking and fighting were alleged to be all too common among new-comers. Commercial Irish dance halls were seen as the principal source of such 'problems'. Despite being described by members of the clergy as 'a disgrace to the name of Catholics' these halls had proliferated in number to serve the influx of young immigrants. During the 1950s priests were still warning recent immigrants that their actions were ruining the reputation of both faith and nation. As in the 1890s, the Church was too poor to provide this expanding group of adherents with more spiritually uplifting alternatives and was forced to leave them to the tender mercies of the market.[7]

New and more profound developments also underfoot before the war only came to full but destructive fruition after 1945. In the early 1930s Manchester Corporation was one of a number of local authorities to propose the clearance of inner-city slum districts. This threatened to destroy life in working-class areas where the Church had slowly, and at considerable cost, established an institutional presence. The fear among clerics was that years of effort would be thrown away if Catholics were despatched to distant estates, leaving churches and schools empty and useless. After the Council published its plans, the Bishop of Salford issued a pastoral letter, which demanded that Catholics be rehoused only within existing parish boundaries. Concern was particularly intense in the recently-established parish of St Malachy's, Collyhurst, at least half of whose residents were to be relocated. Although the Church was principally protecting its own interests, it also reflected popular hostility to rehousing. Generations of working-class families raised in places such as Ancoats were uneasy at the prospect of losing all that was familiar. In Collyhurst Catholics and Protestants even temporarily overcame their differences and made a joint protest to councillors.[8]

Although Manchester Council chose to ignore these objections, it was nevertheless unable to implement its scheme due to lack of funds. As a consequence, the destruction of Irish Catholic communities established in the nineteenth century was deferred until the later 1950s and 1960s. However, when it did take place dispersal was on a scale impossible to envisage before 1939. Residents were scattered as far afield as Knutsford in the south and Middleton in the north. Thereby the cultural props that had sustained a sense of apartness among descendants of Irish Catholic immigrants were fatally shattered. This pattern was repeated across the length and breadth of urban England.[9] After 1945 a new cohort of Irish immigrants entered Manchester, drawn in by reconstruction work and the promise of a new prosperity. On their arrival they settled in areas in which few Irish Catholics had lived before the war. Instead of going to now-flattened Ancoats or Angel Meadow they moved to former middle-class districts such as Moss Side. The new Irish were part of a more heterogeneous wave of immigration. Instead of neighbours who shared a common Irish ancestry and Catholic faith, they lived side-by-side with workers from the West Indies. In Northampton they also worked with Ukrainians and Poles, and some married Lithuanians.[10]

Just as the 'fortress church' lost some of its geographical homogeneity and insularity so theological uniformity and certainty was replaced by doubt. In the 1960s Vatican II and the rise of ecumenism meant that Catholic and non-Catholic lost many of their distinctive attributes. In marriage, sex, divorce, contraception and social standing they were almost indistinguishable. Thus, the nineteenth century 'ghetto', such as it was, hardly existed by the end of the 1970s.[11] As a consequence of these developments the Church's grip upon the political loyalties of adherents began to slip. Even during the war it failed to mobilize them against proposals contained in the 1944 Education Act, which gave the state a greater voice in the administration of Catholic schools. Most Catholics seemed to consider that in 1944 they faced a greater threat than R.A. Butler the emollient Education

Minister. Despite this, many of those on the Left continued to view the Church in diabolic terms. *Socialist Commentary* described its schools as 'the breeding ground for blind bigotry, dogmatism and cynicism.' In response to even limited Catholic pressure it called for the exposure of 'the danger inherent in this factional work by people who get their orders from an alien authority.' Although hoping to challenge the 1944 Act during the 1950 general election campaign Catholic authorities were again unable to set adherents alight with anger. Even the later 1967 Abortion Act failed to move many Catholics.[12]

The Labour Party remained the preferred political choice of both the Irish-born and those of Irish descent. As late as the 1970 general election over 80 per cent of Irish voters supported Labour. This was not simply because most Irish immigrants were working class: during the 1960s both middle- and working-class Catholics were more likely to vote Labour than their non-Catholic counterparts. This was despite the anti-socialism of many priests and their opposition to the Wilson government's permissive reforms. Thus, Catholicism still seemed to promote Labour voting: paradoxically regular attenders at mass actually favoured Labour more than nominal Catholics.[13]

The reluctance of immigrants in England to pursue explicitly Irish issues after the creation of the Free State was maintained. This was demonstrated by their response to the IRA bombing campaign of 1939. An admittedly ill-conceived affair, its results were none the less deadly – especially in Coventry. Those directly responsible for the campaign were strangers to the country and had only recently moved from Ulster with the specific intention of committing acts of violence. In Manchester, for example, the conspirators operated from an empty shop and had lived in the city for a matter of weeks. In contrast to the bombings of the early 1920s, there was little or no support for the IRA among those who had settled in England. The young conspirator Brendan Behan alleged that the crowd that booed him on his arrest in Liverpool contained many compatriots 'trying to prove their solidarity with the local stock.' The only person put to trial in Manchester who was not of Irish birth used this fact as part of his defence and was eventually discharged.[14]

After 1945 Nationalist organizations continued to arouse little support. The Connolly Association urged Irish workers in England to follow the socialist teachings of James Connolly. Although not formally anti-clerical the Association was condemned from the pulpit for its close links with the Communist Party. Despite the enthusiasm of its leaders the Association only enjoyed modest success.[15] The Anti-Partition League, which sought to reunite Ireland, also failed to impress. In the 1950 general election the League stood four candidates, three in Glasgow and one in Bootle, who described themselves as pro-Labour on all but the Irish issue. Despite this tactic they each lost their deposit. One former League organizer in the late 1950s considered that there was 'a striking absence of national sentiment' amongst the Irish-born. As one, admittedly bitter, agitator claimed in the 1960s, 'All they're good for now is cursing the English on Saturday nights with their free National Health teeth.' Thus, lack of Nationalist fervour was blamed on immigrants placing their own well-being before the interests of Ireland. Just as in the late nineteenth century, they stood accused of having been corrupted by English ways.[16]

The most striking continuity connecting the periods divided by the Second World War was the way that the English viewed immigrants. The anti-Irish Catholic bias remained endemic.[17] Even the English middle class, a body that took its own tolerance for granted, exhibited deep-seated prejudices. In 1939 Mass-Observation asked members of its National Panel, a predominantly liberal, educated and professional group, whether the IRA campaign of that year had changed their attitude towards Irish people. Over 80 per cent declared that it had not. This was principally due to the fact that the Irish were held in such low esteem that it was impossible for the bombings to bring them down any further. Panelists suggested that such actions merely confirmed their impression that the Irish were unbalanced, untrustworthy, vicious and stupid. A Sussex doctor stated:

> I have always thought the Irish wanting in a sense of reality, and since I have studied Psychology I have considered them paranoiac, although I have good friends who are Irish. These latter are, how-ever, Protestants, which in my opinion means greater intelligence.[18]

Some even felt that the Irish were incapable of organizing such a campaign on their own. They suggested that a more sinister – German – hand was at work. Similar sentiments had been expressed by J.B. Priestley six years earlier during his English journey. Priestley was a politically progressive figure who came to embody radical wartime feeling, supported the Labour Party and helped form the Campaign for Nuclear Disarmament in the 1950s. Nevertheless, on visiting Liverpool's 'Irish quarter' he wrote:

> A great many speeches have been made and books written on the subject of what England has done to Ireland. I should be interested to hear a speech and read a book or two on the subject of what Ireland has done to England. If we do have an Irish Republic as our neighbour, and it is possible to return her exiled citizens, what a grand clearance there will be in all the Western ports, from the Clyde to Cardiff, what a fine exit of ignorance and dirt and drunken-ness and disease. The Irishman in Ireland may, as we are so often assured he is, be the best fellow in the world, only waiting to say good-bye to the hateful Empire so that, free and independent at last, he can astonish the world. But the Irishman in England too often cuts a very miserable figure. He has lost his peasant virtues, whatever they are, and has acquired no others. These Irish flocked over here to be navvies and dock hands and casual labourers, and God knows that the conditions of life for such folk are bad enough. But the

English of this class generally make some attempt to live as decently as they can under these conditions; their existence has been turned into an obstacle race, with the most monstrous and gigantic obstacles, but you may see them straining and panting, still in the race. From such glimpses as I have had, however, the Irish appear in general never even to have tried; they have settled in the nearest poor quarter and turned it into a slum, or, finding a slum, have promptly settled down to out-slum it. And this, in spite of the fact that nowadays being an Irish Roman Catholic is more likely to find a man a job than to keep him out of one.[19]

In the 1950s Irish immigrants continued to be met by signs declaring, 'No Irish, No Blacks, No Dogs'.[20] Specifically anti-Catholic attitudes also survived the war. David Storey's novel *This sporting life*, first published in 1960, was set in working-class West Yorkshire. The central character considered that a Catholic:

> . . . more or less represented a foreign agent. They might be on your side. On the other hand they might not. It was better to treat them all as enemies, then you could be sure. If you made every one of them a tiger then you couldn't go far wrong.[21]

Anti-Catholicism could spring up in the most unlikely places. The following incident occurred in Stoke during the early 1960s:

> Tony had been walking out with a girl who was training to be a nurse. Suddenly her mother forbade her to see him, not because she had anything personal against him, but because he was a Catholic. Tony was furious, and all the more because he practically never went to mass; his Catholicism meant scarcely anything more to him than his Irish ancestry, about which he was completely vague.[22]

Thus, notwithstanding the increasing rate of inter-marriage after 1945, attitudes more associated with the mid-Victorian period could still on occasion reassert themselves.

Despite such sentiments, the conventional wisdom is that the Irish became less 'alien' to English eyes after 1945. Admittedly, the influx of other more unfamiliar immigrant groups might have had some effect. The way that Irish and English united against Jewish immigrants has already been noted. The same was also true when it came to expressing hostility to the presence of black workers.[23] However, escalating communal tensions in Ulster in the late 1960s and the IRA mainland campaigns of the early 1970s renewed popular antipathy for the Irish in England. As in earlier times they were held to account for violence committed by compatriots. It was no accident that Irish jokes revived in popularity during this period. However, the Troubles also accentuated differences between Catholics from north and south. One Galway construction worker commented of those from Ulster in 1975:

Look at all the money that's been spent on them – unemployment money, the welfare state – the whole lot. Most of them never had a job in their lives – never had to lift a finger. We had to emigrate and work to get where we are. No wonder they turned out trouble-makers – they've had nothing else to do but draw the dole.

By being once again identified more clearly as an outcast group some Irish responded by distancing themselves even further from their national origins. Some even told anti-Irish jokes as a form of defence. Others, however, were radicalized and defiantly celebrated their cultural heritage and asserted their political interests in the face of indigenous hostility. The Irish in Britain Representation Group, which was formed in the 1980s, was one such organization.[24]

The dynamic nature of Irish Catholic immigrant culture was more than confirmed after 1945. As older communities faded or were uprooted new centres of settlement were created. Perhaps those who came after the Second World War were rather less attached to the Church than their predecessors. The Church was, in any case, unable to assert its authority in the way that it had once done. Yet, they possessed no less a sense of apartness. This was more than confirmed when established immigrants fell victim to numerous miscarriages of justice that followed IRA mainland outrages. Such immigrants were also possibly less politically unified and assertive than those before 1914, for the simple verities of Home Rule had collapsed. However, Irish voters were still influenced by the struggle for national independence, as indicated by their continued attachment to Labour. Thus, after 1945 tensions between class and ethnic identities did not usually have the direct and political impact that was so characteristic of the period before 1939. However, as those who have visited an Irish pub in one of England's urban centres and seen photographs of John F. Kennedy behind the bar and heard the Pogues playing on the juke box will confirm, there is little sense that those of Irish birth or descent have abandoned their own distinctive ethnic identity.

Notes

List of abbreviations in footnotes and bibliography

AD	Archives Department, Manchester Central Reference Library
CCM	Corpus Christi Magazine
CF	Catholic Federationist
CH	Catholic Herald
CHWE	Catholic Herald Western Edition
CNWRS	Centre for North-West Regional Studies
DD	Daily Dispatch
DW	Daily Worker
FJ	Freeman's Journal
GMPM	Greater Manchester Police Museum
HNM	Holy Name Messenger
LCH	London Catholic Herald
LHD	Local History Department, Manchester Central Reference Library
LL	Labour Leader
LNV	Labour's Northern Voice
LPACR	Labour Party Annual Conference Report
LPNEC	Labour Party National Executive Committee
LSE	London School of Economics
MC	Manchester Citizen
MCH	Manchester Catholic Herald
MCN	Manchester City News
MEC	Manchester Evening Chronicle
MEN	Manchester Evening News
MFP	Manchester Faces and Places

MG   Manchester Guardian
MSTC   Manchester Studies Tape Collection
PRO   Public Record Office
SCR   Salford City Reporter
SWPM   St Wilfrid's Parish Magazine
TMSS   Transactions of the Manchester Statistical Society
TUCAR   Trades Union Congress Annual Report
WCML   Working Class Movement Library
WH   Wardley Hall

Chapter 1: Interpretations

1 J. Rex, 'Immigrants and British labour: The sociological context', in K. Lunn (ed.), *Hosts immigrants and minorities* (Folkestone, 1980), p. 27.
2 D. Thompson, 'Ireland and the Irish in English radicalism before 1850', in J. Epstein and D. Thompson (eds), *The Chartist experience* (Cambridge, 1982), pp. 125–9; R. O'Higgins, 'The Irish influence on the Chartist movement', *Past and Present*, **20** (1961).
3 J. Foster, *Class struggle and the industrial revolution* (London, 1974), pp. 212–19; N. Kirk, 'Ethnicity, class and popular Toryism, 1850–70', in Lunn, *Immigrants*, pp. 92, 95; N. Kirk, 'Class and fragmentation: Some aspects of working-class life in south-east Lancashire and north-east Cheshire, 1850–70', unpublished PhD thesis, University of Pittsburgh (1974), p. 378.
4 L.H. Lees, *Exiles of Erin. Irish migrants in Victorian London* (Manchester, 1979), pp. 241–3; S. Gilley, 'English attitudes to the Irish, 1780–1900', in C. Holmes (ed.), *Immigrants and minorities in British society* (London, 1978), pp. 105–6; M.A.G. O'Tuathaigh, 'The Irish in nineteenth century Britain: Problems of integration', in R. Swift and S. Gilley (eds), *The Irish in the Victorian city* (Beckenham, 1985), p. 30.
5 J. Walvin, *Passage to Britain* (Harmondsworth, 1984), p. 59.
6 E. Hobsbawm, *Industry and empire* (Harmondsworth, 1969), p. 311.
7 E. Hobsbawm, 'The making of the working class, 1870–1914', in E. Hobsbawm, *Worlds of labour. Further studies in the history of labour* (London, 1984), p. 207.
8 R. Hoggart, *The uses of literacy* (Harmondsworth, 1958), pp. 72–101.
9 E. Hobsbawm, 'The formation of British working-class culture', in Hobsbawm, *Worlds of labour*, p. 178.
10 J. White, *The worst street in north London* (London, 1986), p. 108; G.S. Bain, R. Bacon and J. Pimlott, 'The labour force' in A.H. Halsey (ed.), *Trends in British society since 1900* (London, 1972), pp. 123–4.
11 B. Tillett, *Memories and reflections* (London, 1931), pp. 158–9; E. Hobsbawm, 'Working classes and nations', *Saothar*, **8** (1982), p. 79.
12 R. McKibbin, 'Why was there no Marxism in Great Britain?', in R. McKibbin, *Ideologies of class* (Oxford, 1991).
13 O. MacDonagh, 'The Irish in Australia: A general view', in O. MacDonagh and W.F. Mandle (eds), *Ireland and Irish Australia: Studies in cultural and political history* (London, 1986).
14 C. Holmes, *John Bull's Island. Immigration and British society, 1871–1971* (London, 1988), pp. 3–15; J. Cheetham, 'Immigration', in Halsey, *British society*, p. 452.

15 J. Cheetham, 'Immigration', p. 469.

16 B. Williams, *The making of Manchester Jewry, 1740–1875* (Manchester, 1976), pp. 44–5.

17 E.R. Norman, *Anti-Catholicism in Victorian England* (London, 1968), p. 13.

18 G. Rudé, 'The Gordon riots: a study of the rioters and their victims', *Transactions of the Royal Historical Society*, 5th series, **6** (1956); *The Catholic; or, Christianity not popery*, 24 November, **1** (8 December 1821).

19 E.P. Thompson, *The making of the English working class* (Harmondsworth, 1968), pp. 28–58.

20 J.C.D. Clark, *English society 1688–1832* (Cambridge, 1985), pp. 349–424; G.I.T. Machin, *The Catholic question in English politics* (London, 1964), p. 194; G.F.A. Best, 'The Protestant constitution and its supporters 1800–1829', *Transactions of the Royal Historical Society*, 5th series, **8** (1958).

21 W.L. Arnstein, 'Victorian prejudice re-examined', *Victorian Studies*, **12** (1968–9) and 'The Murphy riots: a Victorian dilemma', *Victorian Studies*, **19** (1975–6); G.F.A. Best, 'Popular Protestantism in Victorian Britain', in R. Robson (ed.), *Ideas and institutions of Victorian Britain* (London, 1967), pp. 134–42.

22 Hoggart, *Uses of literacy* p. 118.

23 M. Hechter, *Internal colonialism. The Celtic fringe in British national development, 1536–1966* (London, 1975); W.R. Jones, 'England against the Celtic fringe: A study in cultural stereotypes', *Journal of World History* **13** (1971); E. Snyder, 'The wild Irish: A study of some English satires against the Irish, Scots and Welsh', *Modern Philology*, **17** (1920).

24 Anonymous, *Incipient Irish revolution. An exposé of Fenianism to-day* (London, 1889), pp. 10–15.

25 J. Belchem, 'English working-class radicalism and the Irish, 1815–50', in Swift and Gilley, *Victorian city*, pp. 93–4.

26 D.C. Duggan, *The stage Irishman* (London, 1937); J. Nelson, 'From Rory and Paddy to Boucicalt's Myles, Shaun and Conn: The Irishman on the London stage 1830–1860', *Eire-Ireland*, **13** (1978).

27 M. Tebbutt, 'The evolution of ethnic stereotypes: An examination of stereotyping with particular reference to the Irish (and to a lesser extent the Scots) in Manchester during the late nineteenth and early twentieth centuries', unpublished MA thesis, University of Manchester (1982), pp. 60–6.

28 L.P. Curtis, *Apes and angels: The Irishman in Victorian caricature* (Newton Abbot, 1971), pp. 94–108.

29 *MG*, 18 February 1895.

30 D. Dorrity, 'Monkeys in a menagerie: The imagery of Unionist opposition to Home Rule 1886–1893', *Eire-Ireland*, **12** (1977).

31 L.P. Curtis, *Anglo-Saxons and Celts: A study of anti-Irish prejudice in Victorian England* (Bridgeport, 1968); L. Curtis, *Nothing but the same old story* (London, 1984).

32 K. Marx and F. Engels, *On Britain* (Moscow, 1962), pp. 551–2.

33 J. Bedoe, *The races of Britain* (London, 1885), pp. 139–42.

34 A.M. McBriar, *Fabian socialism and English politics, 1884–1918* (Cambridge, 1962), p. 119; E.D. Steele, 'Imperialism and Leeds politics, c. 1850–1914', in D. Fraser (ed.), *A history of modern Leeds* (Manchester, 1980), p. 349.

35 Gilley, 'English attitudes', pp. 84–5.

36 G.S. Jones, *Languages of class* (Cambridge, 1984); J. Obelkevich, 'New perspectives on the history of the Labour party, 1918–45', *Bulletin of the Society for the Study*

of Labour History, **47** (1983); A. Reid, 'Class and organisation', *Historical Journal*, **30** (1987).

37 R. Samuel, 'The Catholic Church and the Irish poor', in Swift and Gilley, *Victorian city*, p. 290.

38 L.H. Lees, *Exiles*, pp. 164, 197, 246–9; D. Feldman, 'There was an Englishman, an Irishman and a Jew . . . immigrants and minorities in Britain', *Historical Journal*, **26** (1983), pp. 185–94.

39 J.H. Treble, 'O'Connor, O'Connell and the attitude of Irish immigrants towards Chartism in the north of England, 1838–48', in J. Butt and I.F. Clarke (eds), *The Victorians and social protest* (Newton Abbot, 1973).

40 W.J. Lowe, 'The Lancashire Irish and the Catholic Church, 1846–71: The social dimension', *Irish Historical Studies*, **20** (1976), p. 129; E.D. Steele, 'The Irish presence in the north of England, 1850–1914', *Northern History*, **22** (1976).

41 Williams, *Manchester Jewry*, p. 279.

42 D. Fitzpatrick, 'A curious middle place: The Irish in Britain, 1871–1921', in R. Swift and S. Gilley (eds), *The Irish in Britain, 1815–1939* (London, 1989); O'Tuathaigh, 'Irish in Britain', pp. 13–14.

43 B. Williams, 'The Jewish immigrant in Manchester, the contribution of oral history', *Oral History*, **7** (1979), p. 44.

44 T.M. Endelman, *The Jews of Georgian England, 1774–1830: Tradition and change in a liberal society* (London, 1979), pp. 3–11.

45 A. O'Day (ed.), *A survey of the Irish in England (1872)* (London, 1990), pp. 125–6.

46 C. Pooley, 'Segregation or integration? The residential experience of the Irish in mid-Victorian Britain', in Swift and Gilley, *Irish in Britain*, p. 61; Fitzpatrick, 'Irish in Britain', pp. 10–12, 44.

47 J. Denvir, *The Irish in Britain. From earliest times to the fall and death of Parnell* (London, 1892), p. 462.

48 The classic account of the Irish in America is to be found in: S. Thernstrom, *Poverty and progress. Social mobility in a nineteenth century city* (Cambridge, Mass., 1964); S. Thernstrom, *The other Bostonians. Poverty and progress in the American metropolis, 1880–1970* (Cambridge, Mass., 1973).

49 J. Abrahamson, *Ethnic diversity in Catholic America* (London, 1973), pp. 173–82; E.H. Levine, *The Irish and Irish politician* (Notre Dame, 1966), pp. 8, 70–3.

50 J. Buckman, *Immigrants and the class struggle. The Jewish immigrant in Leeds, 1880–1914* (Manchester, 1983), pp. 156–67.

51 K. O'Connor, *The Irish in Britain* (London, 1972), pp. 68–9.

52 M. Turner, *Collyhurst then* (no date), deposited *LHD*, p. 21.

53 S. Thernstrom (ed.), *The Harvard Encyclopedia of American ethnic groups* (Cambridge, Mass., 1980), p. 528.

54 J. Denvir, *The life story of an old rebel* (Dublin, 1910), p. 2; Denvir, *Irish in Britain*, p. 430.

55 L.H. Lees, 'Patterns of lower class life: Irish slum communities in nineteenth century London', in S. Thernstrom and R. Sennet (eds), *Nineteenth century cities* (New Haven, 1969), p. 377; J.O. Power, 'The Irish in England', *Fortnightly Review*, **27** (1880), p. 417.

56 B. Kennedy, *Slavery: Pictures from the abyss* (London, 1905), pp. 60–1; J. Sexton, *Sir James Sexton. The life story of an agitator* (London, 1936), pp. 18–19; J. Toole, *Fighting through life* (London, 1935), p. 160.

57 M. Lennon, M. McAdam and J. O'Brien (eds), *Across the water. Irish women's lives in Britain* (London, 1988), p. 148; MSTC 271, 484, and 794.

58 G. Brown, *In my way* (Harmondsworth, 1972), pp. 18–19; *MCN* 13 January 1912.
59 J.R. Clynes, *Memoirs*, 1 (London, 1937), p. 27.
60 *MCH* 12 November 1910.
61 T. Barclay, *Memoirs and medleys. The autobiography of a bottlewasher* (Leicester, 1934), pp. 23–4; B. Naughton, *On the pig's back* (Oxford, 1988), p. 76; A. Bartlett, 'From strength to strength: Roman Catholicism in Bermondsey up to 1939', in *The Church and the people. Catholics and their church in Britain, c. 1880–1939* (Warwick Working Papers in Social History, 5, Centre for the Study of Social History, 1988), p. 39.
62 J. London, *The people of the abyss* (London, 1977), pp. 64–6.
63 P. O'Mara, *The autobiography of a Liverpool–Irish slummy* (London, 1934), pp. 111–12.
64 R. Roberts, *The classic slum* (Harmondsworth, 1983), p. 110.
65 Guardian of the Poor, *The Irish peasant. A sociological survey* (London, 1892), p. 18.
66 J. Devoy, *Recollections of an Irish rebel* (New York, 1929), p. 114; D. MacAmlaigh, *An Irish navvy. The diary of an exile* (London, 1964), p. 9; O'Day, *Irish in England*, pp. 3, 32–3, 50; Power, 'Irish in England', *Tablet* (5 December 1885), p. 412.
67 Community History Press, *The Irish in exile. Stories of emigration* (London, 1988), p. 4; Lennon et al, *Across the water*, p. 150.
68 F.S.L. Lyons, *Ireland before the famine* (London, 1981), pp. 226–9; W.F. Mandle, *The Gaelic Athletic Association and Irish nationalist politics, 1884–1924* (London, 1987); Lees, *Exiles*, p. 234.
69 Lees, *Exiles*, pp. 189–90.
70 *MCH* 9, 23 February 1906, 23 March 1906, 5 October 1906.
71 N. Richardson, *The pubs of old Ancoats* (Swinton, 1987), p. 11; *MCH* 21 September 1900.
72 *MCH* 29 April 1904, 23 March 1906, 5 October 1906.
73 *MCH* 29 January 1904, 16 July 1910, 30 August 1919.
74 *MCH* 5 February 1904, 1 January 1907, 3 May 1907.
75 *MCH* 26 February 1904, 26 April 1907, 13 August 1910, 15 October 1910.
76 *MCH* 5 September 1931, 16 January 1932, 8 September 1934.
77 Barclay, *Memoirs*, pp. 95–6, 101; Lees, *Exiles*, pp. 234–5.
78 *LCH* 19 January 1924.
79 D. Feldman, 'How Jewish were the Jews?', paper delivered to the Economic History Society Annual Conference, Liverpool University, March 1990; Williams, 'Jewish immigrant', pp. 43, 50–1.

Chapter 2: Social context

1 C. Pooley, 'Irish settlement in north west England in the mid-nineteenth century: A geographical critique', *North West Labour History*, **16** (1991).
2 J.A. Jackson, *The Irish in Britain* (London, 1963), pp. 1–5; A. Redford, *Labour migration in England, 1800–50* (Manchester, 1975), pp. 134–51.
3 J.H. Treble, 'The place of the Irish Catholics in the social life of the north of England, 1829–51', unpublished PhD thesis, University of Leeds (1968), pp. 2–15.

4 C.M. Arensberg and S.T. Kimball, *Family and community in Ireland* (Cambridge, Mass., 1940), p. 98; Jackson, *Irish in Britain*, p. 5.

5 Guardian of the Poor, *Irish Peasant*, p. 104.

6 T.W. Freeman, 'Emigration and rural Ireland', *Journal of the Statistical Society of Ireland*, 17 (1945), pp. 404, 409–10; Arensberg and Kimball, *Family and community*, pp. 148–9; Jackson, *Irish in Britain*, p. 26.

7 R.S. Walshaw, *Migration to and from the British Isles* (London, 1941), p. 78.

8 O'Day *Irish in England*, p. 1; MSTC 85.1, 122(2).

9 C. O'Grada, 'A note on nineteenth century immigration statistics', *Population Studies*, 29 (1975), p. 148.

10 Walshaw, *Migration*, pp. 69–70, 73, 78.

11 S. Glynn, 'Irish immigration to Britain, 1911–51: patterns and policy', *Irish Economic and Social History*, 8 (1981), p. 51.

12 D. Fitzpatrick, 'Irish emigration in the later nineteenth century', *Irish Historical Studies*, 22 (1980), pp. 130–7.

13 B. Lancaster, 'Who's a real Coventry kid? Migration into twentieth century Coventry', in B. Lancaster and T. Mason (eds), *Life and labour in a twentieth century city. The experience of Coventry* (Coventry, 1986), pp. 71–3; B.M. Walter, 'Time–space patterns of second-wave Irish immigration into British towns', *Transactions of the Institute of British Geographers*, new series, 5 (1980); Jackson, *Irish in Britain*, p. 15; Glynn, 'Irish immigration', pp. 57–8; Walshaw, *Migration*, p. 73.

14 P. Gallagher, *My story. By Paddy the Cope* (London, 1939), pp. 71–3; Lennon et al, *Across the water*, pp. 36–7.

15 B. Naughton, *Saintly Billy* (Oxford, 1989), pp. 84, 125; History Press, *Irish in exile*, p. 6; Naughton, *Pig's back*, pp. 73–5, 109.

16 P. MacGill, *The rat-pit* (London, 1915), p. 307.

17 T.P. O'Connor, *Memoirs of an old Parliamentarian*, 1 (London, 1929), pp. 28–9.

18 G. Orwell, *Collected essays, journalism and letters*, 1 (Harmondsworth, 1970), p. 76.

19 W.N. Hancock, 'On the equal importance of the education, poor-law, cheap law for small holders and land questions, at the present crisis' and 'Some further information as to migratory labourers from Mayo to England, and as to importance of limiting law taxes and law changes in proceedings affecting small holders of land', *Journal of the Statistical and Social Inquiry Society of Ireland*, 8 (1880), pp. 53, 63, 75; F. Thompson, *Lark Rise to Candleford* (Harmondsworth, 1973), pp. 235–6; Gallagher, *My story*, p. 51; Guardian of the Poor, *Irish Peasant*, p. 103; O'Day, *Irish in England*, p. 63; Jackson, *Irish in Britain*, p. 193.

20 P. MacGill, *Children of the dead end* (London, 1914), pp. 116–17; Gallagher, *My story*, p. 79; History Press, *Irish in exile*, pp. 94–7; Naughton, *Pig's back*, pp. 172–3; Turner, *Collyhurst then*, p. 27; O'Grada, 'Nineteenth century immigration', p. 147; MCH 10 December 1917.

21 M. Burke, *Ancoats lad* (Swinton, 1985), p. 3; Jackson, *Irish in Britain*, p. 11; MCH 5 April 1907; SWPM May 1911.

22 I. Babcock, 'Angel Meadow: a study of a migrant community in Victorian Manchester', unpublished dissertation, for BA, Manchester Polytechnic (1980), p. 59; Thernstrom, *Encyclopedia*, p. 529.

23 Jackson, *Irish in Britain*, pp. 67–70, 192; Lennon et al, *Across the water*, pp. 21–4; Freeman, 'Emigration', p. 419; Glynn, 'Irish immigration', p. 52.

24 Arensberg and Kimball, *Family and community*, p. 149; Memo by the Home Secretary, Appendix C, 20 February 1929, CAB/24/201/45, PRO; MSTC Crawley transcript, 122(1), 273.
25 Lennon et al, *Across the water*, p. 49.
26 P. Horn, *The rise and fall of the Victorian servant* (London, 1975), p. 106; M. Ebery and B. Preston, *Domestic service in late Victorian England, 1871–1914*, Geographical Papers, 42 (University of Reading, 1976), pp. 74–8; MSTC 266, 271 and 1024.
27 E. Osman, *Salford stepping stones* (Swinton, 1983), pp. 51–2.
28 Anonymous, 'The Irish in London', *Blackwood's Edinburgh Magazine*, **170** (July 1901), pp. 125–6; C. Booth, *Life and labour of the people in London. Volume Three. Blocks of buildings, schools and immigration* (London, 1892), pp. 91, 96; Guardian of the Poor, *Irish peasant*, pp. 140–1.
29 S. Richardson (ed.), *The recollections of three Manchesters in the Great War* (Swinton, 1985), p. 4.
30 A. Wright, *Disturbed Dublin* (London, 1914), pp. 171–2.
31 Mass-Observation, *The pub and the people* (London, 1970), pp. 151–3; MacGill, *Dead end*, pp. 243–5; Naughton, *Pig's back*, p. 59; MSTC 122(1), 823(1) and 1024.
32 D. Gittins, *Fair sex. Family size and structure, 1900–39* (London, 1982), p. 100; J. Lewis, *Women in England 1870–1950: Sexual divisions and social change* (Brighton, 1984), pp. 15–20; Mass-Observation, *Britain and her birth-rate* (London, 1945), p. 185; J. Haslett and W.J. Lowe, 'Household structure and overcrowding among the Lancashire Irish, 1851–71', *Histoire Sociale*, **10** (1977), pp. 46–51.
33 J. Herson, 'Irish immigration and settlement in Victorian England: a small-town perspective', in Swift and Gilley, *Irish in Britain*, pp. 93–7.
34 P.J. Waller, *Democracy and sectarianism. A political and social history of Liverpool, 1868–1939* (Liverpool, 1981), pp. 237–41; T. Gallagher, 'A tale of two cities: Communal strife in Glasgow and Liverpool before 1914', in Swift and Gilley, *Victorian City*; J. Smith, 'Labour traditions in Glasgow and Liverpool', *History Workshop Journal*, **17** (1984).
35 Toole, *Fighting*, pp. 139–44.
36 B. Murray, *The old firm* (Edinburgh, 1984); T. Mason, 'The Blues and the Reds', *Transactions of the Historic Society of Lancashire and Cheshire*, **134** (1984), pp. 123–6; G. Green, *There's only one United* (1978), pp. 189–202.
37 F. Engels, *The condition of the working class in England* (London, 1979), pp. 87–94; J.M. Werley, 'The Irish in Manchester, 1832–49', *Irish Historical Studies*, **17** (1973), pp. 345–50.
38 Thompson, *Working class*, pp. 469–85.
39 Pooley, 'Segregation', pp. 79–81.
40 J.E. Mercer, 'The condition of life in Angel Meadow', *TMSS*, 1897, pp. 169–75; Babcock, 'Angel Meadow', p. 47.
41 'The Irish in Manchester (by one of them)', 1887, Manchester Cuttings Collection, LHD.
42 F.W.S. Craig, *British parliamentary election results, 1885–1918* (London, 1974); P.F. Clarke, *Lancashire and the new Liberals* (Cambridge, 1971), p. 431.
43 *MG* 14, 16, 17, 18, 19, 20 and 24 November 1885, 26, September 1891, 6 October 1909; *MCN* 10 October 1891.
44 Figures derived from the *Salford diocesan almanac*, Manchester, 1890–1939 and the 1900 Lenten visitation returns, WH.

45 F. Finnegan, 'The Irish in York' and D. Large, 'The Irish in Bristol in 1852: A census enumeration', in Swift and Gilley, *Victorian City*, pp. 40 and 63; Lees, *Exiles*, pp. 55–87; Booth, *Schools and immigration*, Table A.

46 B.M. Walter, 'The geography of Irish migration to Britain since 1939 with special reference to Luton and Bolton', unpublished PhD thesis, University of Oxford (1978), pp. 400–2; Fitzpatrick, 'Irish in Britain', pp. 14–15; Finnegan, 'Irish in York', pp. 74–5; Mercer, 'Angel Meadow', p. 161.

47 *HNM* January 1929; MSTC 268(2).

48 Pooley, 'Segregation', p. 75.

49 Thernstrom, *Poverty and progress*, pp. 157, 200–1; Thernstrom, *Other Bostonians*, pp. 133–5.

50 Roberts, *Slum*, p. 17.

51 Haslett and Lowe, 'Household structure', pp. 48–52; Lees, *Exiles*, pp. 87–122; Finnegan, 'Irish in York', p. 75; Fitzpatrick, 'Irish in Britain', pp. 20–3.

52 Denvir, *Irish in Britain*, p. 431.

53 P. Joyce, *Work, society and politics* (Brighton, 1982), p. 252.

54 H. Clay and K.R. Brady, *Manchester at work. A survey* (Manchester, 1929), p. 91; J.K. Walton, *Lancashire. A social and economic history, 1558–1939* (Manchester, 1987), pp. 208–9; University of Manchester Economic Research Section, *Readjustment in Lancashire* (Manchester, 1936), p. 7, 37–8.

55 C. Rowley, *Fifty years of Ancoats loss and gain* (London, 1899), p. 4; C. Rowley, *Fifty years of work without wages* (London, 1912), p. 196.

56 J. Inman, *Poverty and housing. Conditions in a Manchester city ward* (London, 1934), pp. 12–14; Manchester University Settlement, *Ancoats. A study of a clearance area* (Manchester, 1945), p. 15; E.D. Simon and J. Inman, *The rebuilding of Manchester* (London, 1935), pp. 58–68; M. Stocks, *Fifty years of Every Street* (London, 1945), p. 55; M. Fitzgerald, 'Ancoats clearance area. Sociological study, May 1937 to March 1938', p. 5, Misc/847, AD; F. Scott, 'The condition and occupations of the people of Manchester and Salford', *TMSS* 1888–9, pp. 101–2.

57 *MFP* 10, 1899; *MCN* 26 September 1891; *MG* 21 October 1904.

58 T.R. Marr, *Housing conditions in Manchester and Salford* (Manchester, 1904), p. 61; MSTC 87.

59 M. MacAskill, 'Paddy's Market' (Centre for Urban and Regional Research Discussion Paper 29, University of Glasgow, 1987); Lees, *Exiles*, pp. 96–7; Treble, 'Place', p. 85; *MG* 17 April 1908.

60 Burke, *Ancoats*, p. 4, 43.

61 M. Bertenshaw, *Sunrise to sunset* (Manchester, 1980), p. 57; MSTC 821.

62 D.M. Clarke, *The Irish in Philadelphia* (Philadelphia, 1973), p. 146; Booth, *Schools and immigration*, p. 98; J.B. Freeman, 'Irish workers in the twentieth century United States: the case of the Transport Workers' Union', *Saothar*, 8 (1982), pp. 25–6; Levine, *Irish politician*, pp. 112–3; *MCH* 19 October 1906, 25 March 1922; MSTC 794.

63 F. Doran, *Down memory lane*, undated, page unnumbered, LHD; S.J. Davies, 'Classes and the police in Manchester, 1829–1880', in A.J. Kidd and K.W. Roberts (eds), *City, class and culture* (Manchester, 1985), p. 34.

64 *SWPM* February 1912; *CF* July 1913.

65 *Harvest* December 1913.

66 *MG* 27 April 1912.

67 Lenten visitation return, WH; M4/20/13, AD.

68 Booth, *Schools and immigration*, p. 199.
69 Tebbutt, 'Stereotypes', p. 205; *MCN* 22 April 1899.
70 J. Davis, 'From "rookeries" to "communities": Race, poverty and policing in London, 1850–1985', *History Workshop Journal*, **27** (1989), p. 71; 'Irish in Manchester', cuttings, LHD.
71 Walter, 'Bolton', pp. 397–8; M278, /5/3, /6/5,6,10, AD; MSTC 518.
72 P. Lane, *The Catenian Association, 1908–83* (London, 1983), pp. 18–19.
73 A. Burgess, *Little Wilson and big God* (London, 1987), p. 14.
74 Roberts, *Slum*, pp. 10, 13–14, 17–18, 19–23, 30, 110, 159, 170, 183.
75 C. Forman, *Industrial town* (London, 1979), p. 146; R. Hoggart, *Local habitation* (Oxford, 1988), pp. 84, 132–3; M. McCarthy, *Generation in revolt* (London, 1953), pp. 21–2; Tebbutt, 'Stereotypes', p. 22.
76 Roberts, *Slum*, p. 26, 171.
77 Lennon et al, *Across the water*, p. 146; MSTC 780; tape in author's possession.
78 F. Neal, 'English–Irish conflict in the north west of England: Economics, racism, anti-Catholicism or simple xenophobia?', *North West Labour History*, **16** (1991), pp. 17–19; MSTC 82.
79 S. Humphries, *Hooligans or rebels?* (Oxford, 1981), pp. 189–90; Forman, *Industrial town*, p. 172; Mr F1P, CNWRS.
80 R.J. Cooter, 'The Irish in County Durham and Newcastle, c. 1840–1880', unpublished MA thesis, University of Durham, 1972, pp. 239, 266, 269–70.
81 H. Senior, *Orangeism in Ireland and Britain, 1795–1836* (London, 1966), pp. 151–5, 305; F. Neal, 'Manchester origins of the English Orange Order', *Manchester Region History Review*, **4** (1990–1); G.P. Connolly, 'Little brother be at peace: The priest as Holy Man in the nineteenth century ghetto', in W.J. Sheils (ed.), *The Church and healing* (Oxford, 1982), p. 199.
82 Tebbutt, 'Stereotypes', p. 7; Waller, *Democracy*, p. 95; *Federationist* August 1922.
83 *MG* 9, 13 July 1988; *MCN* 14 July 1988; *Manchester Saturday Half-Penny* 14 July 1988.
84 Richardson, *Old Ancoats*, p. 11; MSTC 87, 122(1), 794 and Crawley transcript.
85 C.A. Bolton, *Salford Diocese and its Catholic past* (Manchester, 1950), p. 204; Turner, *Collyhurst*, p. 25; *MCH* 16 February 1924, 2 July 1927, 14 April 1934.
86 Manchester City Watch Committee Minutes, 22, 24, 25 November 1897, AD; *LCH* 25 January, 1 February 1930.
87 Treble, 'Place', p. 66; Kirk 'Ethnicity', pp. 83–6; Kirk, 'Class and fragmentation', p. 339.
88 E.H. Hunt, *Regional wage variation in Britain, 1850–1914* (Oxford, 1973), pp. 288–99; Gallagher, 'Two cities', pp. 110–11.
89 Cooter, 'County Durham', p. 191.
90 Booth, *Schools and immigration*, pp. 88–92.
91 Forman, *Industrial town*, p. 34.
92 Liberal leaflet 1516, no date, Irish Question Collection misc. 28, LSE.
93 W. Greenwood, *There was a time* (London, 1967), p. 65; MSTC 794.
94 H.W. Benjamin, 'The London Irish: A study in political activism, 1870–1910', unpublished PhD thesis, University of Princeton (1976), pp. 307–8; Tillett, *Memories*, p. 94; MSTC 85(1), 87, 266; Mr F1P, CNWRS.
95 White, *Worst street*, p. 105; Bartlett, 'Bermondsey', p. 34; Forman, *Industrial town*, p. 174.

96 J.E. Handley, *The Irish in modern Scotland* (Cork, 1947), p. 302.
97 *MCN* 29 July 1922; MSTC 745.

Chapter 3: Church and people

1 Bolton, *Salford*, p. 205; A. McCormack, *Cardinal Vaughan* (London, 1966), pp. 130–6; G.P. Connolly, 'Catholicism in Manchester and Salford, 1770–1850', unpublished PhD thesis, University of Manchester (1980), pp. 63–5; Walton, *Lancashire*, p. 222; *Harvest* October 1894, December 1912, August 1922; MSTC 794.
2 Denvir, *Irish in Britain*, p. 431; *Harvest* January 1897, July 1899; *MCN* 22 April 1899; *MCH* 20 March 1920.
3 J. Bossy, *The English Catholic community, 1550–1850* (London, 1975), p. 303, 309, 424; Bertenshaw, *Sunrise*, p. 57.
4 Bolton, *Salford*, pp. 131–4; Levine, *Irish politician*, pp. 73–4; *MCH* 21 November 1925.
5 'Souvenir brochure of the twenty-first anniversary of St Anne's, Crumpsall' (Manchester, 1938); *MCH* 19 March 1932.
6 D.J. Holmes, *More Roman than Rome: English Catholics in the nineteenth century* (London, 1978).
7 P. Sidney, *Modern Rome in modern England* (London, 1906), pp. 311–16.
8 C.C. Martindale, *Father Bernard Vaughan: A memoir* (London, 1923), p. 60; E.R. Norman, *The English Catholic Church in the nineteenth century* (Oxford, 1984), p. 351; A.E. Dingle and B. Harrison, 'Cardinal Manning as a temperance reformer, *Historical Journal*, **12** (1969), p. 499; Burgess, *Little Wilson*, p. 85; *MG* 7 March 1908.
9 *MG* 21 June 1897, 29 January 1936.
10 *MG* 17 April 1893.
11 L.C. Casartelli, *Sketches in history* (London, 1906), pp. 238–40; J. O'Dea, *The story of the old faith in Manchester* (Manchester, 1910), pp. 152–3; *LCH* 3 March 1939.
12 Naughton, *Pig's back*, p. 131; Bartlett, 'Bermondsey', p. 39; Benjamin, 'London Irish', p. 293.
13 *MG* 6 September 1919; *MCH* 6 February 1926; MSTC 87.
14 *MCN* 27 October 1906.
15 J.G. Snead-Cox, *The life of Cardinal Vaughan*, **1** (London, 1910), p. 473; McCormack, *Vaughan*, pp. 215–16.
16 *Federationist* July 1910, September 1910; *MCH* 2 April 1921, 27 August 1921, 19 March 1932.
17 *MCH* 29 March 1924.
18 *MCH* 27 July 1935.
19 Dingle and Harrison, 'Cardinal Manning', pp. 488, 502; *MG* 18 March 1881, 18 March 1882, 2 September 1896.
20 *MG* 18 March 1882, 18 March 1901; *Harvest* March 1922.
21 Tebbutt, 'Stereotypes', p. 249.
22 P.H. Bagenal, *The priest in politics* (London, 1893); E. Benson, *To struggle is to live* (Leeds, 1979), p. 58.
23 J.S. Supple, 'The Catholic clergy of Yorkshire, 1850–1900: A profile', *Northern History*, **21** (1985), pp. 221–3; Snead-Cox, *Vaughan*, p. 441.

24 H. McLeod, *Religion and the working class in nineteenth century Britain* (London, 1984), p. 74, 430–1; L. Kennedy, 'Profane images in Irish popular consciousness', *Oral History*, **2** (1979), pp. 34–5; Bartlett, 'Bermondsey', pp. 36–7.

25 Burgess, *Little Wilson*, p. 119.

26 F. Boulard, trans. M.J. Jackson, *An introduction to religious sociology* (London, 1960), pp. 85–6; Letter from unnamed priest, Ep. 1/9, WH.

27 R.B. Walker, 'Religious change in Liverpool in the nineteenth century', *Journal of Ecclesiastical History*, **19** (1968), pp. 200–1.

28 Letter from Ruddin, 20 January 1904 and letter from members of the Confraternity of the Christian Doctrine, c. 1910, St Patrick's Box, WH.

29 P. Doyle, 'The Catholic federation, 1906–29', in W.J. Sheils and D. Wood (eds), *Voluntary religion* (London, 1986), pp. 465–7; *MCH* 10 May 1907; *Federationist* June 1910; *MG* 12 January 1910.

30 McCormack, *Vaughan*, p. 175.

31 MSTC 87; Mr F1P, CNWRS.

32 B.S. Rowntree and G.R. Lavers, *English life and leisure: A social study* (London, 1951), pp. 349–50; Letter to Bilsborrow, 19 April 1893, St Michael's box, WH; MSTC 271.

33 Booth, *Life and labour*, pp. 241-2; Burke, *Lad*, p. 9.

34 *Harvest* March 1893.

35 MSTC 271.

36 MSTC 487(1), 821; Burke, *Lad*, p. 9.

37 MSTC 484.

38 *LCH* 17 January, 7 February, 1931.

39 MSTC 457.

40 MSTC 821.

41 F. Roberts, *Memories of a Victorian childhood and working life in Miles Platting, Manchester* (Swinton, 1983), p. 9; H.E. Sheen, *Canon Peter Green* (London, 1965), p. 34; MSTC 780.

42 MSTC 516.

43 O'Mara, *Slummy*, pp. 66–7.

44 MSTC 271.

45 Booth, *Life and labour*, p. 243; O'Mara, *Slummy*, p. 69; *MFP*, 2, 1890, p. 26; *MCH* 19 October 1907.

46 *The story of St Anne's, Ancoats* (Manchester, 1948); *MCH* 18 March 1892, 26 October 1907.

47 Booth, *Life and labour*, p. 244.

48 E. Larkin, 'The devotional revolution in Ireland, 1850–75', *American Historical Review*, **77** (1972); Lees, *Exiles*, pp. 164–97.

49 P. Hughes, 'The English Catholics in 1850' in G. Beck (ed.), *The English Catholics* (London, 1950), p. 80; G.P. Connolly, 'Irish and Catholic: Myth or reality? Another sort of Irish and the renewal of the clerical profession amongst Catholics in England, 1791–1918' in Swift and Gilley, *Victorian city*, p. 231, 336–7; S. Gilley, 'Catholic faith of the Irish slums. London, 1840–70' in H.Y. Dyos and M. Wolff (eds), *The Victorian city: Images and realities* (London, 1973); Walker, 'Liverpool', p. 202; Bartlett, 'Bermondsey', p. 31.

50 1900 Lenten visitation returns, WH.

51 MSTC 457.

52 MSTC 60; Turner, *Collyhurst*, p. 24.

53 Cooter, 'County Durham', p. 86.

54 D.C. Jones, *The social survey of Merseyside*, 3 (Liverpool, 1934), pp. 325–6; Bartlett, 'Bermondsey', p. 33.
55 Snead-Cox, *Vaughan*, 2, pp. 396–9; *Harvest* November 1901, April 1909, March 1913; *CCM* February, April 1936.
56 St Andrew's, Ancoats, statistical returns on parochial work, 1894–1903, M45/1/6/1–3, AD.
57 Boulard, *Introduction*, pp. 134–5; F. Finnegan, *Poverty and prejudice: A study of Irish immigrants in York, 1840–1875* (Cork, 1982); Jones, *Merseyside*, 3, pp. 330–31; B.S. Rowntree, *Poverty. A study of town life* (London, 1901), pp. 345–9; B.S. Rowntree, *Poverty and progress. A second social survey of York* (London, 1941), pp. 417–19, 422; Rowntree and Lavers, *Life*, p. 344.
58 Jones, *Survey*, pp. 330–1; Rowntree, *Poverty and progress*, pp. 417–19; Rowntree and Lavers, *Life*, p. 344.
59 Burgess, *Little Wilson*, pp. 25, 138; *MCH* 1 March 1924.
60 *CCM* May 1936.
61 *St Anne's souvenir*, *HNM* September 1929; *MCH* 28 May 1910.
62 Turner, *Collyhurst*, p. 24; *MFP*, 2, 1890, p. 26.
63 Derived from figures included in various issues of the *SWPM*.
64 H. McLeod, 'White collar values and the role of religion' and R.Q. Gray, 'Religion, culture and social class in late nineteenth and early twentieth century Edinburgh', both in G. Crossick (ed.), *The lower middle class in Britain, 1870–1914* (London, 1977).
65 *HNM* April 1929, November 1929.
66 McCormack, *Vaughan*, p. 175; Snead-Cox, *Vaughan*, 1, pp. 432–3; 1900 Lenten visitation returns, WH.
67 Kennedy, *Slavery*, pp. 206, 210–15; MSTC 481(1), 509.
68 Kennedy, *Slavery*, p. 210; O'Mara, *Slummy*, pp. 63–4; MSTC 487(1).
69 McLeod, *Religion*, p. 76; 1900 Lenten visitation returns, WH.
70 MSTC Crawley transcript; tape in author's possession.
71 Holy Family mission log book, available St Augustine's church; *MCH* 23 August 1908; MSTC 60, 266.
72 Barclay, *Memoirs*, p. 36; Bertenshaw, *Sunrise*, p. 6; O'Mara, *Slummy*, p. 90.
73 McLeod, *Religion*, p. 77; Rowntree and Lavers, *Life*, p. 47; tape in author's possession.
74 M. Kerr, *The people of Ship Street* (London, 1958), p. 137; H. McLeod, 'New perspectives on Victorian working-class religion: the oral evidence', *Oral History*, 14 (1986); Barclay, *Memoirs*, p. 9; Bertenshaw, *Sunrise*, p. 5; O'Mara, *Slummy*, p. 117; Sexton, *Agitator*, p. 20; MSTC 556.
75 M.C. Bishop, 'The social methods of Roman Catholicism in England', *Contemporary Review*, 39 (1877), p. 610; Bertenshaw, *Sunrise*, p. 25; Burgess, *Little Wilson*, pp. 48–9; Toole, *Fighting*, 1935, p. 12; Turner, *Collyhurst*, p. 82.
76 Greenwood, *Time*, p. 19.
77 Barclay, *Memoirs*, p. 27; Burke, *Lad*, pp. 5, 16.
78 J.F. Champ, 'Bishop Milner, Holywell and the cure tradition', in Sheils, *Church and healing*, p. 162; *MG* 7 September 1896; *MCH* 28 June 1924.
79 *MCH* 31 May 1924, 18 August 1934.
80 *Harvest* February 1903.
81 Martindale, *Vaughan*, pp. 45–6; Snead-Cox, *Vaughan*, pp. 400–1.
82 Kennedy, *Slavery*, p. 56.
83 *Harvest* June 1897.

Chapter 4: Catholicism and popular culture

1 SWPM August 1910.
2 S. Gilley, 'The Roman Catholic Church and the nineteenth-century Irish diaspora', Journal of Ecclesiastical History, 35 (1984), pp. 195–6; H. McLeod, 'Building the "Catholic ghetto": Catholic organisations 1870–1914', in Sheils and Wood, Voluntary religion, p. 431; McLeod, Religion, p. 77; Thernstrom, Poverty, p. 179.
3 Casartelli, Sketches, p. 254; SWPM June 1911, February 1912; MG 23 September 1912; LCH 10 January 1931.
4 Dingle and Harrison, 'Cardinal Manning', pp. 496–8.
5 C. Booth, Life and labour of the people in London. Third series: Religious influences. Summary (London, 1903), p. 241; Bishop, 'Catholicism in England', p. 607; O'Day, Irish in England, pp. 97–8, 129.
6 J. Lewis, 'The working-class wife and mother and state intervention, 1870–1918', in J. Lewis (ed.), Labour and love. Women's experience of home and family, 1850–1940 (London, 1986), pp. 99–100.
7 In P. Coman, Catholics and the welfare state (London, 1977), p. 23.
8 Harvest June 1894; 1906 Lenten Pastoral, pp. 9–10, WH; MG 2 November 1891, 25 August 1930.
9 Lewis, Women in England, p. 36; Lewis, 'Wife and mother', pp. 113–14; CF October 1919.
10 Harvest August 1904.
11 Coman, Welfare state, p. 18; Harvest January 1899.
12 1900 Lenten visitation return, WH.
13 Harvest May 1897; MG 25 November 1912; CF January 1919; MSTC 87.
14 Doyle, 'Federation', p. 476.
15 Harvest February 1909; LCH 22 February 1922.
16 Champ, 'Milner', pp. 153–4; Tebbutt, 'Stereotypes', p. 155; MCH 11 May 1900, 11 May 1929.
17 Lewis, 'Wife and mother', pp. 101–3.
18 Arensberg and Kimball, Family and community, pp. 47–50.
19 Excerpts taken from MacGill, Dead end and MacGill, Rat-pit.
20 Letter to Bilsborrow, 19 April 1893, St Michael's Box, WH.
21 CF January 1919, January 1920; MCH 12 February 1921; transcript, Christmas Day sermon 1919, WH.
22 F.P. Cobbe, 'Wife torture in England', contemporary Review, 32 (1878), p. 222; O'Mara, Slummy, pp. 33, 36, 44.
23 McLeod, 'Catholic ghetto', pp. 434–5.
24 MG 21 October 1912.
25 F.M. Mason, 'The newer Eve: The Catholic women's suffrage society in England, 1911–23', Catholic Historical Review, 52 (1986); Harvest August 1910, November 1910; MG 28 October 1910.
26 Clark, Philadelphia, pp. 98–9; Levine, Irish politician, pp. 80–2; Thernstrom, Poverty, p. 179.
27 Snead-Cox, Vaughan, 1, p. 110.
28 Bertenshaw, Sunrise, p. 34; MSTC 60.
29 F. Bealey and H. Pelling, Labour and politics, 1900–1906 (London, 1958), p. 47; E.A. Knox, Reminiscences of an octogenarian, 1847–1934 (London, 1935), p. 239.
30 D. Barber, 'School accommodation problems in Manchester, 1919–39',

unpublished MEd thesis, University of Manchester (1960), p. 18 and Appendix C.1; *Manchester Council Proceedings*, **3**, 1904–5, map and list of available school accommodation.

31 McCormack, *Vaughan*, p. 170; Snead-Cox, *Vaughan*, **2**, p. 89.
32 St Edmund's School Log Book, 27 December 1893, 7 December 1897, 28 January 1932, 22 August 1932, 13 September 1932, available from the school.
33 *Educational statistics of the diocese of Salford* (Manchester, 1905), WH; St Anne's School Log Book, 18 January 1923, available from the school.
34 Clarke, *Lancashire*, pp. 53–75; Kennedy, *Slavery*, pp. 52–4; Naughton, *Billy*, pp. 57–8; O'Mara, *Slummy*, pp. 74–5; *Harvest* February 1908, April 1908.
35 E. George, *From mill boy to minister* (London, 1919), pp. 15–23; Turner, *Collyhurst*, pp. 23–4; St Edmund's Log Book, 23 December 1932; St Michael's School Log Book, 19 March 1890, M66/133/Box 1, AD; MSTC 60, 487(1), 507, 540.
36 Norman, *Catholic Church*, pp. 174–5.
37 Rowntree and Lavers, *Leisure*, p. 350; St Edward's School Log Book, 29 August 1928; *MCH* 7 February 1925.
38 Levine, *Irish politician*, p. 183; Thernstrom, *Other Bostonians*, p. 174.
39 Bertenshaw, *Sunrise*, p. 87; Burke, *Ancoats*, p. 9; Turner, *Collyhurst*, p. 74; MSTC 457, 481(1), 487(1) and 823(1).
40 Jones, *Survey*, p. 329.
41 C. Booth, *Life and labour of the people in London. Third series: Religious influences* (London, 1903), p. 251; Mass-Observation, *Puzzled people* (London, 1947), p. 42, 44–6, 67.
42 MSTC 87 and 787(4).
43 P. Summerfield, 'An oral history of schooling in Lancashire, 1900–1950: Gender, class and education', *Oral History*, **15** (1987); Levine, *Irish politician*, pp. 82–4; Thernstrom, *Poverty*, p. 48.
44 Burgess, *Big Wilson*, pp. 28–9; Doran, *Memory lane*, pp. 7–8; MSTC 469 and 780.
45 J. Springhall, *Youth, empire and society. British youth movements, 1883–1940* (London, 1977), pp. 14–15, 45–6; W.G. Jackson, 'An historical study of the provision of facilities for play and recreation in Manchester', unpublished MA thesis, University of Manchester (1940), pp. 87–98; *Harvest* October 1899, January 1901, March 1902.
46 *Harvest* February 1911.
47 A. Davies, *Leisure, gender and poverty: Working-class culture in Salford and Manchester, 1900–1939* (Buckingham, 1992), Chapter 4; J. Liddington and J. Norris, *One hand tied behind us* (London, 1984), pp. 47–63.
48 *A history of the Heyrod Lads' Club, 1889–1910* (Manchester, 1911), p. 5.
49 *Harvest* June 1894, January 1902, May 1905, November 1914.
50 *CF* May 1922.
51 The following account is based on *Harvest*, May 1891, March 1893, April 1893, May 1893, March 1894, April 1894, May 1894, July 1894, October 1894, December 1896, January 1897, April 1897, December 1897, January 1898.
52 M. Blanch, 'Imperialism, nationalism and organised youth' in J. Clarke, C. Chrichter, R. Johnson (eds), *Working-class culture. Studies in history and theory* (London, 1979), p. 110; Springhall, *Youth*, pp. 37–9, 121; *Harvest* March 1902, February 1911; *MCH* 7 January 1933.
53 Bolton, *Salford*, p. 202; letter from the Cadet Colonel of Salford diocese, 1924, Societies File, WH.

54 *Harvest* January 1928; letter from Cadet Colonel, 1924, report by Cadet Colonel, 5 September 1930, Societies File, WH.
55 W.A. Richardson, 'The Hugh Oldham lads' club', *Manchester Review*, **8** (1959), pp. 340, 345; Doran, *Memory lane*, p. 11; Turner, *Collyhurst*, p. 29; MSTC 49, 457.
56 F. Carter, 'Youth work in Manchester', *Social Welfare*, **4** (1940), p. 108; D. Fowler, 'The interwar youth consumer in Manchester', paper presented at Manchester History Workshop Day School, May 1986; Jackson, 'Recreation', p. 91.
57 F.T. Moore, 'The Hulme youth problem', *Social Welfare*, **4** (1941), pp. 124–5; Canonical visitation, December 1932, St Wilfrid's Box, WH.
58 H.E.O. James and F.T. Moore, 'Adolescent leisure in a working-class district', *Occupational Psychology*, **14** (1940), pp. 139–40.
59 *LCH* 21 January 1938.
60 R. Roberts, *A ragged schooling* (London, 1984), pp. 67–9, 73–5, 87, 140.
61 E. Roberts, *Working-class Barrow and Lancaster, 1890–1930* (Centre for North West Regional Studies, Occasional Papers, **2**, University of Lancaster, 1976), p. 52; E. Roberts, 'Learning and living – socialisation outside school', *Oral History*, **3** (1975), p. 23.
62 Roberts, *Schooling*, pp. 36–7.
63 Humphries, *Hooligans*, pp. 187–9.
64 Burke, *Ancoats Lad*, p. 15; Humphries, *Hooligans*, p. 188; *MG* 24 June 1892; MSTC 155 and 486.
65 *Sunday Dispatch* 10 March 1935.
66 Humphries, *Hooligans*, pp. 190–3.
67 Roberts, *Schooling*, p. 93.
68 M. Levine, *Cheetham to Cordova* (Swinton, 1984), p. 6; MSTC 115.
69 Societies File, WH.
70 The following account is based on *Harvest* April 1909, February 1911, June 1911, February 1912, February 1913, February 1914, June 1918, March 1924.
71 MSTC 272(2).
72 MSTC 484 and 558.
73 Finnegan, 'York' and Large, 'Bristol' in Swift and Gilley, *Victorian city*, pp. 38–40, 51–2, 60, 74; Herson, 'Stafford', in Swift and Gilley, *Irish in Britain*, p. 96.
74 Fitzpatrick, 'Irish emigration', pp. 136–7.
75 J.L. Thomas, 'The factor of religion in the selection of marriage mates', *American Sociological Review*, **16** (1951), pp. 489–90.
76 Thernstrom, *Encyclopedia*, p. 532.
77 MSTC 271, 273 and Crawley transcript.
78 Burgess, *Little Wilson*, pp. 9, 22.
79 E. Roberts, *A woman's place* (Oxford, 1984), pp. 73–4; D. Thompson, 'Courtship and marriage in Preston between the wars', *Oral History*, **3** (1975), p. 41; Roberts, *Slum*, pp. 22–3.
80 *MG* 2 June 1913; *MCH* 16 February 1935.
81 *MCH* 5 August 1916; MSTC 823(1); tape in author's possession.
82 McCarthy, *Generation*, pp. 4, 13, 22–3, 26; MSTC 87, 165(1), 469.
83 Census by members of St George's, Church of England parish (Hulme, 1927), M383/1/9/2, AD.
84 J. Callaghan, *Time and chance* (London, 1987), p. 22; Bertenshaw, *Sunrise*, p. 113.
85 Bartlett, 'Bermondsey', p. 41; *LCH* 8 March 1930, 10 January 1931, 2 March 1935.

86 Mr B9P, CNWRS.
87 O. MacDonagh, 'Irish culture and Nationalism translated: St Patrick's Day, 1888, in Australia', in MacDonagh et al, *Irish Culture and Nationalism*; T.J. Meagher, '"Why should we care for a little trouble or a walk through the mud": St Patrick's and Columbus Day parades in Worcester, Massachusetts, 1845–1915', *New England Quarterly*, **57** (1985); Clark, *Philadelphia*, p. 109; Thernstrom, *Poverty*, p. 173.
88 *MG* 18 March 1905.
89 *MG* 18 March 1924.
90 Tebbutt, 'Stereotypes', p. 60; *DD* 19 March 1900, 18 March 1901; *MG* 18 March 1901, 18 March 1902.
91 St Wilfrid's Parish Log Book; *MCH* 10 May 1905, 15 June 1906, 2 June 1923.
92 The following discussion is based on: S. Fielding, 'The Catholic Whit walk in Manchester and Salford. 1890–1939', *Manchester Region History Review*, 1 (1987).
93 Toole, *Fighting*, pp. 7–8; A.R. Wright and T.E. Jones, *British Calender Customs. England*, 1 (London, 1936), p. 160.
94 W. Doherty, *Reminiscences of old Manchester and Salford telling how we kept Whitsuntide sixty years ago . . . by an octogenarian* (Manchester, 1887), pp. 10–16; R. Ryan, *A biography of Manchester* (London, 1937), pp. 104–6; J.T. Slugg, *Reminiscences of Manchester fifty years ago* (Manchester, 1881), pp. 308–10; R.W. Malcolmson, *Popular recreations in English society 1700–1850* (London, 1973), pp. 31–3.
95 *DD* 5 June 1928.
96 *HNM* June 1910.
97 *MCN* 14 June 1930; tape in author's possession.
98 C. Bundy and D. Healy, 'Aspects of urban poverty', *Oral History*, **6** (1978), p. 90; R. Heaton, *Salford, my home town* (Swinton, 1985), p. 10; *MEN* 20 May 1932; *MCH* 21, 28 May 1932.
99 Kennedy, *Slavery*, pp. 117–18; *MCH* 28 May 1910, 8 April 1922.
100 Bertenshaw, *Sunrise*, p. 93; *MG* 13 June 1935.
101 *MEN* 8 June 1900; *MCH* 15 June 1900.
102 Turner, *Collyhurst*, p. 84; *MEN* 16 May 1921; MSTC 457.
103 Turner, *Collyhurst*, p. 58.
104 *MCH* 19 May 1934; MSTC 457, 492.
105 Burke, *Ancoats*, p. 5; Turner, *Collyhurst*, p. 25; MSTC 457.
106 Anon., 'London Irish', p. 133.

Chapter 5: The politics of home rule

1 An earlier version of this chapter can be found in S. Fielding, 'Irish politics in Manchester, 1890–1914', *International Review of Social History*, **33** (1988).
2 K.D. Wald, *Crosses on the ballots* (Princeton, 1983).
3 D.G. Boyce, *Nationalism in Ireland* (London, 1982), p. 203; M.W. Walker, 'Irish immigrants in Scotland: Their priests, politics and parochial life', *Historical Journal*, 15 (1972), p. 663; Gilley, 'English attitudes', pp. 104–6; Tebbutt, 'Stereotypes', p. 208.
4 E. Hobsbawm, 'Twentieth century British politics', *Past and Present*, 11 1957, pp. 106–7.

5 C. Wrigley, 'Labour and the trade unions', in K.D. Brown (ed.), *The first Labour Party, 1906–1914* (Beckenham, 1985), p. 152; White, *Campbell Bunk*, p. 108.
6 Benjamin, 'London Irish', pp. 222, 274; *FJ* 19 May 1902.
7 P.B. Ellis, *A History of the Irish working class* (London, 1985), pp. 197, 201; F.S.L. Lyons, 'The political ideas of Parnell', *Historical Journal*, 16 (1973), pp. 760–2.
8 Buckman, *Class struggle*, pp. 76–7; Clynes, *Memoirs*, 1, pp. 38–9; George, *Mill boy*, pp. 29–30; Sexton, *Agitator*, pp. 81–2; *LL* 15 June 1895.
9 A. O'Day, *The English face of Irish nationalism* (Dublin, 1977), pp. 118–25; A. O'Day, 'The Irish influence on parliamentary elections', in Swift and Gilley, *Victorian city*; A. O'Day, 'The political organisation of the Irish in Britain, 1867–90', in Swift and Gilley, *Irish in Britain*; P. Thompson, *Socialists, Liberals and Labour. The struggle for London, 1885–1914* (London, 1967), pp. 25–7.
10 Benjamin, 'London Irish', p. 219.
11 H. Pelling, *The social geography of British elections, 1885–1910* (London, 1967), p. 284; H.C.G. Matthew, R.I. McKibbin and J.A. Kay, 'The franchise factor in the rise of the Labour party', *English Historical Review*, 91 (1976), p. 752; Clarke, *New Liberalism*, pp. 6–11, 18.
12 R.L. Greenall, 'Popular Conservatism in Salford, 1868–86', *Northern History*, 20 (1974); J. Hill 'Manchester and Salford politics and the early development of the Independent Labour Party', *International Review of Social History*, 26 (1981), p. 175; N. Mansergh, 'The Unionist Party and the union, 1886–1916', in O.D. Edwards and F. Pyle (eds), *1916. The Easter rising* (London, 1968), pp. 79–80.
13 *MG* 28 June 1892, 1 November 1906.
14 G.S. Law, 'Manchester's politics, 1885–1906', unpublished PhD thesis, University of Pennsylvania (1975), p. 166; O'Tuathaigh, 'Irish in Britain', p. 29.
15 Unionist pamphlet, N.U. 551, 1906, M137/8/2/8, AD; *MG* 25, 30 June 1892, 26 August 1900; *SCR* 18 February 1955.
16 E.P.M. Wollaston, 'The Irish Nationalist movement in Great Britain, 1886–1908', unpublished MA thesis, University of London (1958), p. 76; O'Day, 'Political organisation', p. 185.
17 *MCH* 7 May 1910.
18 H. McLeod, 'Catholicism and the New York Irish, 1880–1910', in J. Obelkevich, L. Roper, R. Samuel (eds), *Disciplines of faith. Studies in religion, politics and patriarchy* (London, 1987), pp. 346–7; Denvir, *Old rebel*, p. 258; Wollaston, 'Irish Nationalist movement', p. 11.
19 D. Hopkins, 'The membership of the Independent Labour Party, 1904–10: A spatial and occupational analysis', *International Review of Social History*, 20 (1975), pp. 191–3.
20 For Boyle: *St Patrick's jubilee souvenir* (Manchester, 1961); *MFP*, 3, 1897; *MCH* 8 June 1900; *MEC* 12 November 1906; *MCN* 22 August 1925. For McCabe: *CF* November 1913; *Harvest* March 1895, November 1919, May 1922; *MFP*, 8, 1897; *MEC* 28 January 1907; *MCN* 13 January 1912.
21 *MCH* 7 May 1910; *MG* 18 March 1896, 18 March 1925.
22 O'Day, 'Political organisation', p. 205.
23 Naughton, *Pig's back*, pp. 119, 125; Naughton, *Saintly Billy*, p. 11.
24 P. Rose, *The Manchester martyrs* (London, 1970), p. 124; *MCH* 6 September 1919; MSTC 87 and 1024.
25 Benjamin, 'London Irish', pp. 183–4; Clarke, *New Liberalism*, p. 34; Law, 'Manchester's politics', pp. 210–11.
26 *MG* 18, 23 March 1906; *MCH* 30 March, 20 April, 30 May 1906.

27 *MC* 26 July, 12 August 1892.
28 St Luke's ward Liberal party minute book, 13 April 1919, M2383/5, AD; *MG* 14 April 1908.
29 T. Regan, 'Labour members of Manchester City Council, 1895–1963', BRF/ 352/04273/RE1, AD; *MCH* 12 February 1904, 20 April 1906, 9 November 1907, 1 January 1910.
30 T.P. O'Connor, *The Parnell movement* (London, 1886), p. 557.
31 F.S.L. Lyons, *Culture and anarchy in Ireland, 1890–1939* (Oxford, 1979), pp. 85–92.
32 McCarthy, *Generation*, p. 24; Sexton, *Agitator*, pp. 30–2, 81; *MCH* 28 September 1906, 17 March 1913.
33 *MCH* 26 February, 11 March 1904.
34 *MG* 20 March 1900.
35 K.R.M. Short, *The dynamite war. Irish–American bombers in Victorian Britain* (Dublin, 1979); J. Parry, 'The Tredegar anti-Irish riots of 1882', *Llafur,* **3** (1983).
36 H.V. Brasted, 'Irish nationalism and the British empire in the late nineteenth century', in O. MacDonagh, W.E. Mandle and P. Travers (eds), *Irish culture and nationalism, 1750–1950* (London, 1983); *MG* 3 January 1893, 17 March 1911.
37 *MG* 2 February 1892, 7 June 1897, 20 March 1900, 23 August 1910.
38 *MC* 8 April 1892; *MG* 18 March 1890, 20 March 1899, 18 March 1901, 19 March 1906.
39 Denvir, *Old rebel,* p. 253.
40 J.H. Fowler, *Bombs and their reverberations* (London, 1939), pp. 2, 15.
41 For an account of this period see F.S.L. Lyons, *The Irish parliamentary party, 1890–1910* (London, 1951).
42 D.A. Hamer, *Liberal politics in the age of Gladstone and Rosebery* (Oxford, 1972), p. 153.
43 D.A. Hamer, 'The Irish question and Liberal politics, 1886-1894', *Historical Journal,* **12** (1969), pp. 513–20; C. Harvie, 'Ideology and Home Rule: James Bryce, A.V. Dicey and Ireland, 1880–1887', *English Historical Review,* **91** (1976), pp. 300, 310; A. O'Day, 'Irish Home Rule and Liberalism', in A. O'Day (ed.), *The Edwardian age: Conflict and stability, 1900–14* (London, 1979), p. 128.
44 C.H.D. Howard, 'The Parnell manifesto of 21 November 1885 and the schools question', *English Historical Review,* **62** (1947), p. 49.
45 *MG* 20 December 1890, 9, 18 March 1891.
46 *Manchester Courier* 19 March 1894; *MG* 25 March 1893, 20 March 1899.
47 B. O'Connell, 'Irish Nationalism in Liverpool', *Eire–Ireland,* **10** (1975); Smith, 'Labour tradition', p. 46.
48 *MG* 8, 17 February 1897.
49 *MG* 31 January 1891, 23 October 1907.
50 Sexton, *Agitator*, pp. 82–4.
51 McCarthy, *Generation*, pp. 4, 10–13, 24; *MG* 17 May 1899.
52 P. Whitaker, 'The growth of Liberal organisation in Manchester from the 1860s to 1903', unpublished PhD thesis, University of Manchester, 1956, pp. 196, 260–1; O'Connor, *Parnell movement*, pp. 546–7; *MG* 16 November 1885, 14 October 1891.
53 North-west Manchester Liberal Association minutes, 13 May 1912 and attached letter from Kemp, M283/4/1/1, AD.

54 Cooter, 'County Durham', pp. 262–8.
55 *MCN* 11 October 1919; MSTC 794.
56 H.C. Rowe, *The Boggart Hole contest* (Manchester, 1896); F. Reid, 'Keir Hardie and the "Labour Leader", 1893–1903', in J. Winter (ed.), *The working class in modern British history* (Cambridge, 1983), pp. 24–8; Law, 'Manchester's politics', pp. 37–8, 59–61; *MG* 24 October 1896.
57 Clark, *Irish in Philadelphia*, pp. 136–42; Levine, *Irish politician*, pp. 112–13.
58 *MG* 25 October 1895, 22 October 1907.
59 *MCH* 10 December 1917; *MG* 27 October 1900, 19 October, 1 November 1906; MSTC 794.
60 *FJ* 8 June 1906.
61 *MG* 18 March 1898; *MCH* 7 May, 11 June 1921.
62 Booth, *Religious influences*, p. 246; *MCN* 26 September 1891, 28 October 1905.
63 Benjamin, 'London Irish', p. 293; *Tablet* 23 July 1892; *MG* 10 January 1910.
64 *MG* 28 November 1898, 13 February 1899.
65 Gilley, 'Irish diaspora', pp. 202–3.
66 A.C.F. Beales, 'The struggle for the schools', in G.A. Beck (ed.), *The English Catholics* (London, 1951).
67 M.J. Daunton, *Coal metropolis. Cardiff, 1870–1914* (Leicester, 1977), p. 145.
68 *MCH* 1 June 1906, 19 April 1907; *HNM* October 1907.
69 *MG* 16, 18 April 1908.
70 *MG* 20, 22, 23, 30 April 1908; *MCH* 25 April 1908.
71 *MCH* 25 April 1908; *MG* 22, 23 April 1908.
72 *MCH* 16, 23, 30 May, 13 June 1908.
73 *MCH* 29 January 1910.
74 *MCH* 5, 12 March 1910.
75 *MCH* 22, 29 October 1910; *SWPM* March 1911.
76 E. Biagini and A. Reid, 'Currents of radicalism, 1850–1914', in E. Biagini and A. Reid (eds), *Currents of radicalism* (Cambridge, 1991).
77 *MC* 12 February 1892.
78 *Clarion* 30 June 1894.
79 S. Shipley, *Club life and socialism* (London, 1983), p. 41.
80 *MG* 11 July 1895.
81 Benjamin, 'London Irish', p. 320; *LL* 12, 19 January 1895, 30 March 1895.
82 N. Reid, 'The Manchester and Salford ILP', *North West Labour History Society Bulletin*, 5 (1979–80), pp. 26–9; Woolerton, *Labour Movement*, p. 8.
83 D. Howell, *British workers and the Independent Labour Party, 1888–1906* (Manchester, 1983), p. 214.
84 *Clarion* 21 April 1894.
85 K.O. Morgan, *Keir Hardie. Radical and socialist* (London, 1975), p. 80; *LL* 20 July 1895.
86 D. McDermott, 'Labour and Ireland' in Brown, *Labour Party*, pp. 260, 265; *MG* 19 March 1906.
87 Denvir, *Old rebel*, p. 272.
88 MSTC 87.
89 *MG* 24 November 1910.
90 *MG* 8 January 1910.
91 *MG* 25 October 1909.
92 Howell, *British workers*, p. 210.
93 Guardian of the Poor, *Irish peasant*, pp. 93, 134.

94 P.F. Clarke, 'The progressive movement in England', *Royal Historical Society Transactions*, 5th series, **24** (1974), pp. 175–7; T.W. Heyk, 'Home Rule, radicalism and the Liberal party, 1886–1895', *Journal of British Studies*, **13** (1974), pp. 68–9; *MG* 10 January 1910.

95 *MG* 11 May 1912.

96 *LL* 2 December 1910.

97 *MG* 24, 25, 28, 30 November 1910.

98 N. Blewett, *The peers, the parties and the people* (London, 1972), pp. 324, 352; I. Maclean, *The legend of Red Clydeside* (Glasgow, 1983), pp. 193–4.

99 Blewett, *Peers*, pp. 24–9; *MG* 14 January 1910; *MCH* 15 January 1910; *LL* 21 January 1910.

100 T.W. Moody, 'Michael Davitt and the British labour movement, 1882–1906', *Royal Historical Society Transactions*, 5th series, **4** (1953).

101 Hill, 'Manchester and Salford', p. 172.

102 Manchester Liberal Federation general committee minutes, 7 July 1911, 6 June 1913, M283/1/4/1, AD.

103 L.W. Brady, *T.P. O'Connor and the Liverpool Irish* (London, 1983), pp. 233–5; *MCH* 10 October 1914; *MG* 4 August, 23 November 1914.

104 F. Lavery (ed.), *Irish heroes in the war* (London, 1917), p. 77; T.P. O'Connor, 'The Irish in Great Britain', in F. Lavery (ed.), *Great Irishmen in war and peace* (London, 1920), pp. 21–9.

105 F.S.L. Lyons, 'The decline and fall of the Nationalist party' in Edwards and Pyle, *1916* p. 38; *MCH* 6, 20 May 1916.

106 S. Gilley, 'Pearse's sacrifice: Christ and Cuchulain crucified and risen in the Easter rising, 1916' in Obelkevich et al, *Disciplines of faith*; R. McHugh, 'The Catholic Church and the rising' in Edwards and Pyle, *Easter rising*, p. 200; Naughton, *Pig's back*, p. 119; *MCH* 29 July, 5 August 1916.

107 *MCH* 15 July 1916, 17 May 1919, 27 September 1919; *MG* 31 March 1919.

108 *MCH* 6, 13 September 1919, 19 July 1920.

109 *MCH* 19 January, 7, 14 May 1921, 11 March 1922.

110 Naughton, *Saintly Billy*, p. 36; *MG* 1 November 1920.

111 *MCH* 26 March 1921.

112 *Times* 26, 27 November 1920, 14, 21, 22 February 1921.

113 McCarthy, *Generation*, pp. 42–3; *MCH* 1 July 1916, 2 October 1920, 8 July 1922.

114 Manchester Watch Committee Minutes 1921, 88, item 40, Greater Manchester Police Museum; ASSI 52/331, PRO; *MG* 4, 5 April, 9, 14 July 1921; *MCH* 9 April 1921; *MEN* 4 April 1921; MSTC 794.

115 *MCH* 16 April 1921, 26 April 1930.

116 Miles Platting Liberal Council minutes, 15 April 1919, M283/3, AD; *MCH* 10 May 1919.

117 J.D. Clarkson, *Labour and Nationalism in Ireland* (New York, 1925), pp. 388, 409–12.

118 *MCH* 24 April, 1 May 1920.

119 *MG* 22, 25, 26 November 1918.

120 C. Howard, 'Expectations born to death: Local Labour Party expansion in the 1920s', in Winter, *Working class*, pp. 67–8.

121 *MCH* 8 July 1922.

122 *MG* 3 December 1923.

123 Clynes, *Memoirs*, **2**, p. 66.

124 *MG* 26 November 1923.

125 T. Gallagher, *Glasgow. The uneasy peace. Religious tension in modern Scotland* (Manchester, 1987), pp. 94–7.

Chapter 6: Labour and the church

1 Clarkson, *Labour and Nationalism*, p. 433–4; *Hansard* 5th Series, **36**, Column 1457, 11 April 1912.
2 R.S.W. Davies, 'The Liverpool Labour party and the Liverpool working class, 1900–39', *North West Labour History Society Bulletin*, **5**, 1979–80, pp. 5–10.
3 *CF* January 1922.
4 R. Baxter, 'The Liverpool Labour party, 1918–1963', unpublished DPhil thesis, University of Oxford (1969), p. 211.
5 *MCH* 12 January 1935.
6 *MCH* 2 February 1929.
7 S. MacIntyre, *A proletarian science. Marxism in Britain 1917–1933* (Cambridge, 1980), p. 57; S. MacIntyre, 'British Labour, Marxism and working-class apathy in the nineteen twenties', *Historical Journal*, **20** (1977), pp. 480–1; *MCH* 12 January 1935.
8 *LL* 14 January 1910.
9 E. Oldmeadow, *Francis Cardinal Bourne*, **2** (London, 1940), p. 197.
10 R. Garner, 'Local Labour parties in Manchester and Salford and the Communist question in the 1920s', *Manchester Region History Review*, **2** (1988); MacIntyre, *Proletarian science*, pp. 35–6.
11 R. Hall, *Marie Stopes. A biography* (London, 1977), pp. 271–2; *LCH* 18 January 1930.
12 E. Gibbon, abridged by D.M. Low, *The decline and fall of the Roman Empire* (Harmondsworth, 1960), p. 11.
13 *MG* 23 October 1907.
14 *MG* 22 November 1923; *SCR* 6 September 1924, 25 October 1924, 31 May 1929, 8 May 1931, 16 October 1931.
15 M. Toole, *Our old man* (London, 1948), pp. 36, 88; *MG* 30 November 1923.
16 MSTC 457.
17 *MCH* 7 August 1907.
18 D. Howell, *A lost left. Three studies in socialism and nationalism* (Manchester, 1986), pp. 232–42. See also I. Wood, *John Wheatley* (Manchester, 1990).
19 Bealey and Pelling, *Labour*, p. 149.
20 *MCH* 5 November 1932.
21 Forman, *Industrial town*, pp. 174–5.
22 Shipley, *Club life*, pp. 25, 37.
23 MSTC 584.
24 Toole, *Fighting*, pp. 85, 100.
25 C.D. Greaves, *The life and times of James Connolly* (London, 1961), pp. 107–8.
26 Naughton, *Saintly Billy*, pp. 20–1.
27 D. Hyde, *I believed* (London, 1952), pp. 279–81; Forman, *Industrial town*, pp. 174, 181–2.
28 R. Moore, *Pit-men, preachers and politics* (Cambridge, 1974), pp. 93–119; A.J. Ainsworth, 'Religion in the working-class community and the evolution of socialism in late nineteenth century Lancashire: a case of working-class consciousness', *Histoire Sociale*, **10** (1977), pp. 376–8.

29 Treble, 'Place', pp. 263–6.
30 *MG* 1 September 1913; *MCH* 4 February 1922.
31 *SWPM* October 1910.
32 *MG* 25 January 1897.
33 *MG* 1 September 1913.
34 Snead-Cox, *Vaughan*, pp. 430, 432–3; *MG* 2 October 1899.
35 *MCH* 25 January 1907, 1, 8, 15 February 1907, 26 April 1907.
36 G.P. Connolly, 'The Catholic Church and the first Manchester and Salford trade unions in the age of the industrial revolution', *Transactions of the Lancashire and Cheshire Antiquarian Society*, **135** (1985); J.H. Treble, 'The attitude of the Roman Catholic Church towards trade unionism in the north of England, 1833–1842', *Northern History*, **16** (1970); *MCH* 25 January 1907, 1, 8, 15 February 1907.
37 G.P. McEntee, *The social Catholic movement in Great Britain* (New York, 1927), pp. 302–3; D. Mathew, *Catholicism in England* (London, 1955), p. 243; Oldmeadow, *Bourne*, pp. 218–19, 141.
38 *HNM* February 1910.
39 *MCH* 16 February 1924.
40 *HNM* January 1910.
41 Gallagher, *Uneasy peace*, pp. 115–17; *MCH* 4 April 1931.
42 C.C. Martindale, *Charles Dominic Plater* (London, 1922), p. 291; McEntee, *Social Catholic*, p. 95.
43 Catholic Federation File, Folder 2, WH.
44 *MCH* 26 January 1924, 5 November 1932; *Harvest* November 1933.
45 W. Teeling, *The Pope in politics. The life and work of Pope Pius XI* (London, 1937), p. 165.
46 *LCH* 18 May 1888.
47 J.R. Corbett, 'Recent electoral statistics', *TMSS*, 1906–7, pp. 48, 62.
48 *Harvest* August 1902.
49 E.S. Pankhurst, *The suffragette movement* (London, 1931), p. 130.
50 Tebbutt, 'Stereotypes', pp. 213–16; Wollaston, 'Irish Nationalist movement', p. 160; *Harvest* August 1906, May 1907.
51 *MCH* 15 February 1908, 14 March 1908; *Harvest* March 1908; *Federationist* August 1911.
52 *Federationist* February 1911.
53 *Federationist* May 1910.
54 *Catholic Federationist*, February, May 1912.
55 J.B. Jeffreys, *The story of the engineers, 1800–1945* (London, 1970), pp. 150–73; D. Lockwood, *The blackcoated worker* (Oxford, 1989), pp. 155–61; H. Reid, 'The furniture workers – from craft to industrial union, 1865–1972', unpublished PhD thesis, University of Warwick (1982), pp. 78–86.
56 Wrigley, 'Trade unions', pp. 129, 136–7, 152.
57 *MCH* 14, 21 March 1908, 14 April 1908.
58 B. Simon, *Education and the labour movement, 1870–1920* (London, 1974), pp. 275, 277–8; C. Grigg, 'Labour and education', in Brown, *Labour Party*, p. 169; TUCAR 1906 pp. 175–6; TUCAR 1907 pp. 186–9; TUCAR 1908 pp. 179–82; TUCAR 1909 pp. 193–4; TUCAR 1910 pp. 173–8; TUCAR 1911 pp. 243–6; TUCAR 1912 pp. 175–84.
59 *Federationist* January 1910; *Catholic Federationist*, October 1912, February 1913.

60 NCCTU Standing Committee to Casartelli, 4 April 1918, item 4; agenda for NCCTU Special Conference, July 1918, item 5 both in Folder 2, CF file, WH.
61 Statement on the ballot, undated, item 3, Folder 2, CF File, WH.
62 Burns to Casartelli, 23 September 1918, item 7, Folder 4, CF File; CLP manifesto, WH; *MG* 24 September 1918.
63 P. Doyle, 'Accommodation or confrontation: Catholic response to the formation of the Labour Party,' *North West Labour History Bulletin*, **16** (1991), pp. 65–71.
64 *Catholic Federationist* April 1913.
65 'Observations by the Organisation Secretary on the condition of the Federation', 4 January 1917, Folder 4, CF File, WH.
66 McEntee, *Social Catholic*, p. 136; Martindale, *Plater*, p. 293.
67 Martindale, *Plater*, p. 295; *LCH* 7 April 1923.
68 M. McDermott, 'Irish Catholics and the British labour movement: A study with particular reference to London, 1918–70', unpublished MA thesis, University of Kent (1979), pp. 66–8, 71–2.
69 *MCH* 16 May 1925.
70 *MCH* 31 October, 7 November 1925, 12 November 1932; *MG* 2 November 1925.
71 In Gallagher, *Uneasy peace*, p. 192.
72 J. Lewis, *The politics of motherhood. Child and maternal welfare in England, 1900–1939* (London, 1980), p. 198; McDermott, 'Irish Catholics', pp. 113–15; LPACR 1925 p. 44, 191–2; LPACR 1926 pp. 32–3, 207; LPACR 1927 pp. 54, 232–3.
73 *LCH* 20 July 1929.
74 *LCH* 18 January 1930.
75 *LCH* 25 January 1930.
76 W.M. Walker, *Juteopolis. Dundee and its textile workers, 1885–1923* (Edinburgh, 1979), pp. 207–8.
77 J. Liddington, *The life and times of a respectable rebel, Selina Cooper (1864–1946)* (London, 1984), pp. 325–35.
78 MSTC 774(2).
79 *LCH* 1, 8, 13 November 1930, 28 February 1931, 14 March 1931.
80 McDermott, 'Irish Catholics', p. 142.
81 Waller, *Democracy*, pp. 341–3; *CH* 7 January 1938; *Catholic Worker*, April 1938.
82 *LCH* 16, 30, May 1931.
83 *MCH* 29 March 1919, 5 April 1919, 20 March 1926, 2 April 1926, 22 May 1926.
84 R. Barker, *Education and politics, 1900–1951. A study of the Labour Party* (Oxford, 1972), pp. 57–8; Barber, 'School accommodation', pp. 100–1, 107, 114, 136.
85 *MCN* 27 October 1928; *MCH* 3 November 1928.
86 *MG* 2 November 1928; *LNV* 9 November 1928; *MCH* 12 January 1929; *MCN* 19 July 1930.
87 LPNEC minutes, 17 February 1929; *MCH* 2 February 1929.
88 *LNV* 23, 30 November 1928, 7, 14 December 1928.
89 LPNEC minutes, 11, 20, 26 March, 5 June, 24 July 1929; *MCH* 4, 11 May 1929.
90 LPNEC minutes, 19 December 1928, 17, 20 February 1929.
91 Barker, *Education*, pp. 55–6, 57–8.
92 *MCH* 18 May 1929; *HNM* February, June 1929.
93 *MCH* 13, 20 July 1929; *LCH* 13 July 1929.
94 D.W. Dean, 'The difficulties of a Labour education policy: The failure of the Trevelyan Bill, 1929–31', *British Journal of Educational Studies*, **17** (1969), pp. 293–4; LPNEC minutes, 24 July 1929.

95 Dean, 'Trevelyan Bill', p. 204; Barker, *Education,* p. 48; *HNM* June 1930.
96 *MCH* 3 May 1930, 5, 26 July 1930, 11 October 1930.
97 B. Simon, *The politics of educational reform, 1920–40* (London, 1974), pp. 164–6.
98 *Times* 26 November 1920; *LCH* 4 October 1930.
99 D.E. McHenry, *The Labour Party in transition, 1931–38* (London, 1938), pp. 216–18; Barker, *Education,* p. 21.
100 *LCH* 11 October 1930.
101 *MCH* 4, 13 October 1930.
102 *MCH* 8 November 1930, 6 December 1930.
103 *LCH* 1, 8 November 1930.
104 *MCH* 14 February 1931, 11, 18, 25 April 1931, 2 May 1931; *LNV* June 1931.
105 S. Rawnsley, 'Fascism and Fascists in Britain in the 1930s. A case study of Fascism in the north of England in a period of economic and political change', unpublished PhD thesis, University of Bradford (1981), pp. 192–3.
106 *MCH* 20, 27 June 1931.
107 *LNV* March 1931.
108 *MCH* 15 November 1930.
109 *MG* 14 October 1930; *MCH* 22 November 1930.
110 McDermott, 'Catholics and Labour', p. 117; *CHWE* 28 January 1938.
111 *LCH* 11 January 1930, 6 September 1930, 22 November 1930, 3 March 1939.
112 *MCH* 22 November 1930, 6, 20 December 1930.
113 *MCH* 22 August 1931.
114 *MCH* 17 January 1931.
115 *MCH* 11 May 1935.
116 *MCH* 12, 19 January 1930.
117 Barker, *Education,* pp. 62–3.
118 *MCH* 29 October 1932.
119 *MCH* 8 November 1930; *CCM* March 1936.
120 Gallagher, *Uneasy peace,* p. 196.
121 J. Saville, 'May Day 1937', in A. Briggs and J. Saville (eds), *Essays in labour history, 1918–1939* (London, 1977), pp. 260–70; *CHWE* 2 July 1937.
122 *CH* 29 October 1937.
123 *LCH* 29 October 1935; *CH* 22 October 1937, 29 October 1937, 5 November 1937.
124 C. Bermant, *London's East End* (New York, 1975), pp. 138–9; K. Harris, *Attlee* (London, 1982), pp. 46–7; H. Pelling, *The British Communist Party* (London, 1958), p. 61; Freeman, 'Irish workers', p. 29; McCarthy, *Generation,* pp. 100–1; McDermott, 'Irish Catholics', pp. 165–6.
125 A. Hastings, 'Some reflections on the English Catholicism of the late 1930s' in A. Hastings (ed.), *Bishops and writers. Aspects of the evolution of modern English Catholicism* (Wheathampstead, 1977), pp. 114–20; S. Rawnsley, 'The membership of the British Union of Fascists', in K. Lunn and R. Thurlow (eds), *British Fascism. Essays on the radical right in interwar Britain* (London, 1980); Rawnsley, 'Fascism and Fascists', pp. 192–3, 252–6; Teeling, *Pope in politics,* p. 169.
126 J. Keating, 'Christian Democrat thought in 1930s Britain', paper presented at the Rerum Novarum centenary conference, Hull University, April 1991.
127 *CH* 9 September 1938, 3 February 1939.
128 *DW* 31 August 1938; *CH* 2 September 1938.

Conclusion

1 Holmes, *John Bull,* Part Three.
2 A. Marwick, *British society since 1945* (Harmondsworth, 1982), pp. 226–7.
3 Gallagher, *Uneasy peace,* pp. 227–90.
4 C. Peach, V. Robinson, J. Maxted and J. Chance, 'Immigration and ethnicity' in A.H. Halsey (ed.), *British social trends since 1900* (London, 2nd edition, 1988), pp. 570–6; Jackson, *Irish in Britain,* pp. 27–8; Lennon et al, *Across the water,* pp. 25–8.
5 Brent Irish Mental Health Group, *The Experience of Irish mental illness in London* (London, 1986); J. Jackson, 'The Irish' in R. Glass (ed.), *London. Aspects of change* (London, 1964); O'Connor, *Irish in Britain,* pp. 137–59.
6 J. Rex and R. Moore, *Race, community and conflict* (Oxford, 1969), pp. 84–99; J. Jackson, 'The Irish in East London', *East London Papers,* **6** (1963), p. 105; O'Connor, *Irish in Britain,* pp. 86–92; *New Society* 14 March 1968.
7 *LCH* 23, 31 December 1937, 7, 21, 28 January 1938, 4 February 1938, 6 January 1939; MacAmlaigh, *Exile,* pp. 73–4.
8 *MG* 30 October 1933, 1, 3 November 1933; *MCH* 30 June, 25 August 1933; *MCN* 29 April 1939.
9 Walter, 'Bolton', pp. 400–2; McDermott, 'Irish Catholics', p. 380.
10 R.H. Ward, 'Some aspects of religious life in an immigrant area of Manchester', *Sociological Year Book of Religion,* **3** (1970); MacAmlaigh, *Exile,* pp. 7, 23.
11 M. Hornsby-Smith, *Roman Catholicism in England. Studies in social structure since the Second World War* (Cambridge, 1987).
12 T. Brennan, *Reshaping a city* (Glasgow, 1959), pp. 126–7; E. Moore, 'Catholic Church and elections', *Socialist Commentary* (January 1950), pp. 23–4 and 'The menace of the Catholic education campaign', *Socialist Commentary* (April 1943), pp. 7–11; Coman, *Welfare,* pp. 41–67; O'Connor, *Irish in Britain,* pp. 102–3; Beales, 'Struggle for schools', p. 404.
13 D. Butler and M. Pinto-Duschinsky, *The British general election of 1970* (London, 1971), p. 408; J.M. Bochel and D.T. Denver, 'Religion and voting: A critical review and a new analysis', *Political Studies,* **18** (1970); W.L. Miller and G. Raab, 'The religious alignment at English elections between 1918 and 1970', *Political Studies,* **25** (1977).
14 B. Behan, *Borstal boy* (London, 1958), p. 13; L. Fairfield, *The trial of Peter Barnes. The IRA Coventry explosions of 1939* (London, 1953); Explosives Trial Cuttings, GMPM; ASSI 52/485, PRO.
15 C.D. Greaves, 'The Connolly Association', paper presented at the North West Labour History Society annual conference, March 1988.
16 H.G. Nicholas, *The British general election of 1950* (London, 1951), pp. 257–8; S.B. Chrimes (ed.), *The general election in Glasgow, February 1950* (Glasgow, 1950), pp. 81, 100–2; O'Connor, *Irish in Britain,* pp. 118–20, 92.
17 G. Scott, *The RCs* (London, 1967), p. 26.
18 Directive on Race, June 1939, Tom Harrisson Mass-Observation Archive, University of Sussex.
19 J.B. Priestley, *English journey* (Harmondsworth, 1977), pp. 235–6.
20 History Press, *Irish in exile,* pp. 22–4.
21 D. Storey, *This sporting life* (Harmondsworth, 1962), pp. 31–2.
22 M. Jones, *Potbank* (London, 1961), p. 95.

23 N. Evans, 'The South Wales race riots of 1919', *Llafur*, **3** (1980), p. 23; Lennon et al, *Across the water*, p. 219.

24 P. Harrison, 'The Irish English' in P. Barker (ed.), *The other Britain* (London, 1982); P. Ullah, 'Second generation Irish youth: Identity and ethnicity', *New Community*, **12** (1985), pp. 310–22; *New Society* 30 October 1975, 20 December 1979.

Bibliography

Catholic records

Salford Diocesan Archive, Wardley Hall

1900 Lenten visitation returns.
Catholic Federation file.
Educational statistics of the Diocese of Salford.
Parish boxes.
Salford Diocesan Almanac.
Societies file.

School log books

St Anne's, Ancoats, available from school.
St Edward's, Rusholme, available from school.
St Michael's, Ancoats, M66/133/Box 1, AD.

Parish log books

Holy Family, All Saints, available from church.
St Wilfrid's, Hulme, available from church.

Parish magazines

Corpus Christi Magazine, LHD.
Holy Name Messenger, available from church.
St Wilfrid's Parish Magazine, available from church.

Parish histories

'Souvenir brochure of the twenty-first anniversary of St Anne's, Crumpsall' (Manchester, 1938).
The Story of St Anne's, Ancoats (Manchester, 1948).
St Patrick's Jubilee Souvenir (Manchester, 1961).

Miscellaneous

Authorized Official Programme for the Catholic Whitsuntide Procession, 1893–1939, LHD.

Political records

Labour Party

Labour Party Annual Conference Reports.
Labour Party National Executive Committee minutes.
Manchester and Salford (after 1920 Manchester (Borough)), Labour Party Annual Reports, WCML.
Salford Central Labour Party Minutes, WCML.
T. Regan, 'Labour members of the City Council, 1894–1965', BRF/352/04273/RE1, AD.
Trades Union Congress Annual Reports.

Liberal Party

General Council, Manchester Liberal Union minutes, M283/1/1/3, AD.
General Council, Manchester Liberal Federation minutes, M283/1/4/1, AD.
North West Manchester Liberal Association minutes, M283/4/1/1, AD.
Miles Platting Ward Council minutes, M283/3, AD.
St Luke's Ward Council minutes, M283/5, AD.

Miscellaneous

Irish Question Collection, LSE.
Local Fabian Society Collection, LSE.

Censuses

Census of England and Wales, 1841–1931.
St Michael's parish, Angel Meadow, c. late nineteenth century, M330/2/6, AD.
St Luke's parish, Chorlton-on-Medlock, M100/1/7, AD.
St George's parish, Hulme, 1927, M383/1/9/2, AD.
St Andrew's parish, Ancoats, 1937, M45/1/14/1, AD.
Ancoats clearance area 1937–8, Misc/847, AD.
Moston Congregational Church, 1939, M274/2/1/1, AD.

Miscellaneous records

Public Record Office

ASSI 52.
CAB 24.
LAB 2, 101.

Tom Harrisson Mass-Observation Archive, University of Sussex

Directive on Race, June 1939.

Manchester Polytechnic

Manchester Studies Tape Collection.

University of Lancaster

Centre for North-West Regional Studies Tape Collection.

Greater Manchester Police Museum

Watch Committee minutes.
Manchester explosives trial cuttings.

Newspapers and periodicals

Catholic Federationist
Catholic Herald
Catholic Herald Western Edition
Clarion
Daily Dispatch
Daily Worker
Federationist
Freeman's Journal
Harvest
Labour Leader
Labour's Northern Voice
London Catholic Herald
Manchester Catholic Herald
Manchester Citizen
Manchester City News
Manchester Courier
Manchester Evening Chronicle
Manchester Evening News
Manchester Faces and Places
Manchester Guardian

Manchester Saturday Half-Penny
Salford City Reporter
Sunday Dispatch
Tablet
Times

Autobiographies

Barclay, T. *Memoirs and medleys. The autobiography of a bottlewasher* (Leicester, 1934).
Behan, B. *Borstal boy* (London, 1958).
Benson, E. *To struggle is to live,* 1 (Leeds, 1979).
Bertenshaw, M. *Sunrise to sunset* (Manchester, 1980).
Brown, G. *In my way* (Harmondsworth, 1972).
Burgess, A. *Big Wilson and little God* (London, 1987).
Burke, M. *Ancoats lad* (Swinton, 1985).
Callaghan, J. *Time and chance* (London, 1987).
Community History Press, *The Irish in exile. Stories of emigration* (London, 1988).
Denvir, J. *The life story of an old rebel* (Dublin, 1910).
Devoy, J. *Recollections of an Irish rebel* (New York, 1929).
Doherty, W. *Reminiscences of old Manchester and Salford: Telling how we kept Whitsuntide sixty years ago . . . by an octogenarian* (Manchester, 1887).
Doran, F. *Down memory lane* (undated, LHD).
Forman, C. *Industrial town* (London, 1979).
Gallagher, P. *My story. By Paddy the Cope* (London, 1939).
Greenwood, W. *There was a time* (London, 1967).
Heaton, R. *Salford, my home town* (Swinton, 1985).
Hoggart, R. *The uses of literacy* (Harmondsworth, 1958).
Hoggart, R. *Local habitation* (Oxford, 1988).
Hyde, D. *I believed* (London, 1952).
Kennedy, B. *Slavery: Pictures from the abyss* (London, 1905).
Knox, E.A. *Reminiscences of an octogenarian, 1847–1934* (London, 1935).
Lennon, M., McAdam, M. and O'Brien J. (eds), *Across the water. Irish women's lives in Britain* (London, 1988).
Levine, M. *Cheetham to Cordova* (Swinton, 1984).
MacGill, P. *Children of the dead end* (London, 1914).
MacGill, P. *The rat-pit* (London, 1915).
McAmhlaigh, D. *An Irish navvy. Diary of an exile* (London, 1964).
McCarthy, M. *Generation in revolt* (London, 1953).
Naughton, B. *Saintly Billy* (Oxford, 1989).
Naughton, B. *On the pig's back* (Oxford, 1988).
O'Connor, T.P. *Memoirs of an old parliamentarian,* 1 (London, 1929).
O'Mara, P. *The autobiography of a Liverpool–Irish slummy* (London, 1934).
Osman, E. *Salford stepping stones* (Swinton, 1983).
Pankhurst, E.S. *The suffragette movement* (London, 1931).
Richardson, S. (ed.), *The recollections of three Manchesters in the Great War* (Swinton, 1985).
Richardson, N. *The pubs of old Ancoats* (Swinton, 1987).
Roberts, F. *Memories of a Victorian childhood and working life in Miles Platting, Manchester* (Swinton, 1983).

Roberts, R. *The classic slum* (Harmondsworth, 1983).
Roberts, R. *A ragged schooling* (London, 1984).
Sexton, J. *Sir James Sexton. The life story of an agitator* (London, 1936).
Slugg, J.T. *Reminiscences of Manchester fifty years ago* (Manchester, 1881).
Thompson, F. *Lark Rise to Candleford* (Harmondsworth, 1973).
Tillett, B. *Memories and reflections* (London, 1931).
Toole, J. *Fighting through life* (London, 1935).
Turner, M. *Collyhurst then* (no date, LHD).

Other published accounts and historical works

Abrahamson, J. *Ethnic diversity in Catholic America* (London, 1973).
Ainsworth, A.J. 'Religion in the working-class community and the evolution of socialism in late nineteenth century Lancashire: A case of working-class consciousness', *Histoire Sociale*, **10** (1977).
Anonymous, 'The Irish in London', *Blackwood's Edinburgh Magazine*, **170** (July 1901).
Anonymous, *A History of the Heyrod lads' club, 1889–1910* (Manchester, 1911).
Anonymous, *Incipient Irish revolution. An exposé of Fenianism to-day* (London, 1889).
Arensberg, C.M. and Kimball, S.T. *Family and community in Ireland* (Cambridge, Mass., 1940).
Arnstein, W.L. 'Victorian prejudice re-examined', *Victorian Studies*, **12** (1968–9).
Arnstein, W.L. 'The Murphy riots: A Victorian dilemma', *Victorian Studies*, **19** (1975–6).
Aspinwall, B. 'The welfare state within the welfare state: The Saint Vincent de Paul Society in Glasgow, 1848–1920', in Sheils, W.J. and Wood, D. (eds), *Voluntary religion.*
Bagenal, P.H. *The priest in politics* (London, 1893).
Bain, G.S., Bacon, R. and Pimlott, J. 'The labour force' in A.H. Halsey (ed.), *British society.*
Barker, P. *The other Britain* (London, 1982).
Barker, R. *Education and politics, 1900–1951. A study of the Labour Party* (Oxford, 1972).
Bartlett, A. 'From strength to strength: Roman Catholicism in Bermondsey up to 1939', in *The church and the people. Catholics and their church in Britain, c. 1880–1939* (Warwick Working Papers in Social History, **5**, Centre for the Study of Social History, 1988).
Beales, A.C.F. 'The struggle for the schools', in G.A. Beck (ed.), *English Catholics.*
Bealey, F. and Pelling, H. *Labour and politics, 1900–1906* (London, 1958).
Beck, G.A. (ed.), *The English Catholics* (London, 1951).
Bedoe, J. *The races of Britain* (London, 1885).
Belchem, J. 'English working-class radicalism and the Irish, 1815–50', in R. Swift and S. Gilley (eds), *Victorian city.*
Bermant, C. *London's East End* (New York, 1975).
Best, G.F.A. 'The Protestant constitution and its supporters 1800–1829', *Transactions of the Royal Historical Society*, 5th series, **8** (1958).
Best, G.F.A. 'Popular protestantism in Victorian Britain', in R. Robson (ed.), *Ideas and institutions of Victorian Britain* (London, 1967).
Biagini, E. and Reid, A. 'Currents of radicalism, 1850–1914', in Biagini, E. and Reid, A. (eds), *Currents of Radicalism* (Cambridge, 1991).

Bishop, M.C. 'The social methods of Roman Catholicism in England', *Contemporary Review*, **39** (1877).

Blanch, M. 'Imperialism, nationalism and organised youth', in J. Clarke, C. Chritcher and R. Johnson (eds), *Working-class culture. Studies in history and theory* (London, 1979).

Blewett, N. *The peers, the parties and the people* (London, 1972).

Bochel, J.M. and Denver, D.T. 'Religion and voting: A critical review and a new analysis', *Political Studies*, **18** (1970).

Bolton, C.A. *Salford Diocese and its Catholic past* (Manchester, 1950).

Booth, C. *Life and labour of the people in London. Volume Three. Blocks of buildings, schools and immigration* (London, 1892).

Booth, C. *Life and labour of the people in London. Third Series: Religious influences* (London, 1903).

Booth, C. *Life and labour of the people in London. Third Series: Religious influences. Summary* (London, 1903).

Bossy, J. *The English Catholic community, 1550–1850* (London, 1975).

Boulard, F. trans. Jackson, M.J. *An introduction to religious sociology* (London, 1960).

Boyce, D.G. *Nationalism in Ireland* (London, 1982).

Brady, L.W. *T.P. O'Connor and the Liverpool Irish* (London, 1983).

Brasted, H.V. 'Irish Nationalism and the British Empire in the late nineteenth century', in O. MacDonagh, et al (eds), *Irish culture and Nationalism.*

Brennan, T. *Reshaping a city* (Glasgow, 1959).

Brent Irish Mental Health Group, *The experience of Irish mental illness in London* (London, 1986).

Briggs, A. and Saville, J. (eds), *Essays in labour history 1918–1939* (London, 1977).

Brown, K.D. (ed.), *The first Labour Party, 1906–1914* (Beckenham, 1985).

Buckman, J. *Immigrants and the class struggle. The Jewish immigrant in Leeds, 1880–1914* (Manchester, 1983).

Bundy, C. and Healy, D. 'Aspects of urban poverty', *Oral History*, **6** (1978).

Butler, D. and Pinto-Duschinsky, M. *The British general election of 1970* (London, 1971).

Butt, J. and Clarke, I.F. (eds), *The Victorians and social protest* (Newton Abbot, 1973).

Carter, F. 'Youth work in Manchester', *Social Welfare*, **4** (1940).

Casartelli, L.C. *Sketches in history* (London, 1906).

Champ, J.F. 'Bishop Milner, Holywell and the cure tradition', in W.J. Sheils (ed.), *Church and healing.*

Cheetham, J. 'Immigration', in A.H. Halsey (ed.), *British society.*

Chrimes, S.B. (ed.), *The general election in Glasgow, February 1950* (Glasgow, 1950).

Clarke, D.M. *The Irish in Philadelphia* (Philadelphia, 1973).

Clarke, J.C.D. *English society 1688–1832* (Cambridge, 1985).

Clarke, P.F. *Lancashire and the New Liberals* (Cambridge, 1971).

Clarke, P.F. 'The progressive movement in England', *Royal Historical Society Transactions*, 5th series, **24** (1974).

Clarkson, J.D. *Labour and nationalism in Ireland* (New York, 1925).

Clay, H. and Brady, K.R. *Manchester at work. A survey* (Manchester, 1929).

Cobbe, F.P. 'Wife torture in England', *Contemporary Review*, **42** (1878).

Coman, P. *Catholics and the welfare state* (London, 1977).

Connolly, G.P. 'Little brother be at peace: The priest as Holy Man in the nineteenth century ghetto', in W.J. Sheils (ed.), *Church and healing.*

Connolly, G.P. 'Irish and Catholic: Myth or reality? Another sort of Irish and the renewal of the clerical profession amongst Catholics in England, 1791–1918', in R. Swift and S. Gilley (eds), *Victorian city.*

Connolly, G.P. 'The Catholic Church and the first Manchester and Salford trade unions in the age of the industrial revolution', *Transactions of the Lancashire and Cheshire Antiquarian Society,* **135** (1985).

Corbett, J.R. 'Recent electoral statistics', *TMSS* (1906–7).

Craig, F.W.S. *British parliamentary election results, 1885–1918* (London, 1974).

Crossick, G. (ed.), *The lower middle class in Britain, 1870–1914* (London, 1977).

Curtis, L. *Nothing but the same old story* (London, 1984).

Curtis, L.P. *Apes and angels* (London, 1971).

Daunton, M.J. *Coal metropolis. Cardiff, 1870–1914* (Leicester, 1977).

Davies A. *Leisure, gender and poverty: Working-class culture in Salford and Manchester, 1900–1939* (Buckingham, 1992).

Davies, R.S.W. 'The Liverpool Labour party and the Liverpool working class, 1900–39', *North West Labour History Society Bulletin,* **5** (1979–80).

Davies, S.J. 'Classes and the police in Manchester, 1829–1880', in A.J. Kidd and K.W. Roberts (eds), *City.*

Davis, J. 'From "rookeries" to "communities": Race, poverty and policing in London, 1850–1985', *History Workshop Journal,* **27** (1989).

Dean, D.W. 'The difficulties of a Labour education policy: The failure of the Trevelyan Bill, 1929–31', *British Journal of Educational Studies,* **17** (1969).

Denvir, J. *The Irish in Britain. From earliest times to the fall and death of Parnell,* (London, 1892).

Dingle, A.E. and Harrison, B. 'Cardinal Manning as a temperance reformer, *Historical Journal,* **12** (1969).

Dorrity, D. 'Monkeys in a menagerie: The imagery of Unionist opposition to Home Rule 1886–1893', *Eire–Ireland,* **12** (1977).

Doyle, P. 'The Catholic Federation 1906–29' in W.J. Sheils and D. Wood (eds), *Voluntary religion.*

Doyle, P. 'Accommodation or confrontation: Catholic response to the formation of the Labour party,' *North West Labour History Bulletin,* **16** (1991).

Duggan, D.C. *The stage Irishman* (Dublin, 1937).

Dyos, H.Y. and Wolff, M. (eds), *The Victorian city: Images and realities* (London, 1973).

Ebery, M. and Preston, B. *Domestic service in late Victorian England, 1871–1914* (Geographical Papers, **42**, University of Reading, 1976).

Edwards, O.D. and Pyle, F. (eds), *1916. The Easter rising* (London, 1968).

Ellis, P.B. *A history of the Irish working class* (London, 1985).

Endelman, T.M. *The Jews of Georgian England, 1774–1830: Tradition and change in a liberal society* (London, 1979).

Engels, F. *The condition of the working class in England* (London, 1979).

Epstein, J. and Thompson, D. (eds), *The Chartist experience* (Cambridge, 1982).

Evans, N. 'The South Wales race riots of 1919', *Llafur,* **3** (1980).

Fairfield, L. *The trial of Peter Barnes. The IRA Coventry explosions of 1939* (London, 1953).

Feldman, D. 'There was an Englishman, an Irishman and a Jew . . . immigrants and minorities in Britain', *Historical Journal,* **26**, 1983.

Fielding, S. 'The Catholic Whit walk in Manchester and Salford 1890–1939', *Manchester Region History Review,* **1** (1987).

Fielding, S. 'Irish politics in Manchester, 1890–1914, *International Review of Social History*, **33** (1988).

Finnegan, F. *Poverty and prejudice: A study of Irish immigrants in York, 1840–1875* (Cork, 1982).

Finnegan, F. 'The Irish in York', in R. Swift and S. Gilley (eds), *Victorian city*.

Fitzpatrick, D. 'Irish emigration in the later nineteenth century', *Irish Historical Studies*, **22** (1980).

Fitzpatrick, D. 'A curious middle place: The Irish in Britain, 1871–1921', in R. Swift and S. Gilley (eds), *Irish in Britain*.

Foster, J. *Class struggle and the industrial revolution* (London, 1974).

Fowler, J.H. *Bombs and their reverberations* (London, 1939).

Fraser, D. (ed.), *A history of modern Leeds* (Manchester, 1980).

Freeman, J.B. 'Irish workers in the twentieth century United States: The case of the Transport Workers' Union', *Saothar*, **8** (1982).

Freeman, T.W. 'Emigration and rural Ireland', *Journal of the Statistical Society of Ireland*, **17** (1945).

Gallagher, T. 'A tale of two cities: Communal strife in Glasgow and Liverpool before 1914', in R. Swift and S. Gilley (eds), *Victorian city*.

Gallagher, T. *Glasgow. The uneasy peace. Religious tension in modern Scotland* (Manchester, 1987).

Garner, R. 'Local Labour parties in Manchester and Salford and the Communist question in the 1920s', *Manchester Region History Review*, **2** (1988).

George, E. *From mill boy to minister* (London, 1919).

Gibbon, E. abridged by Low, D.M. *The decline and fall of the Roman Empire* (Harmondsworth, 1960).

Gilley, S. 'Catholic faith of the Irish slums. London, 1840–70', in H.Y. Dyos and M. Wolff (eds), *The Victorian city*.

Gilley, S. 'English attitudes to the Irish in England 1789–1900', in C. Holmes (ed.), *Immigrants and minorities*.

Gilley, S. 'The Roman Catholic Church and the nineteenth-century Irish diaspora', *Journal of Ecclesiastical History*, **35** (1984).

Gilley, S. 'Pearse's sacrifice; Christ and Cuchulain crucified and risen in the Easter rising, 1916', in J. Obelkevich et al (eds), *Disciplines of faith*.

Gittins, D. *Fair sex. Family size and structure, 1900–39* (London, 1982).

Glass, R. (ed.), *London. Aspects of change* (London, 1964).

Glynn, S. 'Irish immigration to Britain, 1911–51: Patterns and policy', *Irish Economic and Social History*, **8** (1981).

Gray, R.Q. 'Religion, culture and social class in late nineteenth and early twentieth century Edinburgh', in G. Crossick (ed.), *Lower middle class*.

Greaves, C.D. *The life and times of James Connolly* (London, 1961).

Green, G. *There's only one United* (London, 1978).

Greenall, R.L. 'Popular conservatism in Salford, 1868–86', *Northern History*, **20** (1974).

Grigg, C. 'Labour and education', in K.D. Brown (ed.), *The Labour Party*.

Guardian of the Poor, *The Irish peasant. A sociological survey* (London, 1892).

Hall, R. *Marie Stopes. A biography* (London, 1977).

Halsey, A.H. (ed.), *Trends in British society since 1900* (London, 1972).

Halsey, A.H. (ed.), *British social trends since 1900*, 2nd edn. (London, 1988).

Hamer, D.A. 'The Irish question and Liberal politics, 1886–1894', *Historical Journal*, **12** (1969).

Hamer, D.A. *Liberal politics in the age of Gladstone and Rosebery* (Oxford, 1972).

Hancock, W.N. 'On the equal importance of the education, poor-law, cheap law for small holders and land questions, at the present crisis', *Journal of the Statistical and Social Inquiry Society of Ireland*, **8** (1880).

Hancock, W.N. 'Some further information as to migratory labourers from Mayo to England, and as to importance of limiting law taxes and law changes in proceedings affecting small holders of land', *Journal of the Statistical and Social Inquiry Society of Ireland*, **8** (1880).

Handley, J.E. *The Irish in modern Scotland* (Cork, 1947).

Harris, K. *Attlee* (London, 1982).

Harrison, P. 'The Irish English', in P. Barker (ed.), *The other Britain*.

Harvie, C. 'Ideology and Home Rule: James Bryce, A.V. Dicey and Ireland, 1880–1887', *English Historical Review*, **91** (1976).

Haslett, J. and Lowe, W.J. 'Household structure and overcrowding among the Lancashire Irish, 1851–1871', *Histoire Sociale*, **10** (1977).

Hastings, A. 'Some reflections on the English Catholicism of the late 1930s', in A. Hastings (ed.), *Bishops and writers*.

Hastings, A. (ed.), *Bishops and writers. Aspects of the evolution of modern English Catholicism* (Wheathampstead, 1977).

Hechter, M. *Internal colonialism. The Celtic fringe in British national development, 1536–1966* (London, 1975).

Herson, J. 'Irish immigration and settlement in Victorian England: A small-town perspective', in R. Swift and S. Gilley (eds), *Irish in Britain*.

Heyk, T.W. 'Home rule, radicalism and the Liberal party, 1886–1895', *Journal of British Studies*, **13** (1974).

Hill, J. 'Manchester and Salford politics and the early development of the Independent Labour Party', *International Review of Social History*, **26** (1981).

Hobsbawm, E. 'Twentieth century British politics', *Past and Present*, **11** (1957).

Hobsbawm, E. *Industry and empire* (Harmondsworth, 1969).

Hobsbawm, E. *Primitive rebels* (Manchester, 1977).

Hobsbawm, E. 'Working classes and nations', *Saothar*, **8** (1982).

Hobsbawm, E. 'The making of the working class, 1870–1914', and 'The formation of British working-class culture', in E. Hobsbawm, *Worlds of Labour*.

Hobsbawm, E. *Worlds of Labour. Further studies in the history of Labour* (London, 1984).

Holmes, C. (ed.), *Immigrants and minorities in British society* (London, 1978).

Holmes, C. *John Bull's island. Immigration and British society, 1871–1971* (London, 1988).

Holmes, D.J. *More Roman than Rome: English Catholics in the nineteenth century* (London, 1978).

Hopkins, D. 'The membership of the Independent Labour Party, 1904–10: A spatial and occupational analysis', *International Review of Social History*, **20** (1975).

Horn, P. *The rise and fall of the Victorian servant* (London, 1975).

Hornsby-Smith, M. *Roman Catholicism in England. Studies in social structure since the Second World War* (Cambridge, 1987).

Howard, C. 'Expectations born to death: Local Labour Party expansion in the 1920s', in J. Winter (ed.), *Working class*.

Howard, C.H.D. 'The Parnell manifesto of 21 November 1885 and the schools question', *English Historical Review*, **62** (1947).

Howell, D. *British workers and the Independent Labour Party, 1888–1906* (Manchester, 1983).

Howell, D. *A lost left. Three studies in socialism and nationalism* (Manchester, 1986).
Hughes, P. 'The English Catholics in 1850', in G.A. Beck (ed.), *English Catholics.*
Humphries, S. *Hooligans or rebels?* (Oxford, 1981).
Hunt, E.H. *Regional wage variation in Britain, 1850–1914* (Oxford, 1973).
Inman, J. *Poverty and housing. Conditions in a Manchester city ward* (London, 1934).
Irish in Britain History Centre, *The history of the Irish in Britain. A bibliography* (London, 1986).
Jackson, J. 'The Irish in East London', *East London Papers*, **6** (1963).
Jackson, J. *The Irish in Britain* (London, 1963).
Jackson, J. 'The Irish', in R. Glass (ed.), *London.*
James, H.E.O. and Moore, F.T. 'Adolescent leisure in a working-class district', *Occupational Psychology*, **14** (1940).
Jeffreys, J.B. *The story of the engineers, 1800–1945* (London, 1970).
Jones, D.C. *The social survey of Merseyside*, **3** (Liverpool, 1934).
Jones, G.S. *Languages of class* (Cambridge, 1984).
Jones, M. *Potbank* (London, 1961).
Jones, W.R. 'England against the Celtic fringe: A study in cultural stereotypes', *Journal of World History*, **13** (1971).
Joyce, P. *Work, society and politics* (Brighton, 1982).
Kennedy, L. 'Profane images in Irish popular consciousness', *Oral History*, **2** (1979).
Kerr, M. *The people of Ship Street* (London, 1958).
Kidd, A.J. and Roberts, K.W. (eds), *City, class and culture* (Manchester, 1985).
Kirk, N. 'Ethnicity, class and popular Toryism, 1850–70', in K. Lunn (ed.), *Hosts.*
Lancaster, B. 'Who's a real Coventry kid? Migration into twentieth century Coventry', in B. Lancaster and T. Mason (eds), *Life and labour.*
Lancaster, B. and Mason, T. (eds), *Life and labour in a twentieth century city. The experience of Coventry* (Coventry, 1986).
Lane, P. *The Catenian Association, 1908–83* (London, 1983).
Large, D. 'The Irish in Bristol in 1852: A census enumeration', in R. Swift and S. Gilley (eds), *Victorian city.*
Larkin, E. 'The devotional revolution in Ireland, 1850–75', *American Historical Review*, **77** (1972).
Lavery, F. (ed.), *Irish heroes in the war* (London, 1917).
Lavery, F. (ed.), *Great Irishmen in war and peace* (London, 1920).
Lees, L.H. 'Patterns of lower class life: Irish slum communities in nineteenth century London', in S. Thernstrom and R. Sennet (eds), *Nineteenth century cities.*
Lees, L.H. *Exiles of Erin. Irish migrants in Victorian London* (Manchester, 1979).
Levine, E.H. *The Irish and the Irish politician* (Notre Dame, 1966).
Lewis, J. *The politics of motherhood. Child and maternal welfare in England, 1900–1939* (London, 1980).
Lewis, J. *Women in England 1870–1950: Sexual divisions and social change* (Brighton, 1984).
Lewis, J. 'The working-class wife and mother and state intervention, 1870–1918', in J. Lewis (ed.), *Labour and love.*
Lewis, J. (ed.), *Labour and love. Women's experience of home and family, 1850–1940* (London, 1986).
Liddington, J. and Norris, J. *One hand tied behind us* (London, 1984).
Liddington, J. *The life and times of a respectable rebel, Selina Cooper (1864–1946)* (London, 1984).
Lockwood, D. *The blackcoated worker* (Oxford, 1989).

London, J. *The people of the abyss* (London, 1977).

Lowe, W.J. 'The Lancashire Irish and the Catholic Church, 1846–71: The social dimension', *Irish Historical Studies*, **20** (1976).

Lunn, K. (ed.), *Hosts, immigrants and minorities* (Folkestone, 1980).

Lunn, K. and Thurlow, R. (eds), *British fascism. Essays on the radical right in interwar Britain* (London, 1980).

Lyons, F.S.L. *The Irish parliamentary party, 1890–1910* (London, 1951).

Lyons, F.S.L. 'The decline and fall of the Nationalist party', in O.D. Edwards and F. Pyle (eds), *1916*.

Lyons, F.S.L. 'The political ideas of Parnell', *Historical Journal*, **16** (1973).

Lyons, F.S.L. *Culture and anarchy in Ireland, 1890–1939* (Oxford, 1979).

Lyons, F.S.L. *Ireland before the famine* (London, 1981).

MacAskill, M. 'Paddy's Market' (Centre for Urban and Regional Research Discussion Paper 29, University of Glasgow, 1987).

MacDonagh, O. 'Irish culture and Nationalism translated: St Patrick's Day, 1888, in Australia', in O. MacDonagh et al (eds), *Irish culture and Nationalism*.

MacDonagh, O. 'The Irish in Australia: A general view', in O. MacDonagh and W.F. Mandle (eds), *Ireland and Irish Australia*.

MacDonagh, O. and Mandle, W.F. (eds), *Ireland and Irish Australia: Studies in cultural and political history* (London, 1986).

MacDonagh, O., Mandle, W.E. and Travers, P. (eds), *Irish culture and Nationalism, 1750–1950* (London, 1983).

Machin, G.I.T. *The Catholic question in English politics* (London, 1964).

MacIntyre, S. 'British labour, Marxism and working-class apathy in the nineteen twenties', *Historical Journal*, **20** (1977).

MacIntyre, S. *A proletarian science. Marxism in Britain 1917–1933* (Cambridge, 1980).

MacLean, I. *The legend of Red Clydeside* (Glasgow, 1983).

Malcolmson, R.W. *Popular recreations in English society 1700–1850* (London, 1973).

Manchester University Settlement, *Ancoats. A study of a clearance area* (Manchester, 1945).

Mandle, W.F. *The Gaelic Athletic Association and Irish nationalist politics, 1884–1924* (London, 1987).

Mansergh, N. 'The Unionist party and the union, 1886–1916', in O.D. Edwards and F. Pyle (eds), *1916*.

Marr, T.R. *Housing conditions in Manchester and Salford* (Manchester, 1904).

Martindale, C.C. *Charles Dominic Plater* (London, 1922).

Martindale, C.C. *Father Bernard Vaughan: A memoir* (London, 1923).

Marwick, A. *British society since 1945* (Harmondsworth, 1982).

Marx, K. and Engels, F. *On Britain* (Moscow, 1962).

Mason, F.M. 'The newer Eve: The Catholic women's suffrage society in England, 1911–23', *Catholic Historical Review*, **52** (1986).

Mason, T. 'The Blues and the Reds', *Transactions of the Historic Society of Lancashire and Cheshire*, **134** (1984).

Mass-Observation, *Britain and her birth-rate* (London, 1945).

Mass-Observation, *Puzzled people* (London, 1947).

Mass-Observation, *The pub and the people* (London, 1970).

Mathew, D. *Catholicism in England* (London, 1955).

Matthew, H.C.G., McKibbin, R.I. and Kay, J.A. 'The franchise factor in the rise of the Labour party', *English Historical Review*, **91** (1976).

McBriar, A.M. *Fabian socialism and English politics, 1884–1918* (Cambridge, 1962).

McCormack, A. *Cardinal Vaughan* (London, 1966).
McDermott, D. 'Labour and Ireland', in K.D. Brown (ed.), *Labour Party*.
McDougal, I. (ed.), *Essays in Scottish labour history* (Edinburgh, 1978).
McEntee, G.P. *The social Catholic movement in Great Britain* (New York, 1927).
McHenry, D.E. *The Labour Party in transition, 1931–38* (London, 1938).
McHugh, R. 'The Catholic Church and the rising', in O.D. Edwards and F. Pyle (eds), *1916*.
McKibbin, R. 'Why was there no Marxism in Great Britain?', in McKibbin, R. *Ideologies of class* (Oxford, 1991).
McLeod, H. 'White collar values and the role of religion', in G. Crossick (ed.), *Lower middle class*.
McLeod, H. *Religion and the working class in nineteenth century Britain* (London, 1984).
McLeod, H. 'Building the "Catholic ghetto": Catholic organisations 1870–1914', in W.J. Sheils and D. Wood (eds), *Voluntary religion*.
McLeod, H. 'New perspectives on Victorian working-class religion: The oral evidence', *Oral History*, **14** (1986).
McLeod, H. 'Catholicism and the New York Irish, 1880–1910', in J. Obelkevich et al (eds), *Disciplines of faith*.
Meagher, T.J. ' "Why should we care for a little trouble or a walk through the mud": St Patrick's and Columbus Day parades in Worcester, Massachusetts, 1845–1915', *New England Quarterly*, **57** (1985).
Meisel, M. *Shaw and the nineteenth century theatre* (London, 1963).
Mercer, J.E. 'The condition of life in Angel Meadow', *TMSS*, 1897.
Miller, W.L. and Raab, G. 'The religious alignment at English elections between 1918 and 1970', *Political Studies*, **25** (1977).
Moody, T.W. 'Michael Davitt and the British labour movement, 1882–1906', *Royal Historical Society Transactions*, 5th series, **4** (1953).
Moore, E. 'Catholic Church and elections', *Socialist Commentary* (January 1950).
Moore, E. 'The menace of the Catholic education campaign', *Socialist Commentary* (April 1943).
Moore, F.T. 'The Hulme youth problem', *Social Welfare*, **4** (1941).
Moore, R. *Pit-men, preachers and politics* (Cambridge, 1974).
Morgan, K.O. *Keir Hardie. Radical and socialist* (London, 1975).
Murray, B. *The old firm* (Edinburgh, 1984).
Neal, F. 'Manchester origins of the English Orange Order', *Manchester Region History Review*, **4** (1990–91).
Neal, F. 'English–Irish conflict in the north west of England: Economics, racism, anti-Catholicism or simple xenophobia?', *North West Labour History*, **16** (1991).
Nelson, J. 'From Rory and Paddy to Boucicalt's Myles, Shaun and Conn: The Irishman on the London stage 1830–1860', *Eire–Ireland*, **13** (1978).
Nicholas, H.G. *The British general election of 1950* (London, 1951).
Norman, E.R. *Anti-Catholicism in Victorian England* (London, 1968).
Norman, E.R. *The English Catholic Church in the nineteenth century* (Oxford, 1984).
O'Connell, B. 'Irish Nationalism in Liverpool', *Eire–Ireland*, **10** (1975).
O'Connor, K. *The Irish in Britain* (London, 1972).
O'Connor, T.P. *The Parnell movement* (London, 1886).
O'Connor, T.P. 'The Irish in Great Britain', in F. Lavery (ed.), *Great Irishmen*.
O'Day, A. *The English face of Irish nationalism* (Dublin, 1977).
O'Day, A. 'Irish home rule and liberalism', in A. O'Day (ed.), *The Edwardian Age*.
O'Day, A. (ed.), *The Edwardian age: Conflict and stability, 1900–14* (London, 1979).

O'Day, A. 'The Irish influence on Parliamentary elections', in R. Swift and S. Gilley (eds), *Victorian city.*

O'Day, A. 'The political organisation of the Irish in Britain, 1867–90', in R. Swift and S. Gilley (eds), *Irish in Britain.*

O'Day, A. (ed.) *A Survey of the Irish in England* (1872) (London, 1990).

O'Dea, J. *The story of the old faith in Manchester* (Manchester, 1910).

O'Grada, C. 'A note on nineteenth century immigration statistics', *Population Studies*, **29** (1975).

O'Higgins, R. 'The Irish influence on the Chartist movement', *Past and Present*, **20** (1961).

O'Tuathaigh, M.A.G. 'The Irish in nineteenth century Britain: Problems of integration', in R. Swift and S. Gilley (eds), *Victorian city.*

Obelkevich, J. 'New perspectives on the history of the Labour party, 1918–45', *Bulletin of the Society for the Study of Labour History*, **47** (1983).

Obelkevich, J., Roper, L. and Samuel, R. (eds), *Disciplines of faith. Studies in religion, politics and patriarchy* (London, 1987).

Oldmeadow, E. *Francis Cardinal Bourne*, **2** (London, 1940).

Orwell, G. *Collected essays, journalism and letters*, **1** (Harmondsworth, 1970).

Parry, J. 'The Tredegar anti-Irish riots of 1882', *Llafur*, **3** (1983).

Peach, C., Robinson, V., Maxted, J. and Chance, J. 'Immigration and ethnicity' in A.H. Halsey (ed.), *British social trends.*

Pelling, H. *The British Communist Party* (London, 1958).

Pelling, H. *The social geography of British elections, 1885–1910* (London, 1967).

Pooley, C. 'Segregation or integration? The residential experience of the Irish in mid-Victorian Britain', in R. Swift and S. Gilley (eds), *Irish in Britain.*

Pooley, C. 'Irish settlement in north west England in the mid-nineteenth century: A geographical critique', *North West Labour History*, **16** (1991).

Power, J.O. 'The Irish in England', *Fortnightly Review*, **27** (1880).

Priestley, J.B. *English journey* (Harmondsworth, 1977).

Rawnsley, S. 'The membership of the British Union of Fascists', in K. Lunn and R. Thurlow (eds), *British Fascism.*

Redford, A. *Labour migration in England, 1800–50* (Manchester, 1975).

Reid, A. 'Class and organisation', *Historical Journal*, **30** (1987).

Reid, F. 'Keir Hardie and the "Labour Leader", 1893–1903', in J. Winter (ed.), *Working class.*

Reid, N. 'The Manchester and Salford ILP', *North West Labour History Society Bulletin*, **5** (1979–80).

Rex, J. 'Immigrants and British labour: The sociological context', in K. Lunn, *Hosts.*

Rex, J. and Moore, J. *Race, community and conflict* (Oxford, 1979).

Richardson, W.A. 'The Hugh Oldham lads' club', *Manchester Review*, **8** (1959).

Roberts, E. 'Learning and living – socialisation outside school', *Oral History*, **3** (1975).

Roberts, E. *Working-class Barrow and Lancaster, 1890–1930* (Centre for North West Regional Studies, Occasional Papers, 2, University of Lancaster, 1976).

Roberts, E. *A woman's place* (Oxford, 1984).

Rose, P. *The Manchester martyrs* (London, 1970).

Rowe, H.C. *The Boggart Hole contest* (Manchester, 1896).

Rowley, C. *Fifty years of Ancoats loss and gain* (London, 1899).

Rowley, C. *Fifty years of work without wages* (London, 1912).

Rowntree, B.S. *Poverty. A study of town life* (London, 1901).

Rowntree, B.S. *Poverty and progress. A second social survey of York* (London, 1941).
Rowntree, B.S. and Lavers G.R. *English life and leisure: A social study* (London, 1951).
Rudé, G. 'The Gordon riots: A study of the rioters and their victims', *Transactions of the Royal Historical Society*, 5th series, **6** (1956).
Ryan, R. *A biography of Manchester* (London, 1937).
Samuel, R. 'The Catholic Church and the Irish poor', in R. Swift and S. Gilley (eds), *Victorian city*.
Saville, J. 'May Day 1937', in A. Briggs and J. Saville (eds), *Labour history*.
Scott, F. 'The condition and occupations of the people of Manchester and Salford', *TMSS* (1888–9).
Scott, G. *The RCs* (London, 1967).
Senior, H. *Orangeism in Ireland and Britain, 1795–1836* (London, 1966).
Sheen, H.E. *Canon Peter Green* (London, 1965).
Sheils, W.J. (ed.), *The church and healing* (Oxford, 1982).
Sheils, W.J. and Wood, D. (eds), *Voluntary religion* (London, 1986).
Shipley, S. *Club life and socialism* (London, 1983).
Short, K.R.M. *The dynamite war. Irish–American bombers in Victorian Britain* (Dublin, 1979).
Sidney, P. *Modern Rome in modern England* (London, 1906).
Simon, B. *Education and the labour movement, 1870–1920* (London, 1974).
Simon, B. *The politics of educational reform, 1920–40* (London, 1974).
Simon, E.D. and Inman, J. *The rebuilding of Manchester* (London, 1935).
Smith, J. 'Labour traditions in Glasgow and Liverpool', *History Workshop Journal*, **17** (1984).
Snead-Cox, J.G. *The Life of Cardinal Vaughan*, **1** (London, 1910).
Snyder, E. 'The wild Irish: A study of some English satires against the Irish, Scots and Welsh', *Modern Philology*, **17** (1920).
Springhall, J. *Youth, empire and society. British youth movements, 1883–1940* (London, 1977).
Steele, E.D. 'The Irish presence in the north of England, 1850–1914', *Northern History*, **22** (1976).
Steele, E.D. 'Imperialism and Leeds politics, c. 1850–1914', in D. Fraser (ed.), *Leeds*.
Stocks, M. *Fifty years of Every Street* (1945).
Storey, D. *This sporting life* (Harmondsworth, 1962).
Summerfield, P. 'An oral history of schooling in Lancashire, 1900–1950: Gender, class and education', *Oral History*, **15** (1987).
Supple, J.S. 'The Catholic clergy of Yorkshire, 1850–1900: A profile', *Northern History*, **21** (1985).
Swift, R. and Gilley, S. (eds), *The Irish in the Victorian city* (Beckenham, 1985).
Swift, R. and Gilley, S. (eds), *The Irish in Britain, 1815–1939* (London, 1989).
Teeling, W. *The Pope in politics. The life and work of Pope Pius XI* (London, 1937).
Thernstrom, S. *Poverty and progress. Social mobility in a nineteenth century city* (Cambridge, Mass., 1964).
Thernstrom, S. *The other Bostonians. Poverty and progress in the American metropolis, 1880–1970* (Cambridge, Mass., 1973).
Thernstrom, S. (ed.), *The Harvard encyclopedia of American ethnic groups* (Cambridge, Mass., 1980).
Thernstrom, S. and Sennet, R. (eds), *Nineteenth century cities* (New Haven, 1969).
Thomas, J.L. 'The factor of religion in the selection of marriage mates', *American Sociological Review*, **16** (1951).

Thompson, D. 'Courtship and marriage in Preston between the wars', *Oral History*, **3** (1975).
Thompson, D. 'Ireland and the Irish in English radicalism before 1850', in J. Epstein and D. Thompson (eds), *Chartist Experience*.
Thompson, E.P. *The making of the English working class* (Harmondsworth, 1968).
Thompson, P. *Socialists, Liberals and Labour. The struggle for London, 1885–1914* (London, 1967).
Toole, M. *Our old man* (London, 1948).
Treble, J.H. 'The attitude of the Roman Catholic Church towards trade unionism in the north of England, 1833–1842', *Northern History*, **16** (1970).
Treble, J.H. 'O'Connor, O'Connell and the attitude of Irish immigrants towards the Chartism in the north of England, 1838–48', in J. Butt and I.F. Clarke (eds), *The Victorians*.
Ullah, P. 'Second generation Irish youth: Identity and ethnicity', *New Community*, **12** (1985).
University of Manchester Economic Research Section, *Re-adjustment in Lancashire* (Manchester, 1936).
Wald, K.D. *Crosses on the ballots* (Princeton, 1983).
Walker, M.W. 'Irish immigrants in Scotland: Their priests, politics and parochial life', *Historical Journal*, **15** (1972).
Walker, R.B. 'Religious change in Liverpool in the nineteenth century', *Journal of Ecclesiastical History*, **19** (1968).
Walker, W.M. *Juteopolis. Dundee and its textile workers, 1885–1923* (Edinburgh, 1979).
Waller, P.J. *Democracy and sectarianism. A political and social history of Liverpool, 1868–1939* (Liverpool, 1981).
Walshaw, R.S. *Migration to and from the British Isles* (London, 1941).
Walter, B.M. 'Time–space patterns of second-wave Irish immigration into British towns', *Transactions of the Institute of British Geographers*, new series, **5**, (1980).
Walton, J.K. *Lancashire. A social and economic history, 1558–1939* (Manchester, 1987).
Walvin, J. *Passage to Britain* (Harmondsworth, 1984).
Ward, R.H. 'Some aspects of religious life in an immigrant area of Manchester', *Sociological Year Book of Religion*, **3** (1970).
Werley, J.M. 'The Irish in Manchester, 1832–49', *Irish Historical Studies*, **17** (1973).
White, J. *The Worst street in north London* (London, 1986).
Williams, B. 'The Jewish immigrant in Manchester, the contribution of oral history', *Oral History*, **7** (1979).
Williams, B. *The making of Manchester Jewry, 1740–1875* (Manchester, 1976).
Winter, J. (ed.) *The working class in modern British history* (Cambridge, 1983).
Wood, I. 'Irish immigrants and Scottish radicalism, 1880–1906', in I. McDougall (ed.), *Essays*.
Wood, I. *John Wheatley* (Manchester, 1990).
Wright, A. *Disturbed Dublin* (London, 1914).
Wright, A.R. and Jones, T.E. *British calender customs. England, 1* (London, 1936).
Wrigley, C. 'Labour and the trade unions', in K.D. Brown (ed.), *Labour Party*.

Unpublished theses and papers

Babcock, I. 'Angel Meadow: A study of a migrant community in Victorian Manchester', BA dissertation, Manchester Polytechnic (1980).

Barber, D. 'School accommodation problems in Manchester, 1919–39', MEd thesis, University of Manchester (1960).

Baxter, R. 'The Liverpool Labour Party, 1918–1963', DPhil thesis, University of Oxford (1969).

Benjamin, H.W. 'The London Irish: A study in political activism, 1870–1910', PhD thesis, University of Princeton (1976).

Connolly, G.P. 'Catholicism in Manchester and Salford, 1770–1850', PhD thesis, University of Manchester (1980).

Cooter, R.J. 'The Irish in County Durham and Newcastle, c. 1840–1880', MA thesis, University of Durham (1972).

Feldman, D. 'How Jewish were the Jews?', paper presented at the Economic History Society annual conference, Liverpool University, March 1990.

Fielding, S.J. 'The Irish Catholics of Manchester and Salford: Aspects of their religious and political history, 1890–1939', PhD thesis, University of Warwick (1988).

Fowler, D. 'The interwar youth consumer in Manchester', paper presented at Manchester History Workshop Day School, May 1986.

Greaves, C.D. 'The Connolly Association', paper presented at the North West Labour History Society annual conference, March 1988.

Jackson, W.G. 'An historical study of the provision of facilities for play and recreation in Manchester', MA thesis, University of Manchester (1940).

Keating, J. 'Christian Democrat thought in 1930s Britain', paper presented at the Rerum Novarum centenary conference, Hull University, April 1991.

Kirk, N. 'Class and fragmentation: Some aspects of working-class life in south-east Lancashire and north-east Cheshire, 1850–70', PhD thesis, University of Pittsburgh (1974).

Law, G.S. 'Manchester's politics, 1885–1906', PhD thesis, University of Pennsylvania (1975).

McDermott, M. 'Irish Catholics and the British labour movement: A study with particular reference to London, 1918–70', MA thesis, University of Kent (1979).

Rawnsley, S. 'Fascism and Fascists in Britain in the 1930s. A case study of Fascism in the north of England in a period of economic and political change', PhD thesis, University of Bradford (1981).

Reid, H. 'The furniture workers – from craft to industrial union, 1865–1972', PhD thesis, University of Warwick (1982).

Tebbutt, M. 'The evolution of ethnic stereotypes: An examination of stereotyping with particular reference to the Irish (and to a lesser extent the Scots) in Manchester during the late nineteenth and early twentieth centuries', MA thesis, University of Manchester (1982).

Treble, J.H. 'The place of the Irish Catholics in the social life of the north of England, 1829–51', PhD thesis, University of Leeds (1968).

Walter, B.M. 'The geography of Irish migration to Britain since 1939 with special reference to Luton and Bolton', PhD thesis, University of Oxford (1978).

Whitaker, P. 'The growth of Liberal organisation in Manchester from the 1860s to 1903', PhD thesis, University of Manchester (1956).

Wollaston, E.P.M. 'The Irish Nationalist movement in Great Britain, 1886–1908', MA thesis, University of London (1958).

Index

Abortion Act (1967), 130
Anti-Partition League, 130–1
Ashton-under-Lyne, 123
Asquith, Herbert, 81, 88, 98, 101, 103, 122
Australia, 27, 73

Balfour, Arthur, 82
Band of Hope, 98
Bath, 6
Behan, Brendan, 130
Belloc, Hilaire, 111
Benson, Ernie, 44
Berrel, James, 114
Bertenshaw, Mary, 54, 71–2
Bevin, Ernest, 124
Bilsborrow, Bishop, 40, 41, 110
Birmingham, 22
birth control, 26, 106, 118–19, 128
Bishop, M.C. 57
Blackburn, 39, 71, 98, 116
Blythe, 119
Boer war, 43, 73, 76
Bolton, 39, 49, 51, 84
Booth, Charles, 47, 57, 64, 93

Bourne, Cardinal, 60, 106, 111, 112, 116, 117, 120
Boyle, Dan, 83, 89, 90–2, 94, 104
Bradford, 86, 113, 118
Bristol, 20, 70
British, Union of Fascists, 36, 125–6
Brown, George, 15
Bunyan, John, 6
Burgess, Anthony, 33, 44, 51, 65, 71
Burke, Mick, 54
Burnley, 39, 71
Burns, Thomas, 114, 116, 117, 124
Bury, 49, 51
Butler, R.A., 129–30

Callaghan, James, 72
Campbell, Henry, 114
Campbell-Bannerman, Henry, 88
Casartelli, Bishop, 40, 58, 61, 113, 116
Catentian Association, 32–3
Catholic Boys' Brigade, 66–7
Catholic Church
    and 'English'culture, 17–18, 40–1, 70
    and the family, 58–61

and immigrant culture, 11–12
in Ireland, 48–9
and Irish national identity, 39–40,
  42–3
and the Labour Party, 107, 108,
  112, 124, 125
and parish schools, 61–5, 93–5,
  120–3, 129–30
and social mobility, 33
and trade guilds, 110, 124
and trade unions, 110–11, 113–15
Catholic Emancipation Act (1829), 7
Catholic Federation, 45, 94, 113–17,
  120
Catholic lads' and girls' clubs, 65–6
Catholic Social Guild, 58
Catholic Womens' League, 68
Centre Labour Party, 116
Champion, Henry, 4, 10
Chartism, 2–3, 8, 10, 12
Chesterton, G.K., 111
Clancy, George, 122–3
Clynes, J.R., 15, 63, 80, 98, 104, 107,
  122
Cobbett, William, 6
Communist Party, 6, 106, 108, 109,
  112, 126
Connolly Association, 130
Connolly, James, 101, 109
Conservative Labour Party, 82
Cork, 17, 102
Coventry, 22,
Cumberland, 34
Curran, Pete, 36

Daily Worker, 126
dance halls, 128
Davitt, Michael, 100
Defoe, Daniel, 6
Denvir, John, 15, 30–1, 39, 87
de Trafford family, 39
Devoy, John, 16–17
drink, 43, 44, 57, 77, 85, 128
Dundee, 119

Easter rising (1916), 18, 101
Education Act (1902), 62, 93
  (1936), 119–20
  (1944), 129–30
Engels, Freidrich, 27

family
  and Catholic ideology, 58–60
  and immigrant identity, 15
  intervention of priests in, 46, 58–9
  size of, 26
Fermanagh, 83
First World War, 61, 66, 100–1
Fox, Tom, 71
France, 4
Freeman's Journal, 83

Gaelic Athletic Association, 17–18
Gaelic League, 17–18, 86, 104
General Elections,
  1885, 88, 90
  1892, 98–9
  1895, 82
  1900, 99
  1906, 95, 98, 99
  1910 (January), 84–5, 98, 99–100
  1910 (December), 85, 98, 99
  1923, 104
  1929, 107, 121
  1931, 124
  1935, 125
  1950, 130
Germany, 4
Gladstone, William, 82, 88, 89, 98
Glasgow, 5, 27, 31, 34, 68, 108, 130

Hadow Report, 120, 121
Hall, Leonard, 97
Hardie, Keir, 96, 97–8
Harvest, 40
Heinrick, Hugh, 12, 16
Henshaw, Bishop, 40, 43, 122–3, 129
Hinsley, Cardinal, 126
Holland, 4
Holywell, 54, 60, 92
Home Rule
  economic consequences of, 35–6
  opposition to, 8, 9, 10, 81–2
Home Rule Confederation, 80
Hull, 119

immigrants
  age and gender composition, 24–5,
    70
  occupations and poverty, 31–3,
    35–6, 47

places of settlement, 27–31, 128
pre-Famine, 19–20
reasons for leaving Ireland, 20–2,
    127–8
seasonal, 23–4
second and third generations,
    14–16
Independent Labour, Party, 6, 79, 91,
    95, 96–8, 106, 108, 113
Indian immigrants, 5, 127
inter-marriage, 14, 46, 59, 70–2, 90
Irish Democratic League, 117–18
Irish Free State, 1, 5, 18
Irish in Britain Representation Group,
    133
Irish National Foresters, 83
Irish National League of Great
    Britain, 80, 83, 97
Irish Nationalist movement
    and the Catholic Church, 92–5,
        116
    and the ILP, 96–7
    and the Labour Party, 98–100,
        103–4, 117–18
    and the Liberal Party, 88–90, 95–6,
        98–100, 101–2
    membership, 83–4
    moderation, 85–7
    and publicans, 85
    and working-class politics, 80–1,
        90–1
Irish Republican Army, 87, 127, 130,
    131, 132
Irish Republican Brotherhood, 86
Irish Self-Determination League, 92,
    102–4, 122
Irish Socialist Republican Party, 109
Italian immigrants, 42, 76
Italy, 4

Jarrow, 34
Jewish immigrants, 5, 12, 14, 18, 36,
    68, 125–6

Kelley, G.D., 98
Kemp, Sir George, 90
Kennedy, Bart, 15, 55, 62
Kennedy, John F., 133
Knutsford, 129

Labour Leader, 96, 99, 106
Labour Party, 3–4, 79–80, 95–6,
    96–7, 105–6, 130
Labour Representation Committee,
    79, 97–8, 113
Lansbury, George, 121
Larkin, Jim, 26
Lee, Hugh, 102
Leeds, 10, 14, 33, 44, 72, 80, 113, 125
Lees, Lynn Hollern, 11–12, 30
Leicester, 18
Leo XIII, Pope, 58, 112, 117
Liberal Party, 58, 79–80, 88–90
Lithuanian immigrants, 42, 129
Liverpool, 5, 6, 19, 20, 27, 28, 30–1,
    34, 35, 46, 47, 50–1, 54, 61, 64, 67,
    80, 81, 89, 113, 115, 119–20, 126,
    130, 131
Lloyd George, David, 103
London Catholic Herald, 18, 112, 123
London, 4, 11, 15, 17, 18, 20, 22, 23,
    27, 30, 32, 36, 39, 40, 47, 57, 61,
    70, 72, 93, 96, 97, 108–9, 111,
    125–6, 128
London, Jack, 16
Lourdes, 54
Lundy, Richard, 120–1, 124

McCabe, Dan, 15, 31, 83–4, 90–2, 95,
    96, 98, 99
McCarthy, Mary, 103
MacDonald, Ramsay, 105, 112, 116,
    121, 122
MacGill, Patrick, 22, 26, 60
MacSwiney, Terence, 101
Manchester Catholic Herald, 17, 54, 102,
    112, 121, 124
Manchester Citizen, 95
Manchester Guardian, 9
Manchester Martyrs, 85
Manning, Cardinal, 40, 43, 57, 111
Marx, Karl, 9–10
Mass-Observation, 26, 131
Mayo, 23
men
    attendance at mass, 50–1
    membership, of confraternities, 52
    place in family, 59–60
    occupations, 25–6
Middleton, 129

Morgan, Sean, 103
Morrison, Herbert, 121
Mosley, Oswald, 123, 125–6
mothers' and babies' welcomes, 68–9
Mothers' Defence League, 58
Murphy, William, 7

National Council of Catholic Trade
   Unionists, 115–16
Naughton, Bill, 23, 101, 109
Neafsey, Thomas, 103–4
Nelson, 119
New Party, 123
Newcastle, 15, 34, 35, 49, 70, 101,
   113, 119
Northampton, 129

O'Connor, T.P., 23, 81, 85, 90, 96,
   101, 104, 107, 117
Oldham, 15, 30, 80
O'Mara, Pat, 16, 61, 63
Orange Order, 7, 27, 31–2, 34–5
Oswaldtwistle, 33, 103
Oxfordshire, 23

Parnell, C.S., 81, 83, 86, 87, 88, 89
Phoenix Park murders, 82, 97
Plymouth, 72
Pogues, 133
Polish immigrants, 42, 76, 129
Potato Famine, 2, 20
prejudice
   origins of anti-Catholic, 5–8
   origins of anti-Irish, 8–10
   persistence, 131–3
   at work, 36, 91–2
Preston, 39, 72
Preston Catholic News, 108
Priestley, J.B., 131–2

Ratcliffe, Alexander, 35
Redmond, John, 92, 93, 94, 98
Redmond, Willie, 99
Riley, Edmund, 114
Roberts, Robert, 33, 67, 68, 71
Rochdale, 39
Rosebery, Lord, 88
Rowntree, B.S. 50

Samuel, Raphael, 11
Scotland, 22, 35, 36, 104, 127

Scots, 8, 10
Scurr amendment, 122, 123
Sexton, Sir James, 15, 54, 80, 86, 89,
   115
Shaw, George Bernard, 9
Sheffield, 113
Sinn Fein, 102–4
Slattery, Joseph, 35
slum clearance, 128–9
Social Democratic Federation, 36, 79,
   95, 98, 109
Socialist Commentary, 130
Socialist League, 80
South Africa, 24
Spanish civil war, 109, 119, 125
Stafford, 27, 70
stereotypes of Irish Catholics, 8–9
St Helens, 33, 34, 36, 108, 118–19
Stockport, 15, 83, 104
Stoke, 132
Storey, David, 132
St Patrick's Day, 34, 45, 73, 84, 87,
   104
Strachey, John, 126
street socialisation, 67–8, 69–70, 71–2
Sunderland, 6, 119

Taff Vale judgement, 97
Thorne, Will, 115
Tillett, Ben, 36
Toole, Joe, 15, 27, 107–8, 109
Trevelyan, C.P., 121

Ukrainian immigrants, 42, 76, 129
Unemployed Workers' Union, 108
United Irish League of Great Britain,
   15–16, 24, 80, 83, 101–2
United States, 4, 5, 13, 14, 21–2, 24,
   27, 30, 31, 39, 57, 61, 64, 70–1, 73,
   83, 91, 126
Urmston, 59

Vaughan, Bernard, 43, 47
Vaughan, Cardinal, 40, 42, 45, 52,
   54–5, 58, 62, 93, 110
Victoria, Queen, 41, 87

Wallsend, 119
Webb, Sidney and Beatrice, 10
Welsh, 8, 10

West Indian immigrants, 5, 127, 129
Wheatley, John, 108
Whit walks, 73–7
Whitehaven, 45
Wilson, Harold, 130
Wilson, Sir, Henry, 103
women
    attendence at mass, 50–1
    innocence, 43

occupations, 25
place in family, 59–61
relations with priests, 44
role in Nationalist movement, 83, 84
working-class culture
    interpretations of, 2–4, 10–12
    place of Irish Catholics, 33–4

York, 50–1, 70